Trouble in Paradise

Trouble in Paradise

THE SUBURBAN TRANSFORMATION IN AMERICA

Mark Baldassare

Columbia University Press
New York

Columbia University Press
New York   Guildford, Surrey
Copyright © 1986 Columbia University Press
All rights reserved

Printed in the United States of America

p 10 9 8 7 6 5 4 3 2 1
c 10 9 8 7 6 5 4 3 2

Library of Congress Cataloging-in-Publication Data

Baldassare, Mark.
  Trouble in paradise.

  Bibliography: p.
  Includes index.
  1. Suburbs—United States. 2. Suburban life—United
States. 3. Suburbs—California—Orange County—Case
studies. 4. Suburban life—California—Orange County—
Case studies. I. Title.
HT351.B34 1986   307.7'4'0973   85-19499
ISBN 0-231-06014-9
ISBN 0-231-06015-7 (pa.)

Contents

Preface

The United States is now a predominantly suburban nation. The suburbs are where a plurality of Americans live and work. Our scholarly and lay images of the suburbs, however, are from the 1950s. White, middle class, homeowners, single-family homes, men commuting to city jobs, women at home caring for the children, stable neighborhoods and safety. We learned these images from classic studies of the suburbs which no longer apply. This book offers an up-to-date and more accurate account of suburban communities and their residents.

As the suburbs have emerged as the dominant form, changing forever the American landscape, they too have been transformed. Decades of rapid growth and industrialization in suburbia have created a more diverse population, land-use mix, and activities. These have caused a new life-style and, with it, new problems. There are several constants in suburbia which have made the transition from the past to the present most difficult. One is that the attitudes and preferences of the suburban residents, on issues such as housing and transportation, have not changed to reflect the current situation. The other is that the political and ecological structure of suburbia, perhaps once effective, seems ill suited to problem solving. *Trouble in*

Paradise is about the new suburbia that has emerged in the last two decades. It is especially concerned with the problems which occur when rapid growth and industrialization take place without changes in people's values or the social structure.

Of course, many dramatic changes occurred in American society during the 1970s which had profound impacts on suburbia. The economy shifted from industrial to information and service-oriented work. Housing and energy costs increased dramatically. The nuclear family became less prominent as single life, childless marriages, and divorces grew more commonplace. Civil rights activities lifted some of the barriers that kept races and ethnic groups geographically separated. Confidence in government and its ability to solve problems was shaken. The public monies available to improve community life declined. The meeting of basic service needs has become more complex. These and other fundamental changes in American society also led to the formation of a new suburbia and affected its adjustments to change.

The book is oriented toward changing ideas about suburbia. It uses sociological theories about suburban communities, translates these concepts into testable hypotheses, and then tests them empirically. One source of information is the published reports from the U.S. census, along with government publications and previous scholarly studies. The main source of information, however, is the Orange County Annual Survey, a study of a major California suburban community. I interviewed over 1,000 randomly selected residents of Orange County, California in each of two consecutive years. They are asked about a variety of subjects including housing, transportation, government, services, and the quality of life.

Six challenges that face the suburbia of today are at the core of the book. Each helps to define and explain the suburban transformation in America.

The first is the suburban housing crisis. The demand for land in a rapidly growing and industrializing suburbia has driven up the cost of housing. New residents face steep costs of homeownership, and a basic premise of moving to suburbia, that is, owning a home, has been jeopardized. Suburbia's renters face disillusionment and frustration, since their values and preferences for the single-family home and homeownership are mismatched with the new suburban reality.

The second challenge is the growth controversy, fueled by growth itself and the changing landscape of suburbia. Many residents resist the changes around them and express opposition to future growth. It is evident, though, that those against growth do not speak with one voice.

The third challenge is trust in local government. Suburban government is fragmented and lacks central authority, a fact which hinders strategic planning and encourages a lack of confidence. Further, as suburban places have become more dense, large, diverse, and rapidly changing, these new conditions have increased distrust of local governments.

A fourth challenge is the tax revolt and fiscal strain. At a time in which the suburb's middle class residents became increasingly opposed to taxes, the federal and state governments were short of funds. This threatens service delivery and service expansions already strained by the suburban transformation.

The fifth challenge is the special need for services in the suburbs. The sprawling and politically diffuse nature of the suburbs creates problems for delivering services and meeting needs that are now emerging, such as a transportation network and a more diverse health, education, and welfare program.

The sixth challenge is the "special groups," that is, the increasing social diversity of the suburbs. Individuals are moving to the suburbs today more and more for jobs rather than for housing and a homogeneous residential area. The mix of races, classes, age groups, and life-styles is increasing. With greater social heterogeneity are more difficulties in providing social services, greater possibilities for social conflict, and more problems in offering a good quality of life to all of suburbia's residents.

The book is divided into eight chapters. The first chapter is an overview of the historic trends and the current study. The next six chapters present evidence of the six challenges from the Orange County Annual Surveys. The final chapter summarizes the evidence for a "changing suburbia" in the migrants into and out of suburbia and looks toward the future.

Some may question the generalizability of research on California's suburbs. For this reason I will confirm my conclusions with data and studies from elsewhere in the nation. However, there are some sound justifications for my research site. California's suburbs are trendsetters for the nation and likely to inform us early of widespread future occurrences. These suburbs are also viewed by many as "classic" suburbs and even by some as "utopian." One can thus look to California for evidence of "trouble in paradise," even in the most ideal communities.

Several colleagues worked with me in developing questions for the 1982 and 1983 Orange County Annual Surveys. Stephen and Ann Cole of Social Data Analysts, Inc. conducted the fieldwork and provided many useful suggestions. Ellen Greenberger, Karen Rook, Sarah Rosenfield, Amy Somers, Daniel Stokols, and Roger Teal helped design some of the questions. Ray Catalano, Gilbert Geis, Joseph DiMento, and Henry Pontell offered general advice. Many community leaders in Orange County provided comments, background materials, and reactions to the survey questions and findings.

I received valuable assistance from several individuals in preparing the book. Sarah Rosenfield offered statistical advice, computer assistance, editorial feedback, and many useful ideas. Matt Davis, Karyn Griffin, Connie Keenan, Kathleen Rederscheid, and many other students were involved in the data analysis. Margaret Thomlinson typed several drafts of the book and provided editorial advice. Elizabeth Beck and Kathy Bracy helped in preparing the book for publication. I am very grateful to my editors, John Moore, Maureen MacGrogan, and Karen Mitchell who provided useful ideas, editorial assistance, general wisdom, and encouragement.

The funding for the Orange County Annual Surveys was primarily from a three-year grant for "focused research programs" from the Division for Graduate Studies and Research, University of California, Irvine. Supplemental funding for the 1982 Orange County Annual Survey was provided by the Public Policy Research Organization, University of California, Irvine. The 1983 Orange County Annual Survey was partially supported by foundation, corporate, and public agency contributions.

The materials in this book were influenced by the ideas and writings of several scholars. I especially thank Bernard Barber, and also Terry Clark, Jack Kasarda, Kevin McCarthy, and Gerald Suttles. I learned much from recent conversations with David Dowall, David Easton, Claude Fischer, Larry Long, William Michelson, Peter Morrison, and Max Neiman. I was fortunate to be writing this book at a time, and in a place, in which there was increasing curiosity about the scope and meaning of the suburban transformation in America.

M.B.
Irvine, California

Trouble in Paradise

CHAPTER ONE

National Trends

Suburbia has become increasingly diversified in its activities and in its residents. The turning point for American suburbs was the 1970s. The beginning of the decade marked the first time that more people lived in the suburbs than in central cities or rural areas. A slight population advantage grew into a distinct difference by the middle of the 1980s. What has also transpired is a revolutionary transformation of not only where Americans live and work but, more important, how they live and work.

Three competing prophecies have been debated in the wake of the suburban era, variations of which are frequently voiced by academics, the media, and government officials. I present them here in their simplest form to introduce the current concerns about suburbia.

The "utopian" view argues that because the suburbs are now more accessible, a greater proportion of Americans are provided with new and better lives. No longer is the "American dream" available to only a fortunate few. The suburban existence that is a preferable life-style for the majority has been mass marketed. Society has advanced, and, in the wake of greater technological know-how and increased national wealth, a more desirable quality of life is available. Comsumption patterns in homeownership, automobile use, and leisure activities are evidence of suburbia's utopian characteristics. The result is a suburban evolution that has brought greater happiness to greater numbers of people.

The "contagion" view offers a less optimistic assessment. The suburbs are considered to be no different from the central cities they surround. The boundaries between cities and suburbs are artificial and highly permeable. Existing social and economic problems have not been solved by the relocation of people to the suburbs. Instead, urban problems are being swiftly exported to the suburbs. Supporters of this perspective point to trends in crime, racial tension, pollution, and congestion to prove that the escape to suburbia is a myth, a convenient ploy by civic boosters and real estate developers.

The "suburban transformation" perspective offers a more complex interpretation of current events. This less extreme perspective on suburbia appears the most compelling and is considered in detail in this book. Suburbs have obviously changed after decades of rapid growth and industrialization. But they are neither a utopian invention nor an extension of the central city. They are unique in their organization, in the use of land, and in their residents' expectations. Clearly, there have been innovations in viewing the relationship between workplace and dwelling place. As a result of the experimentation with new forms, some improvements have been passed on to suburban residents. However, new problems and old problems in somewhat different forms have also emerged. One can see, for example, weakness in local government, social values in opposition to realities, problems in delivering public services, controversies over future development, and a lack of transportation strategies.

The prospects and problems of suburbia are illuminated by information I have collected and analyzed from a California suburb. I consider this case study to speak to general trends. The foremost goal is to understand the unique social circumstances of suburbia and, by so doing, offer some perspective on the prophecies concerning suburbia's future.

Defining Suburbia

Suburbia is not easy to define. It is the buffer between our central cities and rural areas. What is between these two types of area is rather ambiguous. Suburbia is a residual category and, as such, creates problems for serious analysis. Can we lump together communities with such variation? Are we sure we have eliminated the rural/central city emphasis in separating out the suburbs?

The most widely used definition of the suburbs has been created by the U.S. Census Bureau. They start by delineating "central cities," places containing some threshold of population (usually 50,000). The space beyond the municipal boundaries of the central city but within the county in which the city is located would be defined as the suburb. The places within close reach of the central city are viewed as satellite communities. While their residents live outside the city limits, many work in the city—thus the term "bedroom community." Those who work in the communities surrounding the central city often have jobs tied to the central city economy. They work in branch offices of businesses (e.g., banks, auto parts manufacturing) that have their headquarters in the central city. They may also provide services (e.g., dry cleaning, accounting) for people with central city jobs. In addition, those residing in satellite communities are usually dependent in some way upon the commercial establishments of the city. They frequently visit medical specialists, museums, theaters, foreign restaurants, or major stores in the central city.

This view of the suburbs is now antiquated. Many cities have consciously expanded to the county boundaries in order to merge city and county functions (e.g., San Francisco, Indianapolis, Jacksonville). Sunbelt cities such as Houston and Dallas have continually annexed suburban properties in order to capture white and middle class taxpayers. An extensive and efficient ground transportation system has allowed many central cities to draw their workers from further distances and across county boundaries. Thus, the grasp of today's largest

central cities goes beyond the peripheral areas within given
counties. The U.S. Census Bureau offers a broader definition in
its conception of "metropolitan area": counties adjacent to the
central-city-based county are also considered suburban. These
counties must meet certain requirements to be considered suburban outposts of central cities. For example, the majority of
their economic activities must be nonagricultural, their land
built up to a certain density, and a substantial proportion of
their labor force commuters to a central city workplace. The
suburban communities in counties adjacent to a central city are
viewed as having a similar relationship to the city as the satellite communities within the same county. They are bedroom
communities, contain complementary or branch-office economic activities, and depend upon certain central city functions. Marin County in the San Francisco area and Westchester
County in the New York City area are well-known examples.

     There are bound to be disputes about suburbia's defini-
tion, given the broad and somewhat arbitrary categorizations.
As with many social phenomena, the largest disagreements occur over the boundaries. Suburbs close to the city limits often
have more in common with urban places than with other suburbs. Peter Hall (1977) has noted "graying" inner suburbs,
with housing deterioration, racial conflict, crime, and overcrowding. Such border communities have little in common
with suburbs that are not adjacent to the city limits. Likewise,
satellite communities located on the adjacent counties' outer
boundaries are frequently rural in orientation. Firey (1946)
called these places "rurban," since their life-styles and land use
patterns do not fit into our concept of suburbia. They may
contain argriculture, mobile home parks, industrial ware-
houses, horse farms, tract housing, and junkyards. Some residents commute to city jobs while others work in the town. It is
obvious from these two end points of our definition that the
suburban community has wide parameters.

     Another complication in suburbia's definition is the re-
cent reclassification of suburban adjacent counties into separate
metropolitan areas. Nassau-Suffolk in the New York area and

Orange County in the Los Angeles area are widely used examples. Many social scientists were dismayed that these areas were redefined in the early 1970s. Some claimed foul and favoritism that these heavily Republican counties were given special status by the Nixon Administration. When the dust settled, however, it was clear that the economic activities and population concentrations warranted the metropolitan area status. So did the fact that most of the residents commuted to work within the metropolitan area. A new hybrid was formed, that is, a region which could be metropolitan and yet entirely suburban.

Despite the apparent difficulty in determining what suburbia is, I offer the following characteristics as a working definition. First, suburbia is the area surrounding a major city, either within the same county or in adjacent counties. It is an area in which the primary economic activities are nonagricultural. It is relatively low in density compared to the major central city, yet is highly populated. The suburban area is characterized by political and economic fragmentation. No municipality serves as the main focus for work or commercial activities. Also, many independent local governments operate with little coordination.

Urban Deconcentration
and the Suburban Expansion

Sociologists have monitored the growth of suburbs for more than fifty years. The Chicago school of urban sociology posited theories about suburban expansion during the era of rapid city expansion in the 1930s. Many were based upon a mix of demographic data and ideas about the ecology of human settlement patterns. For instance, Park (1925) noted that new immigrants settled in inner city neighborhoods and displaced the more well-to-do residents towards remoter neighborhoods. He called this process "invasion and succession." It held for some time as the major description of suburbanization. Burgess (1925) posited a "concentric" theory which argued that cities were composed of a series of zones. Each zone had unique social, spatial, and economic characteristics. The five zones— central business district, zone of transition, working class area, middle class area, and commuters' zone—were ordered from less to more desirable. The outer zones offered the lowest densities, best housing choices, fewest poor people, most families, and least deviance and social problems (see also Faris and Dunham 1939; Shaw and McKay 1929). McKenzie (1925) argued that the trend toward suburbia was a demographic and ecological fact that was made possible only by improved transit. Hawley (1950) later described this as a "reduced friction of space" that shortened the travel times between urban locations. Good roadways, cars, and trolleys were thus prime reasons for the move to suburbia.

In its early existence suburbia was viewed as one-dimensional and limited in its functions. It was a domicile or bedroom community for white collar workers employed in the city. Job opportunities, social diversity, and commercial services were extremely limited; one commuted to the central city for all these goods. Some argued that the sameness of the suburbs approached sterility (Dolce 1976; Whyte 1956). Moreover, this uniformity was invented to benefit the middle class employed in the city. The suburbs became equated with the conformity that marked the post–World War II and especially the 1950s era of American history.

A population explosion occurred in the suburbs during the 1960s. Population grew by 33 percent in the suburbs, while it grew by only 1 percent in the central cities (Long and DeAre 1981). The reasons are as multifaceted and complex as that decade was itself. A black and Hispanic population and recent migrants from southern states and Latin America were arriving in central cities. They were forcing the inevitable "invasion and succession" in the inner city neighborhoods. Residents were also moving to the suburbs over issues related to the civil rights movement. School busing, black political power, and rioting stirred up latent racial prejudices and fears. As important, central city residents had increased opportunities to change dwellings. Government subsidies, tax deductions for home mortgages, and mortgage programs, joined with an increasing affluence of the population, resulted in large numbers of potential homebuyers. Massive road building, paid for through a program of long-term interstate highway expansion, facilitated the commute between central city workplace and suburban residence. Large and well-organized development companies, builders, and real estate promoters sold the public on the benefits of suburban living.

The suburbia that had emerged at the close of the 1960s was by many standards a different entity from previous forms. It was the predominant form of American residence. It was massive in geographic and population size. It sprawled long distances at moderate to low densities. It had become socially more complex, as evidenced by Berger's (1960) accounts of working class communities and Gans's (1967) description of lower middle class areas. By and large minorities and the poor still seemed excluded (Danielson 1976; Danielson and Doig 1982). A "family" life-style was pervasive, and job opportunities seemed limited.

During the 1970s the suburbs consolidated their dominance over the large central cities. The movement of employers from central cities to suburbs accelerated (Kasarda 1972). Manufacturers moved in search of lower land rents, local taxes, and labor costs. By 1980, almost twice as many people were employed in manufacturing in the suburbs as in the central cities (i.e., 11 million versus 6 million). More than 400,000 manufacturing jobs vanished in the central cities and over 1.6 million were gained in the suburbs between 1970 and 1980 (U.S. Bureau of the Census 1983c). Not only job replacement but, importantly, economic expansion had moved to the suburbs. The suburb-to-suburb commute was thus becoming the typical journey to work (Kasarda 1978).

Commercial changes have also favored the suburban areas. The regional shopping mall has eliminated the need for many inner city shopping trips. Massive suburban shopping centers have become as complex as some cities' business districts. Specialty stores of all sorts have emerged, and alongside them office buildings are often being constructed. Retail sales and office work have expanded in the suburbs at the cost of many central city businesses (Baldassare 1981).

In all, by 1980 a total of 40 percent of the U.S. population resided in the suburbs, a location clearly preferred over central cities (28 percent) and rural areas (32 percent). In a settlement pattern characterized by urban deconcentration, what were once satellite communities have now become the most common residential form.

The "metropolitan" suburb of today is a direct result of urban deconcentration. In its most developed phase it is represented by places such as Orange County and Nassau-Suffolk. It is different from earlier suburban forms. It is more extensive geographically, typically quite large in population size, and further from the boundaries and influence of the central city. It is not only low-density sprawl, since it contains clusters of high-density development and many areas of moderate density. Land use and activity are commercial and industrial as well as residential. Population characteristics also vary more along class, race, and life-cycle dimensions. Yet, it is also different from the earlier urban forms since it lacks a central place or single concentration of people and activities. The forces that freed many people and enterprises from the old urban form have created a suburban structure that is massive and complicated in nature.

Population Trends
That May Limit Suburban Growth

Not all the recent trends have favored the suburban expansion. Some economic changes have clearly stunted its growth. Other population shifts, it has been argued, have reversed urban deconcentration. Three macrosocial trends are analyzed here, although the evidence suggests that in the final analysis they will have little effect upon the nation's increasing suburbanization.

The growth of the "Sunbelt" received great attention in the 1970s. In simple terms, residents of northeastern and midwestern cities relocated to the metropolitan areas of the South and West, in very large numbers. Beneficiaries were places such as Dallas, Houston, Miami, Phoenix, and San Antonio. The reasons for the Sunbelt explosion are numerous and relate to many new social trends. But the migration is largely accounted for by economics (Perry and Watkins 1977). Southern and western states attracted residents because of lower living costs. Businesses moved because of savings in labor and land costs.

The Sunbelt migration would seem to work to the disadvantage of suburban expansion. First, the "Frostbelt" metropolitan regions as a whole lost population. Since this includes their suburbs, the indication is that residents were uprooted from many northern suburban areas. Second, migrants from the North to the South were moving to Sunbelt cities and not to their suburbs. Finally, the Sunbelt cities were annexing their surrounding lands as they grew, drawing many suburban Sunbelt residents into the central city population.

Suburbs did well despite all these negative trends. The national rate of suburban growth was nearly 20 percent during the 1970s. The growth of the suburbs was almost equivalent to the growth of central cities in the Sunbelt's southern states (42 percent for the cities versus 38 percent for the suburbs). The growth of the suburbs was also substantial, but not as large as the growth of the central cities in the Sunbelt's western states (44 percent versus 29 percent). Remarkably, the Frostbelt suburbs of the northern states had slightly positive growth rates despite a large regional population loss (Long and DeAre 1981). The results suggest that suburbanization continued despite the Sunbelt migration. Southern and western suburbs expanded at a fast rate as the land in the central cities became more precious. Northeastern and midwestern suburbs captured a portion of those fleeing their central cities and grew despite an unfavorable economic climate. So, suburbs grew even though regional trends worked against them.

During the 1970s a much acclaimed "inner city revital-

ization" was discovered that would also seem to reverse suburban growth. Run-down and abandoned neighborhoods were
rehabilitated by private homeowners. A white middle class
population was apparently "gentrifying" areas previously over-
run with poverty, drugs, crime, and unemployed minorities.
Many reasons were offered for the rebirth of urban neighborhoods. There were housing bargains to be had in the inner city.
The energy crisis made the suburb-to-city work commute less
desirable. Childless young professionals seemed willing to risk
urban problems to be near cultural and commercial amenities.

The advent of urban revitalization suggested to many
that migration from the city had been reversed. Middle class
residents and middle class wealth were expected to return to
the city from the suburbs. In fact, this never occured. The majority of gentrifiers were young city residents who were forming
their first households, not return migrants from the suburbs
(Gale 1979). Inner city buildings with dwelling units once occupied by large families were now inhabited by one person or a
couple. There was still an overall population loss. City observers
and elected officials were astonished to learn at the release of
the 1980 census that residents had continued to flee central city
neighborhoods in favor of suburbia. Wealth, moreover, was not
redistributed, as evidenced in the growing gap between city
and suburban median incomes (e.g., almost $10,000 in median
family income in the New York area; New York *Times,* February
27, 1983). When the situation was reassessed, it became obvious that inner city revitalization was a miniscule phenomenon,
limited to some city residents repairing housing in a few central
city neighborhoods. It had no impact upon suburban expansion
(Baldassare 1982a).

Another much heralded trend was the "population turnaround" in rural areas, which was also viewed as a threat to
suburbia's future. Calvin Beale (1975) discovered in the early
1970s that the dormant counties beyond the urban fringe were
beginning to repopulate. Such areas had lost residents to cities
for over a century. Many people hypothesized that a long-
standing preference for rural life and a general anti-urban cli-

mate was at work in this trend (Zuiches and Fuguitt 1972). The view was that metropolitan areas might depopulate as people forsook the city and suburb for the small town and the farm (Long 1980).

There are many parallel events that added up to a reversal of the decline in rural growth. Growth was accentuated by exploration for coal and oil in remote areas. Retirement communities arose in underdeveloped regions as the over-65 population expanded. Most important, however, is a phenomenon called "metropolitan spillover," which takes place when a suburban area bursts out of its existing boundaries into more sparsely developed rural counties. Thus, much of rural growth is a reflection of the suburb's massive expansion into neighboring territory. For example, Riverside and San Bernardino counties have grown in population as open space in Los Angeles and Orange counties has begun to decline. At present the actual rate of rural growth is a significant reversal from historical patterns, but it is quite likely that rural growth in adjacent counties will soon lead to a redefinition of these areas as suburban. This will work to extend the dominance of the suburban form and increase suburban population expansion.

Many factors claimed to be hindering suburbia's expansion have failed to do so. The regional population shifts were no deterrent. The urban renaissance movement was small. The rural turnaround may ultimately increase suburban dominance. Perhaps the attempts to locate roadblocks for suburbanization have represented ambivalence toward this new residential form. Nonetheless, the factors propelling further suburban growth clearly outweigh the countertrends.

Urban Problems Reach the Suburbs

Some problems in our society have a distinctly urban reputation. They are located primarily in cities and considered by many to be caused by city life. These include crime, housing deterioration, population decline, deviance, overcrowding, pollution, and congestion (see Fischer 1984). In recent times these problems have been increasingly sighted in the suburbs. But a unique set of circumstances exists in suburbia that determines the form social problems take and how they will be solved.

Suburbs in some metropolitan areas have begun to lose population, typically areas that border on large central cities. Inner suburbs with notable declines include those of Detroit, Cleveland, Washington, Pittsburgh, Boston, and St. Louis. Each area lost approximately 10 percent during the 1970s. This was an average of 30,000 to 100,000 population decline per inner suburban area (Long and DeAre 1981). Some of these areas failed to hold their residents because of regional employment shifts. Jobs lost in the Northeast, as mentioned earlier, resulted in Sunbelt migrations for suburbanites as well as central city residents. Other suburban areas lost residents to further removed suburbs and nearby rural areas. Still others lost their place as regional commercial centers and distribution points as transportation patterns changed (Listokin and Beaton 1983). Some areas experienced notable physical and social deterioration. Inner suburban neighborhoods went through the invasion and succession process as poor inner city minorities displaced the white working class.

The above-mentioned factors are universal causes of decline that can affect any type of community. There are, in addition, some uniquely suburban factors in population loss. The tract homes that characterize early suburban development do not age well. They have lost much of their value and appeal in a few decades. Also, the many suburban municipalities have begun to compete with each other not only over central city residents but now for current suburban residents. Cost and size of housing, local taxes, school quality, and status are some of the incentives that have resulted in a redistribution of the suburban population. The suburbs' earlier population gains were not merely migratory but were accounted for by the rate of natural increase. But large suburban families have been replaced over time by other individuals, many of whom have fewer children. Thus, a national change in family patterns, a redistribution of the suburban population, and weaknesses in the housing stock have all resulted in some suburban decline.

Crime has recently become a major issue in the suburbs. The number of crimes has increased with recent population gains. More important is the rate of increase in suburban crimes. Of course, the nation as a whole had some increases in crime rates during the 1960s, but there are special factors contributing to the upward trend in suburban personal and property crimes. A diversifying population base accounts in large part for this trend (Farley 1976; Zimmer 1975). The suburbs have become accessible as residential locations for more of the city's poor, disenfrachised, and deviant subcultures. A change in land use patterns is also partially responsible. Commercial institutions have expanded and densities have increased, so that targets of opportunity for property crimes are greater in number and closer together. Another factor unique to suburban crime is the public's response to it. Expectations about safety from crime are quite high in the suburbs, partly because of city residents' reasons for moving to the areas in the first place. Concern about crime is thus high despite what are still relatively low crime rates even after the recent increases. Criminal activity also takes new twists to conform with suburban ecology. Suburbs lack central business districts and the zones of transition around them. The "red light" prostitution districts, concentrations of gambling halls, and areas dominated by criminal activities are thus less prevalent. Illegal activities must take new forms, with outcall massage and gambling rings that use telephone and automobile technology to deliver the illegal services. With criminal activities more diffuse than in the city, police activities obviously become more difficult.

Similarly, the "critical mass" has been reached that allows for deviant subcultures to develop in suburbia. There are sufficient numbers of people to support the emergence of special interest groups. Yet, there are few gay neighborhoods, artists' areas, or radical movement headquarters. The population concentration is obviously present, yet the specialized groups are spread over large areas. The mail, the telephone, and the car allow like-minded people to maintain both identity and a desegregated subculture. This presents new challenges to the subculture's social organization. Coping with the social diffusion of so-called "deviant groups" is also a strain on the suburbs' status quo supporters. Many residents resist a deviation from the white middle class family model of suburbia, yet locating and then eradicating subcultural variations is made difficult by the social diffusion of groups.

A series of environmental concerns has also crept into the suburban consciousness. These include air pollution, land and water pollution, noise, overcrowding, and congestion. Poor air quality in the suburbs is often blamed on cities. Thus, Los Angeles smog is said to invade Riverside or San Bernardino. New York's pollutants are believed to drift over Nassau-Suffolk or Westchester suburbs. In fact, given the industrial diffusion into suburbia and the growing amount of auto traffic in outer metropolitan areas, this perception is outdated. The air quality in the suburbs is often due to the suburbs themselves. Problems emanating from "elsewhere" have become a convenient excuse to deny the need for local solutions. More covert and perhaps worrisome pollution concerns have emerged in the suburbs. Many city industries have disposed of hazardous wastes in outlying regions. There is, at present, a great deal of uncertainty about the whereabouts of illegally buried toxic substances in suburban areas. In short, yesterday's city wastelands are potentially the backyards and playgrounds of today's suburbs.

Sources of urban stress such as noise and congestion are also becoming widespread in the suburbs. Given the necessity of major highways proximate to residential areas, auto-related noise is perhaps especially troublesome. The gradually increasing densities have made noise from neighbors more prevalent. Automobile congestion is an increasing concern. The lack of a central geographic focus avoids the massive rush-hour jams of central city business areas, but in its place is a less predictable and more widely diffused form of traffic congestion. It is a pervasive and not easily solved source of community annoyance. These environmental problems are made more serious by the higher expectations of suburban residents. The people confronted with bad air quality, pollution, noise, and congestion are often those who believed that their move from city to suburbia exempted them from such problems. Their tolerance is much lower than their city counterparts' for so-called urban problems.

Six Challenges in a Changing World

This book identifies several issues that confront suburbia today, evolving from the basic facts and ideas about suburbia already presented. All defy the general "utopian" notion about modern suburbia. Nor are they in line with the "contagion" perspective, since so-called urban problems have unique characteristics when observed in suburban areas. The six challenges in a changing world emanate from national events. Each is complicated by the social values, political structure, and ecological structure of modern suburbia.

It should be noted that the general concern of this book is a departure from earlier generations of suburban research. It goes beyond the mere discovery that suburbia is a diverse social entity (Berger 1961; Kramer 1972; Masotti 1973). It does not attempt a critique or defense of the suburban way of life (Donaldson 1969; Whyte 1968). It does not primarily consider whether other social categories better explain residential attitudes and behaviors than the urban-suburban dimension (Gans 1962; Dorbriner 1958). This book centers on the premise that there are new conditions in suburbia today, caused by increasing industrialization, rapid growth, and several national trends, which create challenges that are different from those of the past. The challenges and their existence, causes, consequences, and possible solutions are the main focus of this book.

The Housing Crisis and New Economic Realities
   People had been lured to the suburbs in the past by housing opportunities. Areas outside the city limits once offered homes for purchase at affordable prices to large segments of the American population. There is evidence that this pattern has changed dramatically in recent years. The price of an owner-occupied home skyrocketed during the 1970s, leaving many potential buyers without hope of future homeownership. Many factors account for this change. Housing demand, home building costs, and investor speculation are among them. If people cannot fulfill the American dream of homeownership then one wonders whether the movement to suburbia will continue. It is possible that city-dwelling renters will remain in place. Suburban renters who have patiently waited to buy homes may flee suburbia in frustration.
   The single-family detached home in a low-density residential setting was an equally important expectation that suburbia provided. It also has become a more elusive reality. The rambling multibedroom home has increased in price to the extent that it is virtually unavailable to the middle income family. The large plot of land, with sizable frontyard and backyard, has also become costly. Suburbia's increased attractiveness has driven up land prices and has resulted in denser settlements. While suburbs are still relatively low density by central city standards, they are not lacking in condominiums and in too-close neighbors. Suburbia has also become a preferred location for industry, and multi-use zoning has replaced the segregated residential suburb. Whether suburbia will continue to remain an attractive location with these changing land uses, especially given Americans' expectations, is thus in question.
   The energy crisis during the 1970s may also have shaken the foundations of suburbia. The metropolitan region is the product of the automobile era. It is based on assumptions of single-party automobile use. Commuting from suburban residence to central city workplace is one example. Trips from home to shopping facilities and services are others. People's residential decisions are partially based on the notion that com-

muting costs are minimal. Energy costs have risen and, with them, the expense of a suburban residence. The periodic disruptions in energy supply, most notably during the Arab oil embargo and the Iranian revolution, made work commuting and travel more difficult. Subsequent rises in utility rates have increased concern about heating, cooling, and powering the large suburban home. But long lines at service stations and higher gasoline prices did the most to shatter the once invulnerable image of suburban living. The issue is whether economic changes in the energy realm will affect the movement of people into and out of suburbia.

There has been much discussion of industrial trends in the United States. The manufacturing of durable goods has certainly become a less prominent feature of our economy. Bell (1973) has argued that our society has entered a postindustrial era in which we emphasize the provision of services to one another. Law, medicine, restaurants, businesses, and the like thus become pervasive. Naisbitt (1982) argued that "high tech/high touch" is the wave of the future. Computers and related information technology will dominate the American economy; educators, disseminators, programmers, and analysts are the new employees. The debate rages as to whether we can, or should, reindustrialize in order to dominate world markets in steel, automobiles, and major appliances. The effects of deindustrialization on the suburbs have rarely been examined. Suburbia has widened its scope through attracting manufacturing from city locations. In fact, suburbia has done remarkably well given the nationwide decline of manufacturing. Perhaps in the short run this has led to economic prosperity. But in the long term suburbia's future may be in jeopardy if U.S. manufacturing plants continue to close their doors and limit their domestic operations. Some employers may relocate in less developed countries or rural U.S. regions, leaving suburban employees without nearby work. The main question is then whether the new wave of computer-oriénted companies will in the future opt for suburban locations. The existence of Silicon Valley suggests the appeal to suburbia, but the evidence is far from conclusive. It is thus essential to determine the numbers and types of peoples and industries moving into and out of suburbia.

Suburbia's landscape and life-styles are thus changing as a result of new economic realities. Housing costs, size, and development patterns have altered. The uncertain energy situation in the 1970s created concerns about geographical mobility. The shift from manufacturing to high technology also left future expansion in doubt. Even worse, it raised possibilities of economic collapse in a significant number of areas. In general, the discontent that reduced the confidence in Americans' futures was also felt in the suburbs. Rounds of inflation, recession, high interest rates, and unemployment had affected the cost of living. The standard of living that suburban residents have come to expect seemed to improve after the economic recession of the early 1980s gave way to an economic recovery, but a sense of insecurity about the future persisted. The extent to which the current suburban form can ride out periodic downward trends and develop a stable economic base has great significance for suburbia's future.

Controversies over Growth

Suburbs have been synonymous with growth for decades. Civic boosters counted the population and cited the rate of migration with pride. Americans had come to equate growth with all that is good in communities and its counterparts of stagnation and decline with all that is bad. It was widely assumed that population growth led to a booming economy, a better quality of life, more job opportunities for average people, a healthier tax base for city governments, and a better housing market for homeowners. After decades of actual growth suburbanites throughout America have begun to vocally question future growth. In some cases they have actually halted community development. The reasons for this collective movement and its meaning for suburbia's future have intrigued social scientists.

The controversy over population restrictions in local

communities is an important philosophical question. Democracies are supposed to allow free movement of residents from place to place. This civil right would be impinged upon if growth in certain areas were restricted. It would force people to stay where they are or at least limit the neighborhoods to which they can move. On the other hand, democracies also pride themselves in local civic participation. People are supposed to have a voice in determining their own destiny. Hence, residents should have a role in deciding what type of community they want to live in. The growth debate has become heated, with, more often than not, people taking extreme positions and showing an unwillingness to compromise. The current growth controversy suffers from a lack of reputable information. Little is known about what cities do, and what their policies actually achieve, in attempting to limit growth.

Growth controversies have often taken the form of battles within communities. The "progrowth" advocates are business and land-baron elites who would benefit directly from property development and industrialization. The "no-growth" supporters are average citizens who have organized because they dislike community change. Government stands somewhere in the middle, pressured by business, yet fearful of citizens' wrath (Molotch 1976).

It is possible to envision some localities as so organized that they can initiate policies to deflect unwanted growth. These well-off communities attract the most prestigious residents and businesses. Other, lower-status suburbs have less control over their destinies. They have ineffective governments and poorly organized citizens. They grow haphazardly at the will of industries and developers (Logan 1978). These are caricatures. Documentation about growth policies and growth's consequences in different communities is very limited.

There are several ways in which suburban cities try to limit growth. Governments commonly use an authority that has been legitimized throughout the twentieth century, that is, zoning. Certain types of development can be eliminated from the city's boundaries through zoning, such as industry or commerce. Apartment complexes and high-density buildings can be ruled out through large lot zoning. Zoning is a process that is supposed to protect the citizens' health and safety. Instead, it is often used to exclude unwanted people and activities.

A variety of more sophisticated approaches toward "growth management" has evolved in recent years. A "cap" can be instituted on population size. Building permits can be limited. Moratoria on building construction can be enforced when rapid growth occurs. Cities can purchase open space and thus reduce the land available for development. Service area boundaries can be drawn so that development outside these territories will not have roads, sewers, or schools. An abundance of growth-limiting procedures has been instituted despite legal challenges to the exclusionary process (Burrows 1978).

Why suburbanites have wanted to limit growth is somewhat of a mystery. Some have claimed that the phenomenon is an outgrowth of the environmental movement. Americans seem more interested than ever before in issues such as pollution, overcrowding, and congestion. It is possible that environmentalism is a more current theme in upper middle class settings, and is therefore frequently voiced as "no growth" sentiment in affluent suburbs. Others claim that growth limits are popular because residents wish to prevent city ills from entering the suburbs. An anti-urban bias thus becomes translated into policies indirectly aimed at preventing crime, garbage, crowds, noise, and pollution.

Still others feel that concerns about growth are fancy pretenses for racism and classism. Suburbanites are really trying to exclude the poor, the working class, blacks, and other ethnic minorities through rather complex land use policies. Some have cited the role of economic self-interest in the support for growth controls. If new housing becomes scarce, then existing homeowners may profit through higher home values. If growth is limited, then taxes need not be raised to pay for more streets, sewers, and schools. It is likely that an array of values and goals accounts for the antigrowth movement. Whatever the reasons,

the ballot initiatives, city planning implementation, legal disputes, citizen groups, and public opinion polls show that controversy surrounds future suburban growth (Baldassare 1981).
What the trend toward growth disputes spells for suburbia is not certain. There is not enough information at present
on the degree of concern about local growth among suburban
residents or under what conditions suburbanites begin to favor
growth restrictions. Even less is known about how citizen concerns affect policy. It is thus hard to predict the spread of
growth controls. It is possible that the enforcement of growth
controls in an increasingly large number of localities will actually subdue the momentum to develop the suburbs. Perhaps
the ways in which suburbs develop will be affected by these
policies. For example, the poor areas may become lower status
as industrial and high-density growth occurs within their
boundaries. The affluent areas may increase in status as they
draw the most sought-after migrants and businesses. The
threat, in sum, is that the controversy over growth may limit
access to the suburbs. Growth limits may affect the general
population or specific undesirable groups and economic activities. Growth may also be redirected if capital flows to communities where development is met with less resistance.

Distrust in Local Government
There are increasing strains in the political relationships
that bind suburbia. Local governments have been in conflict
with each other. Residents have squared off against their local
leaders. Residents have angrily debated other resident groups.
Business interests have opposed local mandates. The era of easy
decisions where everyone goes away a winner seems to have
ended. Suburbia is increasingly a place where zero-sum political games predominate (Thurow 1980). The strains are exacerbated by the fact that suburbs lack a sociopolitical structure for
solving regional issues.
It has been noted that suburbia is composed of multitu-
dinous local governments, each carrying on policy debates and
making important decisions in a relatively autonomous man-

ner. But the suburban world today is highly interdependent. Social and economic decisions in one city affect all the surrounding areas. For example, a municipality seeking expansive growth may overload the streets and roads, and contribute to air pollution, in surrounding areas, despite the fact that surrounding communities may have highly restrictive growth policies. Local governments are thus small, impotent actors in the suburban arena. The result is a history of conflict and competition among suburban municipalities. There is little evidence of collaboration on issues of mutual interest.

Attempts to impose a super-authority on suburban municipal governments have failed. It is true that regional governments have had partial success in other nations (Foley 1972). The United States, however, has a long tradition of home rule and sentiment against big government. So national and state governments have been helpless in solving local disputes. County government could be a replacement for major city government, but in fact, it is not. Unincorporated areas are the county government's major spheres of influence. Otherwise, identification with county leaders or countywide issues in suburbia is often weak or nonexistent. There have been attempts at building metropolitan-wide leagues and other organizational entities for local governments. These are, however, largely symbolic institutions that perhaps best serve as social gathering places and occasional lobbying forces. Their real power pales before the need for authority and coordination in the suburban area.

Fundamental questions have been raised by citizens about the role of American local government. Some believe it should be actively involved in issues related to citizen welfare; local government should thus provide resources and social support for communities. Others claim that local government should do less and stop interfering with citizens' lives. This perspective claims that government is not effective or efficient at managing most human problems. The way should be cleared for private solutions. The new laissez-faire conservatism is clashing with the welfare state liberalism in numerous suburban localities. Municipal governments are usually too confused about their raison d'être to offer perspectives in the dispute. The long-term issues of the role of local government are complex and extremely important. For example, what services will be provided, and what will be the level of care, for those needing public assistance? Further, what will take the place of local government and who will decide what services are needed if local government is reduced in power and influence? Community groups and political organizations are thus disputing the very future of local government activity, at a time when suburbia has real public crises in need of political leadership and solutions. Nonetheless, the vacuum in ideas concerning local government's role continues.

In conditions of weak local government the private sector has increasingly sought status as a legitimate actor. It has always influenced local government, but now it is vying for a larger role in the community. This is evident in discussions of "public-private" partnerships and joint authority over local programs. People in and out of government are considering how the business world might help solve local problems. The private sector has responded in part by asking the local government to reduce regulations. The view has been that planning interferes with the free market's efficient operation. Citizens are wary of private sector involvement. They wonder about the profit motive as a means of meeting local needs and are uncomfortable about new linkages of business interests and politicians. Public-private joint ventures to improve community conditions are thus hampered by the philosophical and legal ground rules for these cooperative efforts.

Through all these conditions local government has been the focus of a confidence crisis. The public has expressed doubts about the honesty of local officials. Significantly, their leadership capabilities, competency, efficiency, willingness to listen to citizens, management skills, and intelligence have also been questioned. Local government has become increasingly "accountable" for its actions. More often it is failing the test of public scrutiny. The lack of confidence could be partly explained by the post-Watergate mood. Perceptions of widespread transgressions may be at work in maxmizing the negative image of politicians. Suburbia is also the site of citizen participation and social movements by citizens for more direct control over community decisions. The downgrading of politicians and government may be the result of a grass-roots campaign to increase the role of citizen activism.

It is perhaps most likely that there is a real feeling that government is not delivering what is needed. The crisis in trust is also a response to the lack of local government's legitimate authority in suburbia. It is a consequence of the weaknesses in political structure, confusion about roles, conflicts between interest groups, and lack of agreed-upon problem-solving mechanisms. These feelings can become self-fulfilling prophecies as local government is further stripped of influence. The complexity of the issues now facing suburbia has highlighted the longstanding fact that suburbia's communities and leadership are divided.

The Tax Revolt and Fiscal Strain

From the Great Depression through the 1960s the powers of local government were slowly usurped by the federal government. The 1970s were a turning point in the return of influence to the local level. Politicians were increasingly arguing that the national government had grown too large, too inefficient, and unresponsive to local problems. American citizens had long communicated this populist argument. Now they began to hear it from presidents, governors, and legislators. In short, more is expected from our local government as authority and decision-making have been transferred from Washington.

Suburban governments have been presented with new responsibilities at a most trying time. Suburbia, after decades of rapid growth and industrialization, is in need of improving and extending services and thus increasing service spending. The federal government may have been willing to expand local government's role, but it has not been forthcoming with adequate financial resources. The national budget has been under intensely difficult circumstances. A weak economy reduced the revenue flow and increased the national debt in the late 1970s and early 1980s. An economic recovery did not alter the fact that expenditures outpaced revenues. A higher priority was placed on new military spending than on increased domestic spending. To some the proposed transfer of power from federal to local sources was thus only a public relations ploy. Others argued that response to local fiscal concerns must now come from local monies. No matter where the fault or solution lies, suburban governments have seen their expenditure needs grow and their revenue sources shrink.

The search for local revenues to support service expansion and transferred responsibilities, unfortunately for suburban governments, has coincided with a tax revolt. Citizens in California voted in 1978 to drastically reduce the amount of property taxes that they pay (California, 1980). Other states subsequently enacted rules to limit sales tax, income tax, and government budgets. These movements were highly popular not only among the wealthy, but in the white middle class and homeowner constituencies. Citizens have told their local governments that they do not want spending decreased and they do not want taxes increased either. They want greater care in spending tax dollars. How to do more for less money is the challenge proposed to modern-day local governments. Suburban municipalities may have suffered disproportionately. Their typical residents have the characteristics and opinions of the tax revolt supporters. Their governments are in a relatively weak position, vis-à-vis large central cities, to lobby effectively to claim funds from state and federal sources. They are also in a more precarious position because many are highly dependent on property taxes. Many suburban areas do not have the diversity of local revenue streams nor the political clout to weather fiscal strain.

There is also a conservative and antigovernment backlash that is particularly evident in the suburbs. People are wondering whether government should involve itself in a variety of social problem-solving endeavors. Some argue that local issues are better left to private concerns than to local public agencies. The extreme view states further that the health and welfare of low-income populations should be the responsibility of religious and charitable institutions. This discussion is often raised in the suburbs because the special populations receiving funding are often in small and isolated pockets. They usually do not constitute large, perceptibly threatening communities. The fiscal conservatives are well organized and more vocal than the suburbs' dependent groups. The increasingly popular belief that problems are not being solved by government intervention has legitimized the tax revolt. In essence, the argument is that the reduced resources of the local government are really inconsequential; the money does little good anyway. This proposition has done much to discourage any attempt to raise local revenues for service provision.

Funding methods have changed, and suburban governments have more limited resources with which to solve specific, pressing problems. There were once a variety of "categorical" grants devoted to certain uses. Examples include interstate highway funds, housing assistance programs, commercial development monies, and special welfare services. The movement has been toward replacing these with "block" grants, undesignated funds to be used as the local government sees fit. This is rationalized as an attempt to transfer decision-making to local authorities. In fact, the funds are often used for solving short-term problems. These include filling potholes, paying utility bills, and meeting administrative payrolls. The needed expansion of the infrastructure or attention to the needs of special groups is left for some future date. Disputes are increasing about where the limited funds should be expended. In such an atmosphere, funds are rarely divided evenly. There are winners and losers, and special interests and lobbyists frequently prevail. One cannot assume that suburban governments are providing for special needs and special groups in distributing funds.

The scenario most likely to result from today's fiscal strain and the tax revolt, in combination with rapid suburban growth and industrialization, is increasing stratification (Logan and Schneider 1981). Some governments will be able to extract federal and state funds through lobbying. Others will not be as successful. Some municipalities will learn how to use existing funds effectively while others will not. Some areas have high property values and good commercial sales while others do not. Finally, politicians in some areas will win the trust of their constituents and will be able to ask for more revenues, while others will not. It is already evident that strategies to overcome fiscal shortfall are used more effectively by some cities than by others (Clark and Ferguson 1983). The consequences, ultimately, will be felt by residents in the less advantaged areas.

Increasingly significant are the long-term consequences of fiscal problems and the responses to them. It is evident that lack of fiscal resources may not be short term. It is a complex political, social, and economic change that may be relatively permanent. Suburbs vary tremendously in size, social composition, and adaptability. For now, it is important to examine the extent of tax revolt sentiment and the degree to which fiscal strain is felt by suburban residents and their leaders.

The Emergence of Special Service Needs

Many people left the central cities because they were dissatisfied with the services provided there. They entered the suburbs with high expectations about the quality of services in their new residences. Schools were to be good, recreation plentiful, the crime rate low, and streets and roads uncrowded. These perceptions were based upon an earlier concept of the suburbs; that is, the early phases of suburban development when the migrations had not reached full stream. Beliefs in the "good life" were also partly a fiction based upon real estate advertisements. Today, the suburbs are in reality complex and cumbersome to manage.

The local services gap—the difference between existing services and residents' expectations—is most evident in the realm of transportation. Highways and arterial streets once delivered commuters to and from work without trouble. Now, the populations of many suburban areas have swelled past the carrying capacity of the road systems. Planning a more expansive transportation grid is a difficult task. An earlier solution might have been to cut major highways between the city and suburbia. Such thinking is obsolete, since suburban residents now drive helter-skelter to a variety of suburban work locations. Some do not even use existing highway systems, but instead, crowd surface streets during business hours. The lack of centrality has caused diffuse traffic congestion that is difficult for planners to contend with using existing technologies.

Mass transit has become a negligible entity in modern suburbia. This was acceptable when most residents were presumed to own cars and when commuting in the suburban area was effortless. That situation no longer exists. Transportation planning is needed for the elderly now residing in the suburbs and often with no driving skills (Wachs 1979). Many other suburban residents, such as poor minorities, the physically handicapped, and young adolescents, need some sort of public bus or railway system to meet their daily needs. With increasing commuting times and traffic congestion a reality, working residents have also called for other means of travel from home to work. The problem lies in the fact that mass transit, to exist, needs certain ecological features which suburbs as presently constructed do not contain. Population densities are not high enough to support a public system. Critical masses are not within reach of transit lines, and bus routes or rail lines cannot be extended. The lack of centrality in work locations has also hampered planning on the destinations of commuter lines. Leaders are reluctant to voice favor for mass transit, since the private automobile has been almost synonymous with the preferred suburban way of life. These obstacles to mass transit burden both commuters and the non-car-owning residents.

Suburbanites are learning that the high-quality school system they expect in their areas is more difficult today to provide. Schools are generally overburdened and underfunded. They are asked to pick up the slack in after-school child supervision, since divorce and dual-career households have increased.

Schools must also increasingly serve special needs. A more diverse suburban population has required bilingual, learning disability, and nutrition programs. These labor-intensive activities are expensive and time-consuming. Suburban schools do not always have the personnel or funds to meet the new challenges.

Police must also contend with an increasingly diverse population. Since land use has intensified and become more industrially and commercially oriented, as was mentioned earlier, suburban areas have become more crime prone. The increasing heterogeneity of residents in the suburbs has also increased the possibilities for property and personal crimes. Moreover, with relatively small and uncoordinated local governments working in large geographical areas, economies of scale are not reached. The police bureaucracies are inefficient, and uneven service results as some small municipalities serve their residents more successfully than others.

There is a growing sense that parks, recreation, and a leisure-oriented life-style have eroded. Open space was once plentiful in the suburbs. Now, it is a precious commodity as land values and the intensity of development have increased. As land fills in with housing, industry, and commerce, the recreational uses of space are often overlooked. Many early suburban developments provided "greenbelts" that assured residents of some place set aside for leisure. Such planning has become less economical, and these luxury items are increasingly available only to the most affluent. This comes at a time when Americans are increasingly enjoying the outdoors and have awakened to the health aspects of sports and recreation. Existing facilities are thus becoming heavily used, even overcrowded. The supply of recreation facilities is not increasing. People thus want more parks and recreation areas when the land shortage suggests that they will get less. The services once associated with a suburban life-style seem likely to be limited to those who can pay for them. The era of free and easy leisure may be drawing to an end.

Private services also suffer difficulties in suburban areas. An increasingly diverse and sophisticated population calls for more specialized facilities. These include, for example, cultural activities, medical specialists, boutiques, and gourmet foods. The chain store in the shopping mall has lost much of its early appeal. It is true that private services are still provided to the satisfaction of suburban residents, but in the future dissatisfaction is likely to increase. How to offer specialties in a large geographic region, where critical markets are not centralized and local advertising is difficult, is a major question even for the most resourceful in the private sector.

Social Diversity in the Population
The suburban image is so strong as to be engraved in America's collective memory. Suburbia is supposed to be a white middle class settlement. Households are to be filled with two parents and two or more children. Their homes are owned or, more accurately, mortgaged. The inhabitants are surrounded with automobiles, appliances, and luxuries. One adult, the male, is working, and the other adult, the female, is engaged in housekeeping and child rearing. This stereotype was always shown to be an inaccurate representation of all suburban residents. It is now fading as a description of most suburbanites, with changes in American society and shifts in the suburban landscape bringing a new awareness.

First, ethnic and racial minorities have been increasing in numbers. Many suburban dwellings are still unattainable to blacks, because of discriminatory land use, zoning, and informal real estate policies. But black suburbanization has nonetheless continually spread (see Schnore et al. 1976). Blacks now comprise about 6 percent of the suburban population, and about one in five blacks lives in the suburbs. The black suburbanite is not as well off as the white suburbanite, in residential or economic terms, but is in better circumstances than the central city black (Clark 1979; Lake 1981). Reasons for this trend include the growing presence of a black middle class and the overflow of minority populations from heavily nonwhite central cities (Spain et al. 1980; Long and DeAre 1981). Third-world immigration has also been present in suburbia. Political refugees from Southeast Asia have been spread throughout the country, and some have been settled in metropolitan fringes. The economic refugees from Latin America and the Caribbean have, likewise, found their way to the suburbs. An increasing Hispanic, black, and Asian presence in the suburbs has shattered previous ideas about the culturally uniform suburban community. Though these groups are still small proportionally, the increasing numbers reveal suburbia's potential ethnic and racial diversity.

Suburbia is no longer solely a middle class domain. Some of the early suburban settlements, notably the lower-middle class tract housing built after World War II, have become prime targets for low-income populations. So-called graying communities have thus emerged in the inner suburbs. Increasing diversity in land use and suburban industrialization have brought about greater residential diversity. Land near manufacturing plants is less valued and becomes used for low-income housing. The creation of blue collar jobs in the suburbs has meant an equivalent need for working class neighborhoods. Thus, occupational heterogeneity has occurred as suburban locations for both work and residence have become more prevalent.

The "nuclear family" has lost its dominance, for many reasons revolving around national demographic trends. The birthrate has declined markedly since the baby boom ended. Many families are choosing to have fewer than two children. In some cases they are having no children at all. Marital dissolution is occurring in all segments of society, and a spiraling divorce rate has also limited the proportion of "complete" families. As a result, suburbia finds itself with growing proportions of female-headed households, divorced couples living alone, and separated singles. A growing proportion of young adults is also remaining unmarried. The numbers of singles living alone and households with unrelated individuals have increased. The nuclear family, in short, is becoming more of a statistical rarity in the suburbs.

The age distribution of suburbia has shifted, with the

elderly and single young adults now more broadly represented. The elderly are in the suburbs because they settled in these areas long ago. Many brought up their children, experienced the "empty nest" syndrome as their children left home, retired, and now comprise the elderly population. They have "aged in place." Others moved to "leisure and retirement" communities in the suburbs specially designed for the elderly. Single young adults have migrated to suburbia because this mobile age group usually follows job opportunities. Employment growth in the suburbs thus spawns age diversity. Some of the children of the suburbs also eventually grow up and start their own suburban households. The challenge for suburban policymakers and observers is to understand the social significance of the transition to a community of many age groups.

The sex role stereotypes that pervade suburban ideology are increasingly inaccurate. As already mentioned, marriage, divorce, and birthrate trends mean that many single women, female-headed households, and childless households now occupy suburbia. Married women are also increasingly present in the workplace, because of both economic necessity and life-style preferences. The male-as-wage-earner family is one that cannot always provide the level of financial support to meet current household needs and suburban expectations. Women are also more often engaging in satisfying full-time careers outside the suburban home. There are, of course, married women who devote themselves to child rearing and housekeeping with the husband as the undisputed head of household. But the increasing diversity of women's social roles is a suburban fact.

Social heterogeneity is also visible in the housing status of suburban residents. There are now more renters in the population who are single, elderly, divorced, and in blue collar occupations. Condominium ownership is also growing, with the ease of maintenance appealing to many non-nuclear-family households. Though hardly by choice, low-income suburbanites are occupying a deteriorating housing stock with conditions reminiscent of inner city abandoned buildings.

Methods and Strategy of This Book

The methods typically used to research suburbia are the case study and the demographic analysis. The case study uses intensive field research to gather data on one community. A researcher lives within a neighborhood, talks regularly with its inhabitants, takes extensive notes, and provides a rather personal account of life in a particular area. A rich tradition of this work exists within urban sociology, perhaps best exemplified by the writings of Gans (1967) and Suttles (1969). The demographic analysis relies upon population and housing data on community areas, usually gathered in the decennial census. It tells us in rather global terms about events in a given region. One might track population growth trends, percentage of minority population, housing values, employment opportunities, or commuting patterns in a suburban county over time in a historical analysis of the data. An alternative approach would be to contrast different suburban regions in a comparative analysis. Good examples of historical and comparative approaches to demographic analysis include the studies by Kasarda (1978) and Logan and Schneider (1981).

This book relies upon a different method that is less commonly used in urban sociology. Existing trends in the suburbs are examined largely through the experiences and opinions of large numbers of inhabitants obtained through the use of community surveys (which will be described below). The survey is a better method for examining suburban life than the case study, since the personal accounts observed in surveys are representative. Residents have been selected randomly and in sufficient numbers. They are all asked the same questions in the same way. Problems of bias, such as who will talk to the field researcher and with whom the field researcher will talk, have been eliminated. The survey methodology increases the study's generalizability.

There are distinct advantages to the survey method, as well, over the demographic analysis. One is timing. Most studies rely upon census data, which is collected every ten

years. They miss opportunities to discover new trends or
watch events unfold over the intervening period. Thus, only
the grossest fluctuations are observed over time. All too often,
the census merely confirms what is already known. The
survey can thus update information since the last census and
help track events as they occur. Many questions about trends
are also left unanswered in demographic analysis. These include why people move someplace, how they feel about the
city they live in, and what their plans are for the future.
Surveys can collect information about attitudes, recollections,
satisfactions, and preferences that in many instances can better
explain and place in perspective a community's current trends.

The research in this book relies upon surveys from one
suburban region. Such surveys even if gathered over sequential
years, as these were, do not always provide enough information to understand the suburban transformation. Census information offers some historical perspective on the area and can
fill in details not gathered during survey interviews. Data from
a specific area is not necessarily generalizable to other regions.
Any given area has unique features, such as its wealth and
growth, that can limit an inquiry's scope. For this reason, I
have included where necessary surveys from other areas in the
1970s and early 1980s. These data, together with the Orange
County Annual Surveys, offer a more comprehensive picture of
the suburbs. Validity, generalizability, replicability, and relevance are increased by the use of mutliple data sets.

The challenges considered in this book must be approached through a uniform strategy that examines each issue
thoroughly. Within such a strategy the first and simplest approach is the descriptive analysis, which merely entails the
counting of various types of individuals, problems, attitudes,
opinions, and so forth. The results are presented as percentages
to represent, as does the census, the prevalence of certain social
phenomena. These are important baseline statistics. They do
not, however, offer much more than the current state of affairs.
But the numbers can offer some surprises as unexpected groups,
beliefs, and perceptions are observed.

A useful approach for a study concerning change is the longitudinal analysis. One can consider those who recently moved to an area and compare them with those who arrived five or ten years ago. This is especially important for analyses of the "new economic realities." For example, how do recent versus long-term residents compare in reasons for moving, housing costs, socioeconomic status, neighborhood perceptions, and desire to stay? Other analyses would examine survey trends over different years of data collection. One could learn, for example, about shifts in perceived growth, service problems, and policy preferences as well as changes in population and housing characteristics.

The next necessity is to examine variations in attitudes and objective circumstances in various segments of the population. The importance of social heterogeneity has been stressed. Comparisons across groups will thus be made in examining the survey data. For instance, singles can be contrasted with marrieds, the old with the young, the Anglos with blacks and Hispanics, and the rich with the poor. The use of this approach speaks to the fact that individuals are diverse in suburban regions, so that the researcher must explore variations in residential opinions, economic resources, policy preferences, self-reports, and social and economic outcomes.

Another analytic approach used in this book is the contextual method. This is an attempt to address the fact that the contexts of people's lives are often important influences on their actions, opinions, and plans. This is rarely accomplished in urban sociology. One can systematically examine the consequences of context, though, by merging different sources of information. For example, growth and housing factors derived from censuses can be combined with survey interviews to better understand why certain attitudes are held. Further, information on financial conditions derived from published reports can be combined with survey interviews to perhaps offer clues to public opinion on taxes, services, and government. The combined data sources provide special opportunities to establish whether differences in suburban community features have become diverse enough to affect decisions and opinions. The precision of outside, objective measures is also beneficial. One could compare communities that vary in specified amounts of growth, income, revenues, or population characteristics and note whether these contextual factors influence the experience of the suburban transformation.

All attempts to explain the causes of suburban phenomena are enormously complex. Many factors operate at once in the real world. Deciding which factor really affects opinions or actions is clouded by the multiplicity of variables. The analyses that follow attempt to control for extraneous factors through various statistical procedures. Variables may include, on the individual level, age, sex, income, occupation, homeownership, race, and length of residence. In addition, statistical methods (to be discussed in chapter 2) are used to assess the relative importance of one causal factor in comparison with others.

The Orange County Annual Surveys

The surveys that comprise this analysis of suburbia were conducted in Orange County, California, in 1982 and 1983. The survey instruments themselves are presented in the appendix.

The same sampling strategies were used in the two surveys. The goal was to contact 1,000 respondents for each survey. The samples are stratified geographically, with half the sample selected from north of the Santa Ana River and half from the south. The interviewing and data coding were conducted by Social Data Analysts, Inc. of New York.[1]

The sample in each geographical area was chosen using a computer program that randomly generates telephone numbers from among working blocks of telephone exchanges. A working block is one that contains numbers in use. The total of telephone numbers generated within an exchange was in proportion to the number of residential phones represented by that exchange in the northern part of the county or the southern part of the county. Using this procedure, in 1982 2,000 telephone numbers from the north and 2,000 telephone numbers from the south were drawn. In 1983 it was 1,800 telephone numbers from the north and 1,800 telephone numbers from the south. This procedure of random digit dialing ensures that unlisted as well as listed numbers are included in the sample. Also, since over 95 percent of the households in Orange County have telephones, random dialing yields a sample representative of the population of the county.

The Troldahl-Carter Method was used in randomly selecting which adult member of the household was to be interviewed (Troldahl and Carter 1964). The total number of adults in the household and the total number of men in the household were enumerated. The age and sex of the person interviewed is then selected from a prearranged grid. (For instance, a household with three persons and two men calls for the youngest man to be interviewed, and a household with three persons and no men calls for the youngest woman to be interviewed.)

The sampling error for surveys of 1,000 respondents is plus or minus 3 percentage points. In other words, if this survey were to be repeated one hundred times, in 95 out of 100 times the answers obtained for a particular question would match those we obtained in this survey within three points. The sampling error for any particular subgroup would be greater. These calculations assume that the data were collected under ideal circumstances. Since there are a large number of practical problems in conducting social surveys, the actual sampling error for any particular result might be slightly larger.

Data Collection

As noted above, the interviewing was done by telephone. Cost considerations and methodological improvements have led to telephone surveys' increased adoption in the social sciences. In addition, several studies show similar quality in telephone and face-to-face interviews (Groves and Kahn 1979; Jordan et al. 1980; Rogers 1978).

Interviewers were closely supervised during the data collection. Interviewers participated in a two-hour training session on the Orange County Survey Instrument. Supervisors were available during the telephone interviewing to answer questions of interviewers or respondents. The telephone system allowed supervisors to monitor interviews to correct for errors in administering the questionnaire.

All interviewing for the 1982 survey was done between August 9 and August 17, 1982. On weekdays, interviewing occurred between the hours of 5:30 and 10:30 p.m., and on Saturday between 10:00 a.m. and 4:00 p.m. For each number in the sample, at least four call-back attempts were made. The resulting sample of 1,009 represents 25 percent of the numbers dialed (4,000 in all). There was a refusal to cooperate for 11 percent of the numbers. The majority of calls not completed (57 percent) was due to nonworking residential phone numbers or to no answers, which may indicate nonresidential phone numbers. The refusal rate for the survey was 30 percent (25 percent completions plus 11 percent refusals divided into 11 percent refusals). This is consistent with the general refusal rate in community surveys, which usually varies between 25 and 40 percent (Frey 1983).

The interviewing for the 1983 survey was done between July 11 and July 27, 1983. Interviewing occurred between the same hours, and again, at least four call-back attempts were made for each number. The resulting sample of 1,003 represents 30 percent of the numbers dialed (3,324 in all). For 11 percent of the numbers there was a refusal to cooperate, and 54 percent of the calls were not completed because of either nonworking phone numbers or no answers. The refusal rate for the survey was 27 percent (30 percent completions plus 11 percent refusals divided into 11 percent).[2]

As a further check on the representativeness of the samples chosen by the above methods, characteristics of the samples were compared to characteristics of the total Orange County population according to the 1980 census. In age, income, sex, marital status, household size, and homeownership, the survey respondents are representative of the population of

Orange County. Characteristics of the 1982 and 1983 survey sample were also compared with each other. Marital status, ethnicity, age, sex, and education were closely comparable in the two surveys.

The Survey Instruments

The 1982 survey included 78 questions. The interview averaged 18 minutes in length. It contained primarily fixed response questions. The questions included personal and household facts and attitudes toward housing, growth, government, politics, taxes, local services, personal circumstances, and transportation. There were three sets of open-ended questions on housing, concerned with reasons for moving into the current residence and reasons for wanting to move out of it. Categories for coding these open-ended questions were developed before the interviewing and then revised on the basis of the first 150 interviews. An additional open-ended question on the respondent's occupation was coded according to a few large census categories to distinguish upper white collar, lower white collar, and blue collar workers. Lastly, there was an open-ended question on zip code of residence that was coded to determine the respondent's city or area.

The 1983 Orange County Survey contained 90 questions. However, a portion of the interview schedule was devoted to elderly respondents only and another section to parents with children in the public schools. The interviews averaged 17 minutes in length. Questions were predominantly fixed response. They involved personal and household facts, many asked previously in 1982, and attitudes toward service spending, transportation, housing, moving, government, politics, growth, schools, and personal well-being. There were no open-ended attitude questions. Zip code of residence was asked as before. In addition, there were open-ended questions on the respondent's occupation, and, if currently married, the spouse's occupation. These responses were again coded using a few of the U.S. Census Bureau's large occupational classifications.

Characteristics of the Survey Respondents

The basic characteristics of the 1982 and 1983 Orange County Annual Survey respondents are shown in table 1.1. Social class and household characteristics are emphasized. Significant changes in demographics from the 1982 survey to 1983 are noted below.

First, in terms of basic demographics, the age range clusters between 25 and 44 years. Almost half the sample falls within this category. The youngest age group, 18–24 years, represents about one-sixth of the sample. The elderly comprise about one-tenth.

The social class composition of the sample is indicated by distributions on family income and education. Income is the most commonly used indicator of socioeconomic status. Results show the relatively high income level in Orange County. In 1983 only 14 percent of families earned less than $15,000. A large majority (63 percent) earned more than $25,000, and 18 percent had incomes over $50,000. Income level in Orange County rose between 1982 and 1983. In the former year a larger percentage (17 percent) earned under $15,000, while fewer (58 percent) made over $25,000. The 1983 educational level showed that only 5 percent of the adult population had not graduated from high school; 69 percent had at least some college. This status indicator also rose between 1982 and 1983. In 1982, 9 percent had not completed high school and 63 percent had some college or were college graduates. Thus, the 1982 and 1983 surveys show Orange County to be relatively high in social class and to be rising in socioeconomic status over time.

In terms of family and residential variables, the distribution of living arrangements for the sample is presented in the table. A majority was married. In 1983 29 percent were married with children and 27 percent were married without children. Seven percent were single living alone. Six percent were one-parent households, and 10 percent were formerly married living alone. The remainder are in a variety of other living

Table 1.1 The 1982 and 1983 Orange County Annual Surveys

	1982 (N = 1,009)	1983 (N = 1,003)
Respondent's Age		
Under 25	17%	15%
25 to 34	25	25
35 to 44	21	23
45 to 54	15	14
55 to 64	11	13
65 or over	11	10
Total	100%	100%
Respondent's education		
Some high school or less	9%	5%
High school graduate	28	26
Some college	32	36
College graduate or more	31	33
Total	100%	100%
Annual household income		
Under $15,000	17%	14%
$15,000 to $25,000	25	23
$26,000 to $35,000	22	21
$36,000 to $50,000	20	24
Over $50,000	16	18
Total	100%	100%
Household arrangement		
Married couple with children	33%	29%
Married couple without children	23	27
Single, living alone	7	7
Formerly married, living alone	10	11
One parent with children	6	6
Other arrangements	21	20
Total	100%	100%
Length of residence		
2 years or less	37%	32%
3 to 5 years	23	23
6 to 10 years	16	18
More than 10 years	24	27
Total	100%	100%
Household size		
1 person	16%	18%
2 people	32	31
3 people	22	21
4 people	18	20
5 or more people	12	10
Total	100%	100%

arrangements. The statistics suggest a minority of nuclear families and great diversity in living arrangements.

The figures on length of residence show that about one-third has lived at the current address for 2 years or less and about one fourth for 3 to 5 years. Half the population has lived at the current address for 6 years or more, with a substantial number in the more than 10 years category. These are indications of both turnover and stability in residential location. Household size indicates that 2-person households are the modal category. About one in six respondents lives alone. However, over half the respondents live in households with 3 or more persons: the average household size is about 2.8 persons. These statistics on household size combined with the figures on parents with children again show a variety of living arrangements and the lack of predominance of the suburban nuclear family.

Statistics from the 1982 and 1983 surveys help provide a further profile of Orange County respondents. The 1982 survey indicated a predominantly white population. Origins were scattered, with only 8 percent of the respondents born in Orange County, 20 percent born in Los Angeles County, 9 percent born in other California counties, 55 percent from other states, and 8 percent foreign-born. Seventy-one percent were employed either full time or part time. Of those who work, 46 percent were in professional white collar jobs. The 1983 survey indicated that the husband as sole wage earner is not the only marital arrangement. In 29 percent of the marriages both spouses worked full time, and in another 15 percent of the marriages one spouse worked full time and the other part time. In one-third of the marriages there was only one wage earner, and the remaining marriages had neither partner working. These findings also point to a white and middle class majority and yet diverse and changing suburban households.

In summary, the Orange County population is characterized by a high socioeconomic level and is rising in status over time. There is also more social heterogeneity than current images of suburbia suggest.

Concluding Comments on National Trends

Urban deconcentration, which has been an ongoing demographic and economic shift for decades, is the root cause of suburbanization. Various countertrends that theoretically could have threatened the suburban momentum have actually had little influence.

There is every indication that the suburbs nationally have reached a new and more complicated stage. They now represent the dominant community form. There are complex versions of the suburbs that stretch previous simplistic definitions. A new round of problems has emerged, some similar to urban problems yet adapted to the suburban landscape. The solutions would seem to require some innovative approaches that reflect the suburban character. All this has raised anew debates about the future of the suburbs. Will they continue to be a viable alternative to cities, or will they more and more resemble the city environments that people left?

This book presents a perspective arguing that suburbs represent a unique community form with many challenges. Neither the utopian image nor the urban decay prophecies seem to fit. Rather, the dominant suburban form today has special features, and special problems associated with them. The six challenges examined in the chapters that follow represent pervasive issues that face the suburbs on a national scale.

What follows in this book is fairly exhaustive research on the modern-day suburbs. Evidence from empirical sources is presented to confirm the existence of these six types of problems. Some of the proof is descriptive; other evidence is longitudinal, comparative, or across groups. The issues addressed call for the examination of census reports, local records, residents' interviews, and government officials' reports of their actions.

Another issue is the approach that intensely analyzes surveys from one major California suburb. Is it proper, first of all, to assume that national trends can be found in a single place? And isn't Orange County different from the rest of the country? I have argued that the six challenges I noted earlier are problems facing all suburban regions. There is no reason to assume that they are not present in California. In fact, Orange County has the bimodal distribution of suburbs found elsewhere. It contains the post–World War II "bedroom communities" serving as central city satellites and the post-1960 "all purpose communities" with a mix of residential, commercial, and industrial functions. California has the varieties of peoples, housing, and activities that are operating in all suburban centers. Orange County, as has been shown, is also socially diverse.

Whether the empirical findings in Orange County, California, can be applied to other areas is an important question that will be addressed throughout the book. Whenever possible, data from other regions and from state and national studies will be considered to help verify the empirical results presented. I will also offer some asides as to problems which I think are more strictly Californian, or Sunbelt in origin, or issues exacerbated by phenomena particular to Orange County. However, for the most part the results of this study represent a scenario for suburbia. Orange County, California, has many advantages in climate, wealth, diversity, innovation, and age over other suburban areas. Thus, concerns that are evident there are likely to be more notable elsewhere. Likewise, problem-solving in this suburb is probably more promising than in the nation as a whole because individuals' personal resources are greater. The discovery of a suburban transformation in this California suburb thus sends a clear signal as to the spread of new concerns. The caution, if any, is that the observations made in Orange County, California, may somewhat understate the more general case.

Notes

1. Fifty seven percent of the Orange County population lives in the north county and 43 percent in the south county. The sample is weighted to reflect the actual

geographic distribution of the population. Further discussion of the methods are found in technical reports dated September 24, 1982, and August 9, 1983, available through the author.

2. After a discovery of possible coding errors, a small number of interviews in 1983 was replaced with data collected on September 22, 1983 with no change in the results. The response rate information is based solely on the July 1983 interviews.

CHAPTER TWO

The Housing Crisis
in Suburbia

Millions of people have moved to the suburbs in the last two decades. Housing developments have replaced the empty wastelands outside the city limits. Shopping centers have taken the place of orange groves and strawberry patches. Major highways and arteries have covered over the country roads. The bulldozer has come to symbolize the suburban revolution, indicating the swiftness, power, and permanence of this change. More recently, rapid growth and industrialization, in combination with ongoing trends in the American economy, have created changes in the basic landscape and goals associated with suburban life. One crucial area of concern is housing. The particular focus of this chapter is housing because it has been a major factor in suburban growth. Evidence is presented that there are recent and major events in the housing realm which can affect suburbia's future.

Burgess (1925) observed more than 50 years ago that residents of the "commuter's zone," outside the central city, had the highest rates of homeownership in the metropolitan area. Suburbia from the 1920s through World War II tended to be white, middle class, family oriented, and socially homogeneous. Land use patterns were low density, nonindustrial, and primarily residential.

The early roots of the mass movement to suburbia for housing can be found in the turmoil of the 1930s and 1940s. A deep economic depression turned back the clock on progress for many Americans, and was followed by a worldwide war. The threat of depression subsided, the soldiers returned from overseas, and attention turned from "guns" to "butter." Great optimism spread about the future, and the strength of our political and economic system. Perceptions focused on outgrowing the past and a search for broader horizons. American consumers expected a better quality of life filled with creature comforts, and had a sense that government and private industry ought to pave the way toward their goal. Suburbia, in a sense, was the Shangri-la, the heart of these exhilarating dreams of post–World War II America.

Beyond the historical events, there are cultural factors that relate to housing. American has a strong rural folklore. Small-town living and the country atmosphere are highly praised. All things urban are considered foreign, unhealthy, and, at the utmost, unnatural. We are a nation of pioneers and immigrants, footloose and willing most of all to break new ground and follow new trails. There is a built-in bias against the crowding of city life. The cultural norm, in fact, is for spaciousness and privacy. Unlike our Western European counterparts, and our economic partners in Asia, the average American disdains the urban world and values land, few neighbors, and owning a house in the country (Fuguitt and Zuiches 1975). Of course, practicalities such as work and transport prevent the cultural value from being fulfilled in most cases. The American suburb was an outgrowth of this fantasy. Housing away from the city was mass-produced to a large and waiting market, and suburbia became the realistic outlet for the American dream.

The basic economic facts that allowed housing development in suburbia cannot be forgotten. The nation after World War II was prosperous, and a good deal of money was spent creating a residential form that is, by world and historical standards, wasteful and opulent. The federal government was on a spending spree that included road building and home mortgages for military service veterans. The private sector, including bankers and developers, had the capital to invest huge sums of money in new homes and communities. The citizens, seeing nothing but good times ahead, were bullish on consumption of housing, automobiles, and all the necessary accoutrements. Such a massive change in developing communities, all the concrete poured and furniture stowed in moving vans, could not have occurred with a weak economy. The surplus of money seeking investments, and a daring spirit guiding its use, fueled the suburban explosion.

At the same time, there was pressure on the housing supply. The returning military were reentering family lives and starting new families, seeking housing in a market that had been flat in the war economy. New household formation fueled the demand for new dwelling units. There also seemed to be an urgency to rebuild the nuclear family, perhaps because children had been postponed during the war years, which grew into what today is called the baby boom era. The growth of the middle class family, with one adult full-time worker, one adult at home, and at least two children, called for a new residential form. The suburbs seemed ideally matched to the nuclear family's housing needs.

In the 1950s, suburban development expanded rapidly. The migration to the suburbs was still white, middle class, and family oriented (Farley 1976). Mass production of owner-occupied dwellings, relatively inexpensive land, increasing salaries and wages, and reasonable financing assured the many home seekers that they could achieve low-density residences and homeownership in suburbia (Baldassare 1981). In fact, lower middle class neighborhoods (Berger 1960; Gans 1967) as well as professional middle class neighborhoods (Whyte 1956) began to emerge. They both reflected the predominance of single-family, owner-occupied dwellings. The goal of owning one's own home and the temporary status of renting were broadly held beliefs.

Suburbia drew even greater number of people during the 1960s. Several factors led to the large suburban migration but most important of them was the housing stock. Much of the movement of the population from city to suburb, in retrospect, appeared to be for larger and better housing rather than for job reasons (Long 1972). As children were conceived or grew older, families outgrew their living quarters and thus became dissatisfied with their city housing (Baldasare 1979; Chevan 1971; Michelson 1976; Morris and Winter 1975; Rossi 1956). In short, the housing in demand by city residents was different from the housing supply that existed in cities. Suburbia offered the housing they most wanted. Its housing was large and affordable because land costs were low. The mass production of new homes made the most modern detached dwellings available to a large market. Coincidentally, banks offered long-term mortgages with low interest rates.

But suburbia began to undergo dramatic social and economic transformations during the 1970s and 1980s that have consequences for both the housing stock and housing costs, the main factors being rapid growth and industrialization. The movement of commerce, manufacturing, and branch offices to suburbia has been well demonstrated (see Kasarda 1972, 1976, 1978, 1980). Employment opportunities once located in central cities relocated or expanded into the surrounding areas. New jobs and regional relocations also occurred with greater frequency in suburban counties. The growth of suburban industry, coupled with a residential population, has meant a change in activity patterns for metropolitan populations. The suburb-to-city commute, for work and goods and services, has gradually given way to predominantly suburb-to-suburb commuting. Suburbs today contain major employers and industries.

Suburban industrialization has had direct repercussions for the dominance of single-family, owner-occupied dwellings. Land costs have increased as competition for existing open space among residential, commercial, and industrial developers has grown. As the price of land rises, pressure for intense resi-

dential development has occurred. Residential densities in suburbia have thus increased at faster rates than in central cities
(Baldassare 1981). The demand for housing created by rapid
growth has also affected costs. Many more people are relocating
to suburbia for job-related reasons, and the supply of housing
has not always kept pace.

There are values and preferences which complicate the
current transformation of housing alternatives in suburbia. This
is despite the fact that the new middle class migrants and many
existing residents are denied easy access to homeownership.
Americans have a long-standing preference for low-density,
single-family homes, and homeownership (Fuguitt and Zuiches
1975; Henretta 1984; Logan and Collver 1983; Perin 1977;
Tremblay and Dillman 1983). Suburban areas offered these
residential amenities earlier and Americans have come to expect them from suburban areas. This value preference is also
evident in the strong prejudice against anything but the single-
family home. Middle class residents have gone so far as to exclude high-density housing and rentals from their communities
(Baldassare and Protash 1982; Danielson 1976; Danielson and
Doig 1982; Frieden 1979). Recent suburban residents have a
dilemma. They are faced with values in favor of the single-
family home and homeownership; yet, increasingly, the economics of the housing market are in opposition.

Suburban Realities:
Homeownership and Housing Costs

The suburbs virtually cornered the market in single-family
dwellings. They have also been frequent sites of large homes
and private outdoor space. This housing package has, until
now, been available to many Americans who desire it. But
current data suggest that the goal has recently become more
elusive.

The price of homeownership, in fact, has dramatically

increased. Nationally new single-family homes sold for $20,000 in 1965 and for $68,900 in 1981. Suburban areas followed this trend, with prices tripling from $20,800 in 1970 to $62,700 in 1980. There has also been a decline of first-time homebuyerrs from 45 percent of all sales in 1976 to 33 percent of all sales in 1980. At the same time, first-buyers' reliance on relatives for down payments increased from 20 percent to 33 percent (U.S. Bureau of the Census 1983). These trends are confirmed in more recent studies of major metropolitan areas (U.S. League of Savings 1984). National events such as inflation, real estate speculation, and the baby boom cohort's search for new housing coupled with suburbia's industrialization and rapid growth have had noticeable effects.

Housing costs increased markedly in California. Between 1967 and 1978 the average price of existing homes rose from $31,700 to $100,200 in Los Angeles. At those times home prices in Orange County were increasing but always lower, that is, $23,300 and $81,100. The cost difference gave a competitive advantage to the housing supply in the suburbs. The factors accounting for the explosive housing prices of California are similar to those found nationally. The 1980s marked the end of the price advantage for the California suburbs. In 1982 the average existing home sale was $131,000 in Orange County, $110,000 in the Los Angeles area, and $101,000 in San Diego (California 1983). The annual principal and interest rates, assuming a 20 percent down payment and a 30-year term, changed from $1,300 to $15,800 between 1965 and 1982. For resale homes housing payments as a percentage of income increased from 14 percent in 1965 to 24 percent in 1977 and, lastly, to 45 percent in 1982 (Center for Economic Research 1983).

One consequence of suburban housing costs must certainly be restricted entry into the ranks of homeowners. In previous times, down payments were relatively small, interest rates were low, and monthly mortgage costs for a 30-year loan were within many people's budgets. Only those in low income brackets could be denied homeownership. Today, all this has changed. Current income does not always cover even the average monthly mortgage cost. Lifetime savings are not always enough for housing down payments. Middle class families who are eager to buy a home, because they want more space or more privacy, are not necessarily able to do so. The chances that one will be a homeowner in the suburbs today more often depend on how long one has been a resident rather than on other social factors or economic circumstances.

A related consequence of the housing price spiral is a "less for more" situation for the new suburban homebuyer. A greater proportion of one's income is devoted to home payments than in the past. The actual house one purchases today probably has less space and amenities than a less expensive house purchased, for example, five to ten years ago. Recent homebuyers making the transition from rentals to homeownership are thus unlikely to experience great improvements in space and amenities after they move. Compared to earlier first-time homebuyers, they must settle for less housing and higher costs. As a result, new homebuyers may also be less satisfied with their residences than longer-term homeowners.

Another factor that has changed markedly is what determines monthly mortgage costs. Differences in housing costs in the past were largely explained by how much individuals or families could afford. Wealthy people would pay more than the less affluent in order to achieve a higher quality of housing. More rooms, a better location, and a detached dwelling would also account for cost differences. All these rules of suburban real estate have been altered by the recent increase in housing prices. How long one has owned a home has much to do with the monthly payment. In brief, the housing costs of suburban homeowners now have less to do with their income or type or size of dwelling than with when the house was purchased.

Thus, financial circumstances, life cycle, and housing character are today less significant factors in explaining ability and costs of owning a suburban home than they once were. The timing of the search for suburban housing with the suburban transformation explains more.

Suburban Dreams: Housing Type and Homeownership

The rising costs of suburban homeownership have certainly placed great economic burdens on new homeowners. But the new homeowners, in some ways, must be considered fortunate, since they have managed homeownership. To many Americans today, this is a major accomplishment.

Owning a single-family home has proved to be more elusive for many categories of people. These are the young singles who, having moved out of their parents' homes, have started work and rented an apartment. These are the young marrieds who are renting and saving their money for future home purchasing. They are also families with young children who, facing a lack of space in their rental unit, are searching for suitable accommodations. From the perspective of the American dream, these are households on the outside looking in.

One would expect a high level of frustration on the part of these renters in search of homeownership. Some will have to wait longer than they have anticipated to reach their housing goal. Others will feel that their housing preferences have to be scaled down considerably. Still others will give up any realistic expectation of obtaining their own home, in any form whatsoever, in the near future. What seems to make matters worse for the relatively deprived renter is that the hope of ownership does not subside much. Even with the greater cost and lesser likelihood of homeownership, the average person, in terms of preferences and desires, still considers the owner-occupied dwelling an important goal. Renting is viewed as temporary, transient, and socially undesirable.

Several factors mentioned earlier about housing costs must discourage the typical American who hopes to become a first-time homebuyer. The news that housing costs are outstripping personal means must be a serious disappointment to many current renters, especially those without great extended family resources, meaningful savings, and potential for large wage increases.

The situation in the suburban housing market affects both potential migrants and current residents. City residents wanting homeownership and single-family housing outside urban boundaries are discouraged. But the frustration may be even greater among the suburban renters. Those present in that setting who do not achieve ownership are likely to feel deprived relative to the city renter and the suburban home-owner. Renting is a more peculiar phenomenon in the suburbs than in the city, and suburban renters are likely to feel more at odds with their surrounding culture. A permanent middle class renting population exists in major cities, but such a class is not considered part of the suburban landscape. Finally, there is one more reason why suburban renting may be particularly frustrating. Many suburban renters are new migrants who, rather than arranging housing before a job-related move, decided to live temporarily in an apartment. The hope, dashed once information about the local housing market became known, was that homeownership will occur within a reasonable time.

A new occurrence, then, is that many suburban renters believe that homeownership is improbable. Nonetheless, most individuals still aspire to the dream. One would also assume that expectations for homeownership vary within the suburban renter population. A life-cycle perspective is usually considered in analyses of changing housing choices (Rossi 1956; Morris and Winter 1975). For instance, young families who rent would be considered primary candidates for homeownership, given their growing need for space and privacy. However, current suburban realities would suggest a new set of priorities. The economic conditions of households, such as family income and two-career household status, would dominate expectations of homeownership. Life cycle would be relatively insignificant.

There is an interesting implication of the desire to own a home being strong and the expectations of achieving it being low. That is the possibility that people will compromise their ideals. It is not likely that the wish for homeownership will disappear. But perhaps people will accept a scaled-down version of their wish to own a single-family home. In other words, the desire to own a home may be strong enough to entice renters to purchase small homes. Stated preferences may not change, but realistic goals may be altered.

Hypotheses

The first hypothesis to be tested is that homeownership by suburban residents is largely a function of the length of residence. The shorter the length of residence, the more likely it is that the suburbanite rents rather than owns a dwelling. Also, suburbanites who have recently made rent-to-own transitions are receiving less in housing and are more dissatisfied than are those who made rent-to-own transitions earlier.

The second hypothesis is that recent homeowners have higher housing costs than other homeowner groups. Monthly housing costs of homeowners are largely explained by length of residence rather than income or housing characteristics. Also, length of residence plays a less significant role in rental costs than in mortgage costs.

The third is that suburban residents continue overwhelmingly to favor the single-family home, and most renters desire to own a home. However, most who desire to own a home are pessimistic that this goal will be reached. Family status and social status are not as important as economic resources and financial satisfaction in accounting for optimism toward homeownership.

The fourth hypothesis is that most suburban renters are willing to compromise their ideal housing for a small and affordable home that they can own. The small owner-occupied home thus has a broad appeal among various social and economic groups.

Methods

The 1982 survey conducted with residents of Orange County, California, contained information about current homeownership, previous homeownership, housing type preference, and renters' attitudes toward homebuying. The 1983 survey included questions about current homeownership, housing costs, and renters' attitudes toward buying a small home.

In many ways the housing conditions in Orange County are symptomatic of suburbs throughout the nation. The growth of population has been rapid. Industrialization has diversified the social groups and land use in the area. Residential densities have increased. The residents are still primarily white, homeowners, middle class, and family oriented. The issue of housing costs, and especially the affordability of homes for first-time homebuyers, is somewhat exaggerated because of the California coastal location. Yet, living costs are comparable to elsewhere and income levels are somewhat higher. The findings from Orange County should be generalizable, and at least forecast what may occur in numerous American suburbs.

Five questions pertinent to the hypotheses about housing in suburbia were asked in the 1982 survey. One asked, "Do you own or rent your present residence?" Those who rented were then asked two attitude questions. The first was, "Do you hope to someday own a home?" Answers were yes or no. For those who answered yes a follow-up question asked, "Realistically, how likely is it that within the next three years you will own your own home?" Possible answers were very likely, somewhat likely, and not at all likely.

Another attitude question was asked of all respondents: "If you had a choice, what type of dwelling would you prefer to live in?" The possible answers were single-family detached house, single-family attached house, apartment, mobile home, and other. The categories corresponded to a question on dwelling type asked elsewhere in the survey.

Finally, questions about the previous residence were asked only of residents who had lived in their dwellings 10 years or less. One question in particular was relevant in this series: "Did you own or rent your previous residence?" Other questions included dwelling size, location, and number of people in the previous dwelling.

The 1983 survey asked four questions that were directly relevant to testing the hypotheses about suburban housing. The first was a repetition of the question on owning versus renting. Then homeowners were asked, "What is the category of your monthly mortgage payment (not including taxes and insurance)?" The categories were under $350, $350–$500, $501–$750, $751–$1,000, $1,001–$1,250, $1,251–$2,000, and more than $2,000. Renters were asked, "What is your monthly rental payment?" The categories were under $250, $251–$500, $501–$750, $751–$1,000, and more than $1,000.

Renters were also asked a homebuying preference question: "Would you buy a small home in Orange County if you could afford the monthly payments?" Answers were yes and no.

The initial task was to understand whether homeownership in suburbia is declining among more recent residents. Homeownership rates were determined among different length-of-residence groups using the 1983 survey. Then, the relative significance of length of residence in explaining homeownership was considered with 8 other factors, through a stepwise multiple regression procedure that entered the most powerful explanatory factor first, the next most powerful second, and each remaining factor in order of significance until all variables were entered into the regression equation. The other factors considered were family income, age, education, marital status, household size, current dwelling type, and number of rooms in the dwelling.

Homeownership attainment was explored further with the subsample of the 1982 survey that made rent-to-own transitions in the last 10 years. Recent homebuyers were contrasted with longer-term homebuyers in terms of their objective characteristics and subjective attitudes. Objective characteristics examined for changes over time included number of rooms, persons per room, and whether there is more room in the current dwelling than was noted for the previous rental dwelling (i.e., a greater number of rooms). Persons per room is calculated simply by dividing the number of persons by the number of rooms. Subjective characteristics include self-reports about how satisfied the respondent was with finances, housing, neighborhood, and family life. Mean scores were determined for each characteristic with different length-of-residence categories. Significant differences due to length of residence were determined through analyses of variance and analyses of covariance.

Housing costs were analyzed from the mortgage payments and rental costs reported in the 1983 survey. The immediate task was to analyze changes over time, using the length-of-residence variable. Then, the relative importance of length of residence in predicting housing costs was contrasted with other factors in the same process used to analyze length of residence as a predictor of homeownership. The stepwise regression procedure was repeated with the same 8 variables to rank-order them as predictors of mortgage payments and then rental costs. These factors were then used as control variables in further assessing the relationship between housing costs and length of residence.

Renters' attitudes toward homebuying were examined in several stages. First, the proportion of renters who wished to own a home in the 1982 survey was measured. Whether the desire to own a home is different within certain population segments was analyzed. The proportion of residents in 1982 who preferred different dwelling types was also examined. The results point to the strength of homeownership and the single-family house in suburbia.

The next renters' attitude to be considered was the expectation of owning a home in the near future. Life cycles and social status, as compared with purely economic resources, were examined as explanations of the perceived likelihood of joining the homeowner ranks. Mean scores in different subgroups were considered and analyses of covariance determined the significant factors.

The last renters' attitude toward homebuying explored was willingness to purchase a small home, through analysis of a 1983 survey question. Predictors of this preference were considered, including life cycle, social status, and housing and economic factors. Each factor was considered separately and examined in an analysis of variance and then an analysis of covariance. The results indicated the extent of support for purchasing a small home and the social groups most favorably disposed toward this particular option.

Findings

The Attainment of Homeownership

In the 1983 survey, 62 percent of households were owner-occupied. This is typical of nationwide homeownership rates in suburban areas. Most interesting is the discrepancy in homeownership rates between different length-of-residence groups. The sample was divided into four groups: most recent residents (2 years or less), recent (3 to 5 years), long term (6 to 10 years), and longest term (more than 10 years). Figure 2.1 shows that recent residents are experiencing very different rates of homeownership. Only 25 percent of the most recent residents are homeowners, contrasted with 66 percent of recent, 79 percent of long term, and 88 percent of longest term.

A stepwise regression involving key factors in predicting homeownership confirmed the importance of recent residence for discouraging owner occupancy (see table 2.1). Eight variables in all were considered. Only dwelling type (i.e., single-family detached versus others) was a better predictor of home ownership. Length of residence was a more important explanation of owner occupancy than family income, number of rooms, age, marital status, educational attainment, or household size.[1] Approximately one-fourth of the total variance for homeownership was explained by length of residence.

In a separate analysis, length of residence was entered

The Housing Crisis in Suburbia

Percent
homeowners

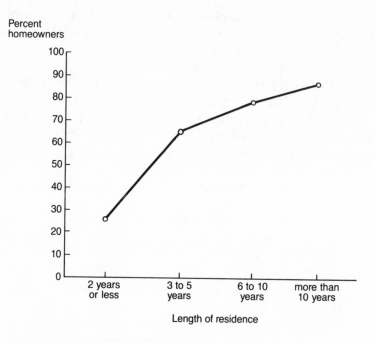

SOURCE is the 1983 Orange County Annual Survey.

Figure 2.1 Homeownership Rates and Length of Residence

first into the eight-variable equation. It accounted accounted
for 25 percent of the total variance. Even when length of residence was entered last, it was still highly significant and explained much of the variance. In sum, low homeownership
rates are strongly related to recent residence.

Other trends in homebuying were evident in the 1982
survey, from which it was possible to analyze all residents who
had made rent-to-own transitions in the last 10 years. There
were 146 respondents who fell into this group, divided into 3
length-of residence categories: 2 years or less, 3 to 5 years, and
6 to 10 years.

Objective characteristics of the homebuying population
considered over time include the average number of rooms,

Table 2.1 Predicting Homeownership and Housing Costs

	Homeownership (N = 1,003)			Mortgage Payment (N = 622)			Rental Payment (N = 381)		
	Step entered	Significance	Variance	Step entered	Significance	Variance	Step entered	Significance	Variance
Family income	3	.001	5.5	2	.001	17.5	1	.001	15.0
Education	7	NS	0.0	8	NS	0.0	7	NS	0.2
Age	5	.001	1.3	7	NS	0.0	8	NS	0.1
Marital Status	6	NS	0.1	4	.01	0.7	5	NS	0.5
Length of residence	2	.001	10.2	1	.001	43.6	2	.001	8.5
Household size	8	NS	0.0	5	.05	0.3	4	.01	1.1
Dwelling type	1	.001	27.3	6	NS	0.0	6	NS	0.3
Number of rooms	4	.001	2.0	3	.001	1.4	3	.001	4.7
Total—all factors	—	.001	46.4	—	.001	63.5	—	.001	30.4

SOURCE is the 1983 Orange County Annual Survey. Statistics reported for the results of a stepwise regression equation with the most powerful variable entered before other variables. Total refers to the final equation including all 8 factors.

persons per room, and whether there were more rooms in the house bought than in the previous rental. Recent homebuyers are living at higher person-per-room densities than earlier homebuyers; .87 to .67 to .62. Recent homebuyers also purchased fewer rooms in their dwellings than earlier homebuyers: 4.45 to 4.91 to 5.15. These findings were significant at .05 or less after controlling for education, sex, marital status, household size, and dwelling type. The other trend did not reach this level of significance but is worth noting. Those reporting that there was more room in the new dwelling declined over time: 56 percent to 63 percent to 82 percent.

The subjective characteristics include 4 items each on 4-point scales on housing, neighborhood, family, and financial satisfaction. Higher scores indicate more dissatisfaction. More recent homebuyers have less housing satisfaction than earlier homebuyers: 1.43 to 1.55 to 1.23. Recent homebuyers similarly have higher levels of neighborhood dissatisfaction: 1.53 to 1.63 to 1.29. It is interesting that recent homebuyers have more family dissatisfaction than those who bought homes earlier: 1.50 to 1.21 to 1.20. All these differences are significant at .02 or less even after education, sex, marital status, household size, and dwelling type are controlled for. Financial satisfaction does not vary with length of residence.

Housing Costs

Monthly housing costs are examined with the 1983 survey. The median mortgage cost is $450 and the median rent is $445. Figure 2.2 details the average rental and mortgage payments for the 4 previously used length-of-residence categories.

The median mortgage costs are respectively $954, $710, $400, and $239. Monthly costs for the most recent owners are four times greater than for the longest-term owners.

Median rental payments over time are respectively, $474, $437, $411, and $308 (see figure 2.2). Rental payments for the most recent residents are only half the monthly mortgage payments for the most recent homeowners. Further, long-term renters actually pay 20 percent more than long-

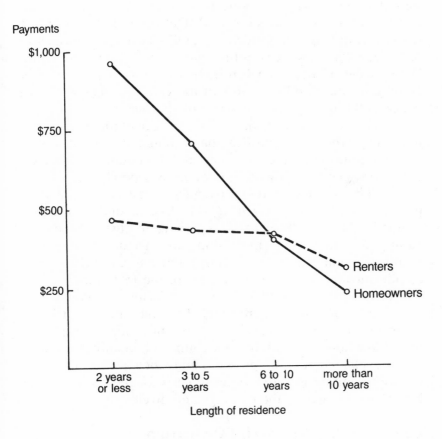

SOURCE is the 1983 Orange County Annual Survey.

Figure 2.2 Housing Payments and Length of Residence

term homeowners. Also, the most recent renters are paying only 50 percent more than the longest-term renters.

Table 2.1 presents the results of an analysis that attempts to predict monthly mortgage payments, by the same regression method used to predict homeownership. The best predictor of one's monthly mortgage payment is the time in the dwelling.

Recent homeowners pay more than others. Two-thirds of the explained variance and 43.6 percent of the total variance, are derived from length of residence. Family income is a weak second, adding 17.5 percent to the total variance explained. Other factors have relatively small roles as causal factors.[2] Even after accounting for all other factors in the equation, length of residence still explains 37.1 percent of the variance. Its unique influence is thus confirmed. The significance of the relationship is startling when one considers that a suburban resident's earnings and housing characteristics are not as important in predicting housing costs as is when the home was purchased.

The predictors of rental payments, analyzed by the same process, are also summarized in table 2.1. The findings are substantially different from those regarding mortgage payments. Family income is the most important factor in predicting monthly rental cost. More affluent renters pay higher rents. Family income explains 15 percent of the total variance and half of the variance explained by all 8 factors. Length of residence accounts for 8.5 percent of the total variance. It is the second most important factor, with recent residents again paying higher housing costs, but it accounts for about half as much of the explained variance as does family income,[3] with number of rooms coming in third. Housing costs for rentals thus seem highly determined by the earnings and dwelling size.

Renters' Attitudes Toward Ownership

The 1982 survey asked all renters (36 percent of the sample) if they hoped some day to own a home. Seventy-eight percent of all renters answered yes. Thus, the belief that residents have adjusted their values to reflect current circumstances is not valid. This high proportion desiring homeownership cuts across most social and economic groups. There were few types of people who wanted to be counted out as house-hunters. The poor, the aged, retired persons, and divorced and widowed persons do not hope for homeownership. One might assume that the increase in single-person households, childless couples, and nonmarried individuals in suburbia would lessen the demand for homeownership. These groups, however, wanted home-ownership to the same extent as others. Those interested in homeownership today represent a broad cross-section of suburbia. It is thus doubtful that housing costs have discouraged desires.

Renters who hoped to own a home were questioned about the likelihood of homeownership in the next three years. Twenty-three percent viewed homeownership as very likely in the near future. Thus, fewer than one in four renters who want to own homes (or one in six of all renters) strongly expect to do so shortly. Thirty percent viewed homeownership as somewhat likely, and 47 percent thought it not at all likely. There is great pessimism about achieving homeownership in the current housing market.

One important issue is the household characteristics of renters who see homeownership in their futures. The housing literature in sociology usually suggests that life cycle and social status determine the shift from renting to homeownership. Young couples and white collar families with children would then be more likely to expect homeownership than others. Accordingly, differences in homeownership expectations were explored.

Table 2.2 summarizes the critical results. Having a child in the home does not increase the expectation of homeownership. Nor does being white collar. Life cycle and social status thus appear somewhat irrelevant. Family income clearly separates those with higher expectations from those with lower expectations. Those with incomes in excess of $35,000 annually were more likely to expect homeownership in the future than those with lower income levels. It is interesting that renters of detached single-family dwellings were also more optimistic than others. Economic resources are the determining factor. These findings remain after controlling for marital status, age, length of residence, education, and sex.

Table 2.2 also suggests that attitude domains are associated with homeownership expectation. Those who are "very" and "somewhat" satisfied with their finances contrast with

Table 2.2 Renters' Attitudes Toward Homeownership

Homeownership Pessimism[a]

		Mean	Significance
Children	No	1.78	
	Yes	1.75	NS
Occupation	Professional	1.77	
	Nonprofessional	1.76	NS
Income	$35,000 or less	1.80	
	More than $35,000	1.53	.001
Type of dwelling	Detached home	1.72	
	Other	1.82	.05
Financial satisfaction	Satisfied	1.74	
	Dissatisfied	1.88	.01
TOTAL SAMPLE (N = 276)		1.77	

Acceptance of Small Homes[b]

		Mean	Significance
Rental payment	$500 or less	1.67	
	More than $500	1.88	.001
Full-time workers	1 or none	1.74	
	2 or more	1.86	.01
Household size	1 person	1.58	
	2 persons	1.78	
	3 or more persons	1.84	.001
Age	18 to 35	1.86	
	Over 35	1.60	.001
Type of dwelling	Detached home	1.81	
	Other	1.69	.01
TOTAL SAMPLE (N = 321)		1.75	

[a]SOURCE is the 1982 Orange County Annual Survey. Higher means indicate lower expectations of homeownership. Significance based upon analyses of variance.
[b]SOURCE is the 1983 Orange County Annual Survey. Higher means indicate more acceptability of small homes. Significance based upon analyses of variance.

those who are "very" and "somewhat" dissatisfied. Those with financial satisfaction felt more positively about achieving home-ownership. This probably reflects their feelings about their earnings, expendable income, and potential for future income gains. The finding remained after controlling for marital status, age, length of residence, education, and sex.

If most renters believe that owning a home is beyond their reach in the current housing market, to what extent are they willing to compromise their optimum goals? In the 1982 survey over 80 percent of all residents said they preferred the detached dwelling. In that year only 57 percent of all residents actually lived in detached dwellings. Many people are already compromising their values.

The following year's survey sought to pursue this topic further. Renters in in the 1983 survey were presented with a housing choice that was a fairly realistic goal given current prices. Renters that year constituted 38 percent of the sample. The question was whether they would purchase a small home in Orange County if they could afford the monthly payments. The definition of "small" is left to the respondent's discretion. Seventy-five percent said they would be interested in buying a small home. This is confirmation that renters in suburbia still desire homeownership and are willing to make compromises in order to achieve it. It also indicates the relative importance of suburban homeownership in contrast with dwelling size.

One is tempted to believe that suburbanites who want small homes must be a special group of people, but numbers in acceptance of the proposition run against this interpretation. So does the analysis conducted, which explored the possibility that interest was among singles, poor people, or those living in small rental units. Family income had no effect on the willing-ness to purchase a small home. Neither did single versus mar-ried status, nor did the size of the current dwelling. The find-ings again reflect the broad appeal of affordable small homes.

There are factors that do predispose individuals who rent to accept purchase of a small home. Some are expected; others are not. The possibility that age, type of dwelling, household size, number of full-time workers, and rental payment affected the willingness to compromise one's housing goals was explored. The results are presented in table 2.2. Those paying rents in excess of $500 per month are more likely to favor a small home purchase than any other group. Economic concerns are also evident in that households with two or more full-time workers are more interested in homeownership. Age also has an effect, with younger persons more willing to purchase a small home than older persons. Household size has a somewhat opposite effect from what one might expect. Households with three or more persons are the most likely to favor small home purchases and one-person households are the least likely. Finally, those already living in detached single-family homes are more interested in homebuying. All these findings remain significant after controlling for length of residence, number of rooms, household size, marital status, and education.

The acceptance of tradeoffs to avoid rentals is fairly widespread. A majority of all groups noted in table 2.2 are interested in purchasing what would appear to be a nonideal housing type. Married couples, those renting larger dwellings, and the affluent are all likely prospects for purchase of small homes. The young nonapartment renters, high-rent households, and dual-worker households are somewhat more eager for small home purchases. The social value of homeownership in suburbia is very strong. People still want to be owners of single-family homes. But the changes in real circumstances and expectations are dramatic.

Concluding Comments
on the Housing Crisis

Suburbia has been a popular alternative to urban living since the 1940s. It will undoubtedly be the predominant residential location for the remainder of this century, for several reasons. Central cities have serious problems. As a result residents have sought other places in the metropolis. Foremost in their selection criteria has been an abundant stock of high-quality, spacious, and reasonably priced housing in suburbia. The American dream of homeownership typically was within reach of many migrants as the suburbs grew. This chapter has suggested a challenge to the almost taken-for-granted lure of suburbia, a threat to suburbia's continued popularity connected to new housing trends.

Suburban industrialization and rapid growth have had profound impacts on housing conditions. Land use has diversified, the population has become more heterogeneous, competition for the land has increased, and higher population densities have resulted. This suburban transformation has had obvious consequences for the housing market. National trends in the economy and housing market have also had an influence. Several new facts have emerged. Costs of owner-occupied dwellings have risen dramatically. Homeownership rates are quite low among the most recent residents. What new homebuyers receive in housing is less than what earlier homebuyers achieved and, apparently, all at a higher cost. The new distinction between the "haves" and "have nots" in suburban homeownership is not based upon income, but rather, upon time of entry to suburbia.

The basic goal of homeownership in suburbia is still prevalent. What is markedly in contrast to these desires is the expectation of owning a home. Most renters are not optimistic about the possibilities. These renters are not only poor families, or single adults, or the elderly, or those who reject the responsibilities of homeownership. Even renter groups we typically expect to join the homeowner population, such as young families with children and professionals, are not hopeful. Only the most economically advantaged believe they have a chance to obtain homeownership. Many who are residing in apartments have simply given up on the prospects of ever owning a home or even moving to a better residence. Housing conditions in California, and especially Orange County, may seem extreme. But in the rising land costs, high mortgage rates, and spiraling housing construction costs they are similar to other suburban areas.

A question that emerges from this study is whether social values toward housing will eventually change as a result of economic realities or, alternatively, whether economic realities can change so as to coincide with existing social values. It is obvious, in housing issues, that there is little room for change. Social values appear to strongly favor homeownership and single-family dwellings, despite the high costs and the unavailability of appropriate choices. And the economic situation in the housing market has reached such extremes in some suburbs that it is doubtful that costs can decline to the extent that the broad spectrum of the middle class can again afford large detached dwellings. Thus there are narrow acceptable and practical limits for those who can act to influence the suburban housing crisis.

A preferred solution to the current crisis is the development of small and affordable owner-occupied dwellings. A remarkable level of approval was noted among the renter population. Strong support was visible not only among the single population, childless couples, and elderly "empty nesters" but also among families and other renter groups for whom owner occupancy has become an impossibility. In suburbia, then, given a choice between space and ownership, the critical variable is ownership. It remains to be seen, of course, whether small homes can be built in sufficient numbers, with acceptable designs, in reasonable locations, and at affordable prices.

A major source of uncertainty involves suburban government's ability to prescribe, implement, and enforce plans for developing affordable and diverse housing. Suburban voters are currently in a fiscally conservative mood. Residents are generally unwilling to expand their government's role into private sector affairs and are even less anxious to commit tax revenues for housing development subsidies. It is also obvious that on any broad public scale the long-term suburban homeowners have little interest in supporting new residents' homeownership. Suburban governments also have structural disadvantages for solving problems within their boundaries. County govern-ments have limited influence outside the unincorporated areas and, in a multiplicity of municipal areas, each sets its own agenda. The opportunities for coordinated efforts to influence the housing supply are thus limited. Suburban government in-tervention in the housing market, such as the inclusionary zon-ing programs (Schwartz and Johnston 1983), have thus had little success.

The major response to the housing crisis in suburbia will thus probably come from the private sector. It is not known whether builders and developers will respond to the mismatch between housing realities and resident's ideals. If the challenge of the housing crisis is not met, migration into suburbia may decline and migration out may increase.

Notes

1. The beta weights for the final regression equation, considering only the sig-nificant factors for homeownership, are: dwelling type = .52; length of residence = .35; family income = .25; number of rooms = .18; and age = .13.

2. The beta weights for the final regression equation, considering only the sig-nificant factors for mortgage costs, are: length of residence = − .66; family income = .42; number of rooms = .14; marital status = .09; and household size = .07.

3. The beta weights for the significant factors from the final regression equation for rental costs are: family income = .39; length of residence = − .29; number of rooms = .25; and household size = .12.

CHAPTER THREE

Growth Controversies

There has been a broad awakening of sentiment against growth, and increasing skepticism that growth offers the average person a better life. This is evident in discussions of the worldwide population explosion, the dangers of environmental pollution, the stresses of urban overcrowding, and the hazards of rapid economic development (Baldassare 1979; Ehrlich 1968; Hirsch 1976; Shumacher 1977). It is also obvious in the writings of social theorists who claim that growth favors elites and landowners rather than the average citizens (Castells 1976; Harvey 1973). The subject of future growth is not unfamiliar to the suburbs. In fact, growth controversies have developed into social movements there in the last two decades.

No clear resolution is in sight. Sides have been chosen and each offers an impressive list of arguments and counterarguments. Some see the debate over future growth as the alignment of forces favoring the "public good" versus those favoring the "private good." The public good refers to the needs and well-being of the average citizen, while the private good in this instance speaks to the plans and profits of entrepreneurs and corporations. Growth must be halted, slowed down, or redirected according to its opponents because it does the general polity no good and perhaps has disruptive repercussions. The proponents reply that limits on development reward the status quo and stunt the prospects of those whose housing and job goals have not yet been reached.

Lurking close to the surface of the "public good" disagreement is a more fundamental question. The issue is the extent to which the government should be involved in the daily activities of citizens and businesses. Some argue that government intervention in the process of growth is a necessity. Without it, the public's welfare would be endangered by rapid and irrational development. The retort has often been that government has no place in the free market system. It can only do harm by interfering with businesses' efficient operations in providing housing and jobs for the people. There is serious strain between those who feel the need for protection from the free market system and the private sector that would like to operate without constraints.

Another facet of the growth conflict has been disagreement about growth's environmental and social consequences. The environmental and Earth Day movements have brought to consciousness the costs of growth. Water pollution, air pollution, toxic wastes, a scarcity of resources, and limits to how many people the land can support have become topics of discussion. The need to save the environmental quality of "Spaceship Earth" and to preserve, keep pure, use wisely, and recycle its material goods has been discussed. An anti-urban bias is sometimes expressed by the environmentalists. Some claim that enough "cityfying" has occurred; we need a "back to nature" and "small is beautiful" movement. Citizens caution the private sector that small, seemingly insignificant growth decisions, when placed together in a longer time frame, can have far-reaching repercussions. Growth's proponents have countered by exclaiming on the unreality of "turning back the clock" on industrial and urban progress.

Government policymakers have become increasingly aware that they directly influence the economy and population trends. Funding projects such as military bases, dams, power plants, roadways, and agricultural projects can make or break regional economies. The federal and state authorities thus have much influence, and so the debate rages as to whether government should consciously set limits and goals for future growth. Likewise, local governments affect growth through zoning practices and infrastructure funding decisions. Land set aside for nonindustrial uses affects the economy and population growth. Only in rare circumstances are American localities not affected by government's role.

The issue is, then, whether governments should conceive their policies' consequences more directly. Local policy-makers have lobbied for a more thoughtful approach to managing growth. In so doing, they have raised concern inside and outside of government about the use of new "growth management" tools. For example, there are very explicit "first generation" techniques for limiting growth, such as permit moratoria, buying open space, preserving privately owned undeveloped land, and instituting planning pauses. "Second generation" growth-control strategies would include creating urban service boundaries and imposing annual ceilings on permits, population, and urban services. Thus, some in government consider uncontrolled growth an anachronism from a more primitive development era and argue for the use of advanced planning methods. Many, however, cite the lack of proven effectiveness of growth management strategies.

The growth controversy, that is, whether or not residents want their community to grow, has become almost synonymous with suburbia. It has been manifest in debates over residential development because of rapid population growth. More recently, the issue of industrial expansion has also created conflicts. Many suburban areas have developed policies to limit size and influence their growth patterns (Alonso 1973; Morrison 1977). Danielson and Doig (1982) present several examples of exculsionary population practices in the New York metropolitan area. The Washington, D.C., suburbs have also been in the forefront of limiting growth and urban development (Dawson 1977). Danielson (1976) has noted exclusionary limitations throughout the suburban landscape in the United States. Perhaps mentioned most frequently are the planning practices, and controversies surrounding them, in Florida, Colorado, and California (Naisbitt 1982). Communities such as Petaluma, Boulder, and Boca Raton have been prototypes for the implementation of growth controls (Burrows 1978). At first, these were considered isolated cases to be understood only in their special local circumstances. As this is no longer the case, interest has increased in why the suburbs have considered and adopted restrictive growth policies (Baldassare 1981; Goddschalk 1977; Scott et al. 1975). The major reason seems to be citizen support for them. Popular support for growth controls has been evidenced in opinion surveys, local elections, and community leadership studies (Baldassare and Protash 1982; Neiman 1980; California 1980). Certain conditions in suburbia have led to antigrowth feelings.

One of the most obvious factors is population dynamics. Suburbs are, after all, where the population is growing. Further, it is evident that many communities are experiencing the kind of rapid growth that turns once-small towns, seemingly overnight, into bustling small cities. The type of growth now entrenched in the suburbs is perhaps cause for alarm as well. Developments have steadily become more dense—in other words, more urban—as condominium and apartment complexes have grown more frequent (Baldassare 1981). With these changing housing patterns has come the industrialization of suburbia, which has meant more mix in land use and more mix in social composition. Suburbs are growing, in short, in a way that is socially transforming. The strictly demographic explanation for growth controls in the suburbs is thus compelling. The prevalence of growth controversies in the most rapidly growing states during the most tumultuous period of suburban development offers crude evidence for this view.

A related explanation is that current rates of growth have had adverse consequences for residents' perceptions of the quality of life. Therefore, suburban residents have been eager to

support programs that limit future growth. There is a long tradition in urban sociology which suggests that growth and urbanization are disliked by residents. Burgess (1925), McKenzie
(1925), and Park (1925) speak of the breakdown of "community" and the emergence of social problems when places grow
rapidly. Larger, denser, more heterogeneous places may cause a
syndrome of declining community quality (Wirth 1938; Fischer
1984). The extent to which rapid growth affects residents' attitudes toward their community has been studied nationally.
Fear of crime and dissatisfaction with neighbors, roads, transportation, and accessibility are brought on by rapid suburban
growth (Baldassare 1981). Growth has had negative consequences for suburban residents who have experienced it. There
is little wonder, then, that they would support limits on future
growth.

Suburbanites' expectations have also been discussed as
reasons for growth controversies. Suburban residents are often
ex–city people who left for specific reasons. These include pull
factors such as improved housing and crime-free neighborhoods and push factors such as the perception that city conditions have deteriorated. These feelings heighten a sensitivity to
community change and a desire for the status quo, so that
there is support for the suburban government's exerting some
control over development. A general anti-urban sentiment may
also be pervasive in the suburbs. If so, residents would be more
likely to oppose all growth, viewing it as a step toward a more
"urban" existence and away from a more "rural" setting of
open space, greenery, and friendly informality.

Another evident factor is metropolitan geography. It is
very possible that suburbs consider the instituting of growth
controls, and so often adopt these tools, as means of countering
the central city's influence. Danielson and Doig (1982) argue
this point for the New York metropolitan area. All suburbs are
cognizant of the fact that central cities export their problems.
Very often central cities also attempt to expropriate, or annex,
suburban land. Various growth control measures are thus attempts to protect the territorial integrity of suburban communi-

ties. Encroachment from central city population per se, unde-
sired groups, unwanted industries, and municipal government
itself is avoided. Thus suburbs surrounding a growing urban
core, or a declining urban core, would rally around antigrowth
policies, though from somewhat different motivations.

Some have argued a related theme, which is that suburban growth controls are no more than sophisticated, covert attempts to be exclusive. Perhaps Frieden (1979) has been the
most vocal spokesperson against what is characterized as segregation through land use policies. In essence, the view is that
growth controls have predecessors in "neighborhood protection" movements to lock out unwanted individuals. The legal
precedent is the maze of zoning laws and building safety codes.
In the name of public health and welfare, these restrictions set
parameters on the housing, economic activities, and social fabric
of a municipality. The social counterpart is in antibusing rallies,
vigilantes, and cross-burnings on lawns, which also seek to discourage specific outsiders from invading the local turf. Growth
controls in the suburbs are thus extensions of what has long
been occurring in middle America. That is, the growth controversy has its roots in maintaining social status, increasing property values of residents' homes, and keeping out certain groups.

Another distinct possibility is that antigrowth movements flourish in the suburbs because of the suburbs' political
fragmentation. It may be fairly easy for citizens to threaten
small, relatively powerless local governments. Small pressure
groups can lead to fear by public officials about reelection and
over other political ramifications. Prodevelopment forces, on
the other hand, may more readily decide to take their growth
plans to some nearby community rather than do battle with
citizen activists. In comparison, for big city governments a
larger and more vocal effort would be required to halt development, and with land scarce the developers would be less inclined to find suitable nearby sites. In the suburbs, the level of
organized efforts may not be enormous and the threshold at
which government and business give in to citizen demands
may be lower.

A common explanation for the suburban movement to limit growth is simply the composition of the population—white, middle class, and family oriented. It is argued that these social groups typically are more environmentally aware and active. Worries about pollution, congestion, and overpopulation are translated into opposition to local growth. This argument seems to oversimplify support for growth controls. It is also based upon the outmoded stereotype of suburbia as a socially homogeneous region. More is said about this later. For now, at the heart of all discussion of suburban growth is one simple fact. Citizen support for growth controls is strong.

Defining Citizen Support
for Growth Controls

It is first necessary to review all the different ways of defining attitudes toward growth controls. Then, the causes of citizen support can be better understood. There are many ways to approach the question, and the precise ways of defining citizen support have important implications. The numbers wanting growth limited and opposing specific policies, and the constituencies they represent, vary with the way citizen support is defined.

Support for Limiting Growth
This refers to negative attitudes about the current rate of local growth. The most general attitude is displeasure with current growth. Residents could also link their displeasure to dissatisfaction with growth-related community problems, such as crowded schools, environmental pollution, crime, traffic congestion, social conflict, and personal stress. Other measures include opposition to population growth per se. Still others involve concern about future growth in the locality and its possible consequences. These sorts of attitude measures have been used in local and national studies (Marans and Wellman 1978). They are

lacking in one important respect. They fail to link feelings with actual calls for policy action.

A better approach is to measure support for growth controls. One way is to ask citizens, in clear terms, whether their municipal or county government should be involved in limiting the growth rate. Displeasure with the current growth rate would seem to be a necessary but not a sufficient attitude for support of growth controls. Residents would also have to agree that local government should be actively involved in regulating population and land use. However, there may be instances in which citizens who do not complain about current growth do support growth limits. In these cases citizens may want growth limits as a preventive measure before problems emerge.

Several specific measures of citizen preference for growth limits would seem most useful. One is to ask whether the resident at this time favors government interventions to limit growth. Another is to determine whether the resident believes that current regulation of population growth by the local government is adequate. Of course, not all those who favor government intervention will perceive current government involvement as inadequate, and likewise, those who perceive current involvement as inadequate may not favor further government activities. The hard-core supporters of growth controls can thus be determined by examining the overlapping attitudes of favoring government involvement and believing that current regulatory efforts are inadequate.

Reasons for Limiting Growth

There are many reasons why citizens may express support for limiting growth. Besides the problems already mentioned, they may be concerned about the lack of open spaces or general deterioration of their neighborhoods. They may fear higher taxes, increased government spending, lower property values, and inadequate staffing of local services. Some may not want new residents at all, while others may be concerned about the increasing presence of renters, minorities, singles, or the lower class. The reasons for wanting growth limited can inform the researcher of the community's current problems, self-perceptions, and worries about the future. There may be little agreement as to reasons even in communities where most residents support growth limits.

Reasons for limiting growth may, in fact, divide the supporters of growth controls. True consensus may not exist once residents are asked to specify their rationale. Support for growth limits may be weakened when different coalitions oppose each other over the purposes of government regulations. Some residents may be worried about environmental issues. Others may be concerned with economic issues. Social and attitudinal differences may underlie these concerns. In some instances, coalitions may develop to further pressure local government to enact growth controls. In other cases, communities can be so badly divided over reasons that they never achieve the growth controls which residents want. It is thus essential to look beyond general support and into the specifics.

Several steps are necessary to identify the reasons for limiting growth. The supporters of growth limits must first be identified. Among this subpopulation, reasons must be ascertained and then grouped. Some will represent broad concerns, while others will be idiosyncratic to the local community. General issues also need to be determined, such as consistent concern with environmental or economic issues. Some of the reasons will be agreed upon by most parties, while others will be named by smaller groups. Sufficient background information on the residents and the community must be collected to establish not only the areas of disagreement but the location in the community of disagreements about the reasons for limiting growth.

Policy Preferences for Limiting Growth

There are many ways to limit growth. Some are highly technical and others are crude. Some are legal while others have failed court tests. Citizens may vary in the approaches they favor in their communities. Some may want to see a halt to all new construction. Others may want to limit residential construction while allowing industrial and commercial development. Residents may favor indirect means of limiting growth, such as restricting infrastructure—roads, sewers, and public services. Some may favor practices that limit apartments and high-density land use. Others may support policies that discourage low-income residents and minorities from migrating to their community. Beneath these policy preferences are stated goals for the community's social and physical character.

There may be consensus on how to restrict development in certain instances. Perhaps a highly residential community will not favor new industries or high-rise buildings. But there seem to be ample opportunities for different groups to support different policies within any given community, partly reflecting specific reasons for wanting growth limited in the first place. There are also varying philosophies as to what areas of community development government should and should not regulate. Residents may differ in knowledge of planning and, therefore, vary in plans that they believe will effectively limit growth. Policy preferences may also be a function of the perceived consequences of limiting growth in a certain manner. For instance, renters may not want to see apartments limited, and commuters may not want to halt road building. In fact, even if citizens agree on the reasons for supporting growth limits they may favor a variety of approaches to actually controlling local growth.

The desirable approaches must therefore be discussed. First, different types of policies must be proposed in attitude questions, reflecting a broad range. Next, the degree of support for varying policies must be ascertained. Some individuals will not have any policies that they favor. Others will strongly favor all policies that limit growth, and thus can be identified as the consistent no-growthers. Many residents will probably strongly favor some approaches, marginally support others, and oppose others. A central function of research in policy preferences is to identify the most favored approaches and, perhaps more important, the groups that support some approaches more than others.

The Causes of Citizen Support

Many factors have been explicitly explored as causes of citizen support for growth controls. Others have been mentioned in passing but have not been empirically tested. Still others are potentially promising but have not been seriously considered. Certain individual and community characteristics that may be related to citizen support should be introduced before specific hypotheses are presented.

Status Characteristics

The most common argument is that the supporters of growth controls are high-status individuals. Status characteristics are often defined in terms of family income, education, and occupation. Upper income residents are viewed as seriously concerned with the land use and other physical consequences of rapid growth (Garkovich 1982). The highly educated, white collar resident is considered the foundation of the "environmental movement." Some argue that pro-environmental sentiments are at the root of support for growth controls (see Molotch 1976). There is evidence that higher-status individuals support environmental safeguards, but little which links this to support for growth controls (Buttel and Flinn 1978; Devall 1970; Harry et al. 1969; Van Liere and Dunlap 1980).

Homeowner status is also supposed to be related to support for growth controls. However, homeowners support growth limits for somewhat different reasons. Some researchers view growth limits as an attempt by homeowners to limit the quality and supply of housing in an effort to increase the property values of their homes (Ellickson 1977). This is an economic motivation which, at root, represents self-interest (Frieden 1979). There are numerous instances in which homeowners attempt to and succeed in limiting growth (Baldassare and Protash 1982; Dowall 1980; Frieden 1979; Maurer and Christensen 1982).

There is undoubtedly an association between an individual's status, measured by numerous dimensions, and support for growth controls. The issue this raises is whether high status explains all support for growth controls or only certain examples of citizen support.

Personal Characteristics

These refer to the individual's age, sex, length of residence, work status, marital status, household size, ethnicity, race, and other so-called demographic features. Age, sex, and length of residence are the only factors that have systematically been tied to support for growth controls.

Age and sex have perhaps the most consistent relation. The young adults appear to be the most environmentally aware and active as an age group. These general concerns are evident in their support for local growth limitations. A "gender gap" also exists, with women expressing more environmental concerns than men. Women's support for growth controls may represent a strong desire to maintain the status quo or to protect the community's current level of safety. There is empirical evidence that younger persons and women are more inclined to favor growth controls (see Gottdiener and Neiman 1981).

Length of residence is often assumed to have a direct relationship. But the direction of the association is subject to question. Long-term residence should make people less likely to favor growth-related change than recent residence. But there may also be times when new residents are those most concerned about the effects of growth on the environment. In actuality the findings are equivocal (Freudenberg 1979; Ploch 1980; Voss 1980; Zuiches 1981).

It is unlikely that personal characteristics in themselves explain support for growth controls. But age, sex, and length of residence can predispose an individual to certain attitudes that can affect reasons and general support for growth limitations. Varying social groups may also differ in policy preferences.

Community Characteristics

Communities' structural features may create a context in which citizens support growth controls. Examples include the local growth rate, the average family income, the typical occupational status, and the proportion of homeowners. There is good evidence linking these features to residents' attitudes toward growth policies.

Perhaps most influential is the rate of growth per se. An influx of new residents in itself could signal the need, and therefore support, for growth controls (Rosenbaum 1978). Rapid growth may lead to a breakdown in service delivery and perhaps some changes in the quality of life. Roads become congested, schools are overcrowded, air pollution develops, and new private and public services are needed. Support for growth limits would then emerge. There is evidence in previous studies of a link between rapid local growth and citizens' opposition to growth (Dowall 1980; Protash and Baldassare 1983).

The concentration of homeowners, high income residents, and white collar residents, of course, creates high-status communities, which may encourage the view among their residents that unregulated growth is risky. Logan (1978) views suburban communities as attempting to increase or, at worst, maintain their status relative to others. Growth controls may be an attempt to remain exclusive, segregated, and physically separated from lower class individuals. Suburban status differences have been found to increase over time, providing indirect evidence that community status results in preferences opposed to growth (Logan and Schneider 1981; Logan and Semyonov 1980). Other studies also find that high status communities are the sites of the antigrowth movement (Dowall 1980; Lyon et al. 1981; Maurer and Christenson 1982; Neiman 1980). The effects of living in a high status area, independent of the individual's attitudes or social position, may thus affect growth attitudes.

Residents' Attitudes

Less often considered as an explanatory factor is residents' attitudes. These include opinions about the community, personal life, and government and politics. In brief, growth controls may seem to be sensible alternatives when residents are unhappy with the conditions surrounding their lives.

Perhaps the most significant attitudes are dimensions of perceived community quality—views about housing, neighborhood, private services, and public services. For instance, if local services are currently inadequate, then growth would seem likely to exacerbate the situation, and residents would support growth limits. In theory negative feelings about current conditions appear to be precursors to growth regulation. Related to views of community quality are perceptions of the local growth rates. Perceived growth is the resident's assessment of current growth as rapid, slow, stable, or declining. Perceptions of growth have been found to be only weakly associated with the actual growth rate. They are more strongly related to individual displeasures with ongoing social changes (Baldassare 1981). Individuals who perceive rapid growth are likely to offer support for growth limits. There is evidence that community problems are often viewed as caused by growth, and therefore indirect evidence that these attitudes stimulate interest in growth controls (Bridgeland and Sofranko 1975; Marando and Thomas 1977; Neiman and Loveridge 1981).

People's attitudes toward their local government and their political orientations can also affect support for growth controls. A lack of confidence in government's abilities to solve local problems can create fears about the future. Concern about competence, ultimately, may cause residents to want the future growth rate carefully regulated if not seriously reduced. Residents may simply be less willing to accept community change if they believe that their local government cannot cope with the outcome.

A fiscally conservative political attitude may result in support for growth controls for economic reasons. It is evident that the suburbs have many middle class residents who want taxes and government spending reduced (Clark 1981; Clark and Ferguson 1983). These same fiscal conservatives may scrutinize the costs of growth, considering the expense of new infrastructure, schools, roads, and public services. Thus there may be some overlap between the "tax revolt" supporters and those who favor growth controls.

Attitudes toward personal life are also potentially important factors. Personal life refers to perceived quality of life as measured by satisfaction with family, friends, organizations, work, health, happiness, and mental health. Ratings of life conditions may predispose individuals to have positive or negative views about the future. As a result, there is a possibility that residents' attitudes toward their personal lives may influence them to support growth controls.

There is one advantage to exploring the less often considered effects of residents' attitudes. The variety and numbers of instances in which the suburban movement to limit growth has occurred suggest the inadequacy of status, community characteristics, and personal characteristics as explanations of the phenomenon. A more plausible view may be that resident dissatisfaction, which can emerge among many types of individuals and communities, is the major causal factor.

Hypotheses

The first hypothesis is that support for limiting growth is substantial in the suburbs. Further, it is best explained by residents' attitudes. Support involves attitudes toward limiting growth in the community and perceptions of the adequacy of current growth regulations. Important attitudes include dissatisfaction with local government's problem solving, specific public and private services, and some domains of personal life, as well as perceptions of rapid growth. Overall, residential attitudes dwarf personal factors and community characteristics in explaining why citizen support for growth controls has emerged in the suburbs.

The second hypothesis is that the reasons for supporting limits to growth are frequently environmental reasons and, to a lesser extent, economic reasons. This is because the population of homeowners and other high-status residents tend to note these particular concerns. One would therefore expect that status factors have an important role in predicting which residents are more environmentally concerned and more economically concerned. Highly educated residents should note environmental reasons for limiting growth more frequently than other residents. Homeowners should offer economic reasons more often than others. The suburban residents who are fiscal conservatives may also be opposed to future growth because of spending issues. Implicit in this hypothesis is that the causes of support for growth controls are distinct from the specific reasons for wanting growth limited. This suggests that many kinds of individuals can agree on the need for growth controls but that specific groups have different reasons for their support.

The last hypothesis is that preferences on policies for limiting growth will indicate strong general support and yet little concensus on which policy is most advantageous. This is because individuals and social groups will vary in their views about how a growth policy will affect them. Homeowners may want to see apartments limited but, if they are commuting to work, may not favor the limiting of new roadways. Women may want to see high-rises limited. Renters may be less inclined to favor apartment limitations. It is probable that certain factors causing support for one policy have no effect on other policy preferences.

Methods

The 1982 Orange County Annual Survey included questions regarding current growth policies, support for growth controls, and reasons for support for growth controls. In the 1983 survey growth attitudes were pursued further by asking residents about the specific policies they preferred.

The survey data from Orange County, California, is relevant to this controversy for several reasons. Many of the residents are affluent, and thus characterize the supporters of growth controls. The median family income is approximately

$35,000; two-thirds of the resident work force is white collar. The area has also experienced rapid growth. The population grew by 500,000 and at a 35 percent rate between 1970 and 1980. Formal growth control policies may be regarded as constants, since no city government has initiatives or referenda to limit growth (California 1981). The 26 municipalities do vary considerably in growth rates, age, affluence, homeownership rates, politics, and population sizes. There have been disagreements over growth, both countywide and in specific localities, that have resulted in public disputes between citizen groups, local government, and private development companies.

Six questions regarding growth limits were asked during the 1981 survey, from which scales were developed to measure local concerns and reasons for growth-limit support. The first question was worded, "Do you think that growth and development in your city should be limited?" Answers were yes or no. Those answering yes were told, "I am going to read you a list of reasons why some people want to limit growth. For each one tell me if this is a reason you would like to limit growth: to avoid an increase in government spending and taxes; to prevent the environment from deteriorating; to prevent an increase in traffic congestion and overcrowding; to maintain present property values." Respondents were again asked to answer yes or no. A final question was worded, "Do you think that government regulations in your city aimed at controlling growth are too strict, about right, or not strict enough?"

One scale was developed to measure overall support for growth controls. Those who both favored growth controls and considered current policies not strict enough were defined as the strong supporters of growth controls. All other respondents were placed in a separate category. This "limit growth" scale was used instead of the individual items to distinguish those who felt strongly about current and future growth policies. Two scales involving only the residents identified as strong growth-control supporters were created to measure reasons for support. The four questions on reasons for limiting growth fell into two groups, environmental reasons (to prevent environmental deterioration and to prevent traffic congestion and over-crowding) and economic reasons (government spending/taxes and property values). Two 2-point scales were created. On the "environmental scale" those who gave both environmental reasons were distinguished from all others who were strong supporters. In the same way, the "economic scale" distinguished those who gave both economic reasons from all others who were strong supporters. There is little overlap in the scales as evidenced by a low correlation ($r = .05$). These scales were used to distinguish those who were consistent in either their economic reasons or environmental reasons for limiting growth from others.

The first explanatory variables represent the status, community, and personal characteristics so often considered in studies of attitudes toward growth controls (Baldassare 1984, 1985). Three in particular are chosen: homeownership, educational status, and the local growth rate. The rate of municipal growth between 1970 and 1980 in the respondents' city of residence was the measure of the local growth rate (U.S. Bureau of the Census 1982). For the purposes of this discussion these three are grouped and referred to as demographic factors.

The second group of causal factors involves resident attitudes which may be associated with growth control sentiments. Five in all are chosen. Three are items from the survey: perceptions of growth, rating of local government, and fiscal conservatism. The four-point perceived growth question was collapsed into two categories, rapid growth versus all others. Perceived Service Problems and Personal Life Ratings are scales developed from survey questions. Perceived Service Problems were measured by summing the scores of questions pertaining to the quality of streets and roads, parks and recreation, hospitals and clinics, and grocery stores and shopping centers. Answers to the original questions were excellent, good, fair, and poor. The last two response categories were collapsed into one category, forming a 3-point scale for each item. The alpha coefficient is .66 for this scale.

Personal Life Ratings were measured by summing the

scores of six items, evaluating housing, family life, friends, finances, mental health, and happiness. Answers to the first five
questions were very satisfied, satisfied, dissatisfied, and very dissatisfied. The last two response categories were collapsed into
one, forming a 3-point scale. The happiness item was coded in
a 3-point scale ranging from very happy to somewhat happy,
and not at all happy. This scale has an alpha coefficient of .68.

The two control variables used in the analysis are respondents' age and sex. Women and younger adults are consistently
more apt to favor growth controls and note environmental and
economic reasons for supporting growth controls. Personal and
community characteristics that had no influence on the growth
attitude questions, and were dropped from the analysis, include
length of residence, occupation, family income, and 1980 municipal median family income.

The statistical methods used were bivariate and multivari-
ate analysis. The independent variables were divided into two
groups, demographic variables and attitudinal characteristics.
The simple correlations between each independent variable and
the measures of overall support for growth controls, environmental reasons, and economic reasons were first considered.
Then, these relationships were reexamined after controlling for
age and sex. The final stage of the analysis accounted for both
control variables and demographic characteristics in analyzing
the effects of each demographic characteristic and each attitudinal characteristic using discriminant analysis.

Four items relevant to policy preferences were taken
from the 1983 survey. The following statement was read to
everyone: "I am going to read you a list of ways in which cities
try to limit growth. For each one, tell me if this is an approach
you favor very much, somewhat, or not at all." The list included limit the number of new apartment buildings, limit the
number of new industries moving in, limit the number of roads
and freeways, and limit the number of high-rise buildings.

Numerous measures were examined to determine if they
had a significant relationship with any of the policy preferences,
including twenty status characteristics, personal characteristics,

community characteristics, and resident attitudes. All of the
items that had at least one significant relationship with a
growth policy preference were further considered. Three demographic measures are significantly related to at least one policy
preference. These are homeownership, sex, and work status.
Four resident attitude items are significantly associated with at
least one policy preference. They are perceived growth, satisfaction with freeways, Orange County's future, and boredom.

The seven characteristics form the set of potential causal
factors for each policy preference. A stepwise multiple regression
was then performed that excluded all the insignificant factors
from the final causal model for each separate policy preference.

Findings

Residents have strong concerns about current and future
growth in the suburban community. Overall support for
growth controls from the 1982 survey is given in table 3.1.
Sixty-five percent of all respondents who answered wanted
growth limited in their city, while 35 percent did not. Forty

Table 3.1 Support for Limiting Growth

	Percent
Favor growth controls	
Yes	65
No	35
Total	100
Perception of current growth controls	
Not strict enough	40
About right	51
Too strict	9
Total	100
Limit growth scale (composite)	
Yes	26
No	74
Total	100

SOURCE is the 1982 Orange County Annual Survey.

percent of the respondents indicated that city growth regulations were currently not strict enough, while 51 percent said
regulations were about right, and 9 percent said regulations
were too strict. The "limit growth" scale indicates that 26 percent both want growth limits and consider current policies not
strict enough.

The causes of support for the "limit growth" group are
next examined. There were only three significant correlations.
The three variables of education, homeownership, and growth
rate are not strongly correlated. Three of the five are positively
correlated with the "limit growth" scale. These are, in order of
significance, a low rating of local government $(r = .24)$, perceived rapid growth $(r = .11)$, and service problems $(r = .08)$.
After controlling for the respondents' age and sex, and then for
the three demographic factors, the three resident attitudes best
explain support for growth control policies, and the demographic characteristics are insignificant.[1]

Reasons for wanting to limit growth are summarized in
table 3.2. The percentages are first calculated including the total
sample. Traffic congestion and overcrowding was given as a
reason by 59 percent of all the 1982 respondents. Environmental deterioration was mentioned by 52 percent. Limiting
growth to maintain property values was noted by 39 percent of

Table 3.2 Reasons for Limiting Growth

	Percent
Total Sample (N = 1,009)	
Environmental deterioration	52
Traffic congestion and overcrowding	59
Avoid government spending and taxes	30
Maintain property values	39
Limit-growth scale subsample (N = 264)	
Environmental reasons scale	85
Economic reasons scale	42

SOURCE is the 1982 Orange County Annual Survey. Percentages for the first
four items are given in terms of the total sample. Percentages for the last two items are
based upon the subsample who both favor growth controls and perceive current
growth controls as "not strict enough."

the total sample. Another 30 percent gave the reason of avoiding government spending and taxes.

The 264 strong antigrowth supporters noted in table 3.1 are used as the basis for two scales, "environmental reasons" and "economic reasons." Both the environmental reasons were noted by 85 percent of the subsample. Both the economic reasons were mentioned by 42 percent. The responses indicate that many of the individuals who want growth limited are very concerned about environmental and economic issues. Twice as many mention environmental concerns as mention economic concerns.

The causes for mentioning both environmental reasons were next examined with reference to the demographic characteristics and five resident attitudes previously mentioned. For the environmental scale, there were two significant associations. Among the demographic variables, it was educational status $(r = .13)$ and among the residential attitudes it was fiscal conservatism $(r = -.15)$. Controlling for age and sex, and then for the demographic characteristics, did not affect these findings. This indicates that, among the supporters of growth controls, the highly educated and the non–fiscal conservatives mention environmental reasons more than others do.[2] Those who are not fiscal conservatives and who are more highly educated tend to note environmental reasons.

The predictors of economic reasons for supporting growth limits were next examined. The same two factors as noted above were significant. Educational status was correlated at $-.16$. and fiscal conservatism at $.21$ with economic reasons for wanting growth limited. These two factors are the only ones that remain significant after controlling for age and sex, and then the demographic characteristics. Among the opponents of growth, low-status residents and fiscal conservatives give economic reasons more than others do.[3]

Policy preferences for limiting growth are examined in table 3.3. Limiting high-rises has the most overall approval. Following closely is citizen support for limiting apartments. Limiting industries is the third ranking in approval. Limiting

Table 3.3 Policy Preferences for Limiting Growth

Limit high-rises	Percent	Mean
Very much	44	
Somewhat	30	
Not at all	26	
Total	100	1.82
Limit apartments		
Very much	29	
Somewhat	44	
Not at all	27	
Total	100	1.98
Limit industries		
Very much	26	
Somewhat	36	
Not at all	38	
Total	100	2.12
Limit roads		
Very much	26	
Somewhat	33	
Not at all	41	
Total	100	2.15

SOURCE is the 1983 Orange County Annual Survey, including all respondents. Higher means indicate less preference for the policy.

roads is the least favored. The percentages "very much" favoring a policy suggest that limiting high-rises has much more support than limiting apartments. However, the "very much" and "somewhat" responses combined show a similar level of support for high-rise and apartment limitations. The link between limiting apartments and limiting high-rises may be concerns with urbanization, density, and diversification.

It is interesting that a sizable majority very much or somewhat favors each policy. However, further analyses suggest that support for all antigrowth policies is limited. Only 7 percent were "very much" in favor of all the growth-limiting strategies. That group would represent the hardcore antigrowth residents. Another 7 percent were "not at all" in favor of any of the strategies. This may be the most progrowth segment. One in three was either "very much" or "somewhat" supportive of all four policies. The percentage is close to the number identified earlier in the "limit growth" scale. The evidence again speaks to the lack of suburban consensus on growth policy. The majority favors some growth-limiting policies and not others.

To predict support for specific policies, seven variables were examined for each policy preference.[4] As mentioned earlier, each factor considered was associated with at least one policy preference. The seven were entered stepwise into a regression equation until all the significant factors had entered. This procedure was repeated for each of the four policy preferences. Four were related to attitudes toward limiting apartments, including homeownership ($r = .14$), perceived growth ($r = .12$), freeway satisfaction ($r = .06$), and Orange County's future ($r = -.07$). Only two were related to a preference for limiting industry. These were sex ($r = -.09$) and boredom ($r = -.06$). Women and those who were less bored were more in favor of limiting industry than others. Three factors explained the preference for limiting roads and freeways. In order of importance these were work status ($r = -.11$), freeway satisfaction ($r = .08$), and rating of Orange County's future ($r = -.07$). Those not employed full time, those satisfied with the freeways, and those who viewed the future more pessimistically supported this policy.

Attitudes toward limiting high-rises were explained by three factors: perceived growth ($r = .13$), boredom ($r = -.10$), and sex ($r = -.10$). Those who perceive rapid growth, those are not bored, and women also preferred limiting industry.[4]

In sum, there is no one factor that is significantly related to all four or even three policy preferences. Several variables are related to two preferences, but none is the best predictor of two growth-control strategies. This again suggests the independence of support for specific policies.

Of all the possible relations examined, the strongest association is between homeownership and support for apartment limits. This relationship reveals a potential clash of residents' interests, and has implications for the suburban transformation; so it is further explored. The homeownership variable was divided into more distinct categories. Thirty-eight percent of the respondents in the 1983 sample were renters, but 16 percent lived in rental houses and only 22 percent lived in rental apartments. Table 3.4 indicates that homeowners are the most opposed to new apartment buildings, while rental house dwellers are only somewhat less opposed. Those currently living in apartments are the group most in favor of new apartments.

Younger people, singles, new residents, and individuals in smaller households were less supportive of apartment limits. But these factors could not explain the differences in policy preferences between apartment renters and house renters and homeowners.

There is an interesting interaction between length of residence and homeownership, displayed in table 3.4. Homeowners become more opposed to apartment development over time. Those who have lived at their residence more than 10 years have the strongest preference for limiting apartments. Apartment dwellers are most supportive of building new apartments with 3–5 years' residence. Support is weaker among the most recent and the long-term residents. Recent residents may perceive apartment renting as temporary and not related to a future apartment supply. Long-term renters may oppose apartment development because they are opposed to community

Table 3.4 Opposition to Apartments

	Mean			
Homeowner				
Owner	1.90			
Rental house	2.05			
Rental apartment	2.16			

Homeowner by length of residence (means)				
	2 years or less	3 to 5 years	6 to 10 years	More than 10 years
Owner	1.98	1.98	1.90	1.85
Rental house	2.15	1.95	2.08	1.81
Rental apartment	2.11	2.51	2.15	1.90

SOURCE is the 1983 Orange County Annual Survey. Lower mean scores indicate more opposition to apartments. Analyses of variance tests are used to determine the significance of mean score differences. Main effect for homeowner is significant at .001. Interaction effect for homeowner by length of residence is significant at .04.

change per se. Only a small segment of the apartment rental population would favor increasing the supply of apartments. Opposition to apartments is widely held.

In conclusion, rapid growth and industrialization are major concerns in the suburbs. Many people want growth limited, consider current growth-control policies inadequate, cite environmental or economic reasons for halting growth, and favor various means of controlling future growth. Citizen support for growth controls emerges among many different types of residents. The suburban movement to limit growth has the characteristics of a coalition rather than true consensus.

Concluding Comments
on Growth Controversies

Growth is a major concern in today's suburban regions. Whether the population will increase or not, and what consequences will accrue, is far from certain. Citizens battle each other, and face off against powerful business interests, in pursuit of policies that will influence the rate and quality of growth. Cities try to compete with their neighboring localities for the "attractive" residents and most lucrative economic activities, enacting programs aimed at capturing desirable growth and diverting unwanted populations and industries.

The evidence confirmed the existence of citizen support for growth limits, and support in general was found to be strong. But the sources of antigrowth sentiments appear to be diverse and, at times, in competition. Residents' attitudes rather than individual and community characteristics seemed to best explain the conditions under which support flourishes. There was no indication that social status or the actual local growth rate significantly affected the desire to limit growth. Thus, support for growth controls can emerge among broad resident groups and not only among narrowly defined poulations. the predictors of a strong preference for growth controls were negative ratings of local government, the perception of growth as rapid, and dissatisfaction with local services. The findings indicate that public policies that attempt to limit growth can gain favor when residents become dissatisfied with community quality. Citizen support for growth-control policies can therefore emerge with many types of residents and communities.

The large majority who supported growth controls, as expected, mentioned environmental concerns. Environmental reasons were especially prominent among high-status residents. The concerns of high-status residents are thus commonly overcrowding, traffic congestion, and environmental deterioration. Those with more fiscally conservative attitudes were also less frequently concerned with environmental reasons for limiting growth than were others. It is important to note that the community attitudes associated with supporting growth controls were not those correlated with mentioning environmental reasons for doing so. The findings indicate that individuals with environmental reasons for limiting growth are somewhat distinct from those who favor growth controls generally.

Economic reasons for limiting growth are noted by a substantial minority of those who favor growth-control policies. As predicted, economic concerns are noted more often by those with more fiscally conservative attitudes. They are also mentioned more often by low-status residents. Low-status residents and politically conservative individuals thus have reasons to support growth controls, though different from those of high-status or politically liberal residents. These results suggest that current conceptions of citizens who favor growth controls need to be expanded.

Another hypothesis confirmed is that there is strong support for specific growth-limiting policies. Large proportions of residents favored limiting apartments and high rises. Others would like to limit roads and industries. There are, however, very few residents who will support any policy that seeks to limit growth. Individuals agree to be selective in their choice of strategies. Further, different policies seem to gather their support from different segments of the population. Preferences seem to be tied to self-interest, perceptions of specific kinds of problems, and tastes for how the suburban landscape should look in the future. Homeowners strongly favored apartment limits. Those who do not work do not mind limits on road building. Still other groups favored high-rise and industry limits. The support for specific policies by different groups suggests that there is some disagreement about how to proceed.

There is no consensus among all residents that one approach is better than another, no more than there is unanimity as to the reasons for limiting growth. Community conflict may emerge, therefore, even if residents want growth limited. The policy chosen could be opposed even by those who support growth controls. The program enacted may not respond concretely to the reasons underlying support by citizens. In the absence of consensus, coalitions against growth may later turn against each other or their government.

This research indicates that citizens' desire to adopt growth controls is motivated by attitudes that may have little to do, in reality, with growth and its consequences. Orange County's residents wanted to limit growth when they were more displeased with local government, dissatisfied with public services, and perceived growth as too rapid. Yet growth per se had little influence on these attitudes as evidenced in weak relationships between city growth rates and government attitudes, public service ratings, and perceived rapid growth. There is thus no reason to believe that growth controls will improve the community conditions that lead residents to call for their imposition (see also Baldassare 1981). Similarly, specific reasons commonly given to limit growth may have little to do with growth per se. Residents may also be responding to unfounded prejudices and ill-conceived priorities when they support certain growth policies. The governmental response to citizen support for growth controls needs in all cases to be carefully considered. The local policy response in some instances should be to solve specific community problems rather than to limit growth.

There is likely to be more, not less, controversy over growth in the future. The findings of this study suggest that suburbs may turn more frequently to restrictive policies. Growth and its related problems will be found in many communities. Fiscal austerity will fuel the need for policies to curb growth. The growing number of fiscal conservatives will point to the costs of growth. The environmentalists will note the erosion of the small-town atmosphere. Average citizens will wonder if the decline in services and community quality can be reversed if growth is halted. The inability of suburban government to solve problems, and influence events around it, may raise louder calls for action. The increasing presence of business and industry on the suburban landscape, as land use becomes more mixed, ensures heated debate over whether and how growth should be controlled.

Notes

1. City government rating was significant at .001, perceived rapid growth at .01, and service problems at .01 based upon a discriminant analysis including all the demographic and control variables.

2. Both fiscal conservatism and educational status were significant at .05 in a discriminant analysis including all the demographic and control variables.

3. Fiscal conservatism was significant at .01 and educational status was significant at .05 based upon a discriminant analysis including all the demographic and control variables.

4. The beta weights from the regression equations which included only the significant variables were as follows: Apartment Limits=homeownership (.15), perceived growth (.13), freeway opinion (.08), and Orange County future (−.07); Industry Limits = sex (−.09), and boredom (−.06); Road Limits = work status (−.10), freeway opinion (.08), and Orange County future (−.08); and High Rise Limits = perceived growth (.11), boredom (−.10), and sex (−.08).

CHAPTER FOUR

Distrust in Local Government

Trust is an essential ingredient in explaining the functioning of communities. The existence of trust means that there is agreement about the rules, actions, intentions, and expectations in local settings. These understandings underlie political rule, business transactions, and ongoing personal relations. One perhaps best appreciates the importance of trust when confronted with its temporary absence. Distrust heightens the possibilities of suspicion, disagreement, and misunderstanding. The result of removing these anchors of the social world can be chaos and paralysis. It is no wonder, then, that trust is an important object of study.

There are several ways in which trust has been examined. They include trust between individuals, between people and their institutions, and trust by people of their society as a whole. The most commonly explored issue is trust among urban individuals (Baldassare 1979, 1981; Fischer 1981, 1984). Less often considered is people's trust in their society (Campbell, Converse, and Rodgers 1976). A final area of investigation is confidence in social institutions, including business, the government, special interests, and voluntary organizations (Lipset and Schneider 1983). The focus here evolves from the last concern, that is, trust in local government. Trust in local government, and its absence, can have important implications for a community's functioning and its individuals' happiness and is thus worthy of serious analysis (Citrin 1974).

Trust in local government in the suburban context has hardly been explored. Trust in government has declined in modern times, coincidentally with the suburban transformation of America. The political structure of the suburbs may heighten distrust in local government. Given the general and specific relevance of the issue to suburbia, it seems imperative that the subject no longer be ignored.

The relevance of the suburban transformation to trust in local government is obvious. Large population size and high density are considered in classic theories to be causes of distrust. Since intense land use and population growth have caused large and dense areas in the suburbs, perhaps such hypotheses should now be applied. Social heterogeneity in communities is viewed as reducing trust in government. Because the suburbs have become more socially diverse, it is possible that this theorem has a suburban application. Rapid growth has also been a characteristic of old community theories about distrust and, of course, of the modern suburbs.

Several political features impinging upon suburban governments deserve more elaboration. First, a suburban area the size of a large central city may be administered by a score of local governments. County governments do not have jurisdiction over the entire territory. Add to this the fact that no one city in an area may be dominant in population size, total area, economic power, or fiscal capabilities. The political structure encourages a diffusion of responsibility. Conflict over resources exists, and most of all, there is a lack of attention to the "big picture." There is no structure, authority, or meaningful coordination of actions among city, county, and other political jurisdictions. Profound difficulties in performance, efficiency, leadership, and representation of citizens' issues can occur in the suburban area. Attitudes toward local government, especially with regard to trust, can suffer.

The study of trust in local government in the suburbs also offers an opportunity to elaborate upon existing urban theories. Several community features are present in the suburbs and absent in other contexts. The role of local government in individual areas can be more varied and more complex. For instance, there are variations in incorporated status and land use not seen elsewhere. A study in the suburban context expands general knowledge on trust and updates past theories by considering trust in what is today the dominant community form.

This investigation will thus go beyond merely noting the current level of suburban distrust. It is important to consider whether some areas in the suburban region have reached demographic thresholds which distinguish them from other areas. Specifically, it is critical to know whether suburban variations in size, density, heterogeneity, and growth cause fluctuations in distrust of government.

Studying Trust in Government

The literature on trust in government has an important place within the social sciences. Its status has been elevated by keen interests in the American public's moods during the Vietnam and Watergate eras. Measuring trust in government, however, is not an easy task, and some scholars have criticized the design of questions, the analysis, and the interpretation of results. Controversy surrounds the topic of Americans' opinions toward government and what variables should be emphasized in analyzing such attitudes.

The fundamental criticism of the trust-in-government research is its lack of specificity. Many researchers have argued for the need to distinguish the dimensions of trust (Abramson and Finifter 1981; Easton 1975; Feldman 1983). Instead, most studies have relied upon trust-in-government "indices" or composite scales that include several dimensions of trust. Atti-

tudes concerning competency, leadership abilities, political alienation, self-interest, and general distrust of institutions are typically combined to form single item measures (Barber 1983:74–
82). The scales have thwarted the development of theories and
valid evidence. Specifically, it is important to know how individuals feel about their governments in very detailed ways.
Whether government is viewed as competent yet insensitive to
citizens' preferences is lost in multiple-question indices. More
to the point, how different aspects of trust are specifically related to the individual or the community has been lost.

Another limitation of research involves the ambiguous
wording of survey questions. Many trust-in-government questions ask people for their opinions about "government." The
lack of a reference point leads individuals to relay feelings toward federal, state, or local government, or perhaps some combination of the three. The existence of unfocused survey items
raises the possibility of errors in understanding during the interview. Ultimately, there are errors in interpreting the results. This
is especially salient to the issue of trust in the local community.
Residents of large urban places have distinctive attitudes toward
the national government (Fischer 1984), and thus relating findings about their trust in government to their trust in local government may be erroneous. Questions ought to reflect attitudes
toward specific levels of government or institutions.

As serious as the measurement issues is the limited attention to the causes of distrust. Many researchers have argued
that there is less confidence in government today than there
was previously. However, few have offered detailed propositions to examine the specific reasons for a decline. Studies in
the United States typically link personal characteristics with
attitudes toward government (see Hoffman and Clark 1979;
Levin 1960; Lipset and Schneider 1983). Factors such as age,
education, sex, income, and occupation of the respondent are
common causal factors, but some have argued that trust in
government is no longer explained by these factors (House and
Mason 1975), leading others to examine the influence of history and public policy (Citrin 1974; Miller 1974). The explana-

tory variables largely ignored are the characteristics of local communities. This is despite the fact that sociological theories stress the importance of structural factors in predicting individuals' trust in institutions.

A final criticism is about the limited structural features explored when community characteristics have been analyzed. Fischer (1975, 1984) considered the urban-rural dichotomy and the effects of size of place on feelings of trust. Many other community features could influence confidence in local government. Theories that will be discussed in the next section point to the potential role of structural factors such as density, social heterogeneity, and rapid growth. By focusing on only a few features, the importance of community context may be understated. Thus, it is necessary to consider a wide range of community features.

The Community Question and Trust

Several theories dating to the early twentieth century are concerned with trust in the local community. Specifically, sociologists have argued that structural features of communities have a fundamental influence on residents' attitudes, normative orientations, and social behavior.

The issue of trust was evident in Emile Durkheim's *The Division of Labor in Society* ([1893] 1933). He raised questions about how social order is maintained in modern society. Trust seemed to be less problematic in the rural-agricultural societies, where individuals shared common work roles, saw each other in numerous contexts, and solved their disputes on an informal basis. Trust in the urban-industrial situation was more difficult. Individuals had mainly superficial relationships with their community's members. Formalities replaced informalities as means of punishing, rewarding, and even interacting with others. Trust would seem hard to acheive, and fragile at best, in modern society. Social normlessness and individual alienation are constant risks. Thus, the themes are laid out for the classic "community question," which ultimately revolves around the issue of trust. The debate about trust has continued for almost a century.

Population size is viewed as having various effects on residents' trust (see Fischer 1984). Cities with large populations are more specialized economically, differentiated socially, and diverse in land use than places with smaller populations. Wirth (1938) posited that this results in social segregation, role segmentation, and anomie. Increasing population size thus results in a decreasing sense of community and decreasing trust in others in the community. Further, the local community and its moral leaders lose influence in the large, differentiated community setting. Large institutions become the focus for social control and problem solving. Yet, these large institutions have narrow tasks and are highly institutionalized. Individuals are likely to feel estranged from them and frustrated by bureaucratic inflexibility. Of course, local government is a central institution that obtains residents' attention. Confidence in local government should thus decline as population size increases.

Population density is also assumed to have a fundamental influence. Wirth (1938) argued that high-density situations increase frustration and competition between individuals, which inevitably reduces feelings of cooperation and trust in the community. Simmel (1905) argued that dense cities create the potential for psychic overload; residents must adapt to overcrowding by becoming oblivious to the surrounding social world. High density thus increases the probability that personal demeanor toward others will be superficial and goal-oriented (Baldassare 1979). The logical outcome is that individuals view blasé attitudes as pervasive in the local population and its institutions. Trust in local government should decline as density increases.

Many urban theorists have focused on the influence of social heterogeneity on residents' attitudes. The term usually refers to ethnic and racial diversity, though researchers occasionally consider income, occupation, life-cycle, and life-style differences. Wirth (1938) suggested that, in the most diverse places, conflicts of values and interests would develop among individuals. Voluntary groups compete with one another to represent the interests of their constituencies. Local institutions become fragmented and lack legitimate authority. Wirth's views about social heterogeneity are in agreement with earlier writings. Park (1925) considered the urban place a mosaic of moral worlds, each with distinguishing values, beliefs, and rules to govern their residents' actions. The setting is unstable and offers little security. Thus social diversity causes residents to feel largely alienated from their social group and estranged from the community at large. Confidence in local government should be weak in socially heterogeneous places because of limited consensus concerning goals, values, and formal actions.

Population growth is considered to have consequences for the stability of the community, its institutions, and its people. Growth in its most extreme form is usually associated with rapid change, industrialization, and urbanization (Baldassare 1981). According to Burgess (1925), the changing community structure brought about by rapid growth causes increases in crime, deviance, and social disorder. These problems shake residents' confidence in local institutions. McKenzie (1925) believed that local institutions often react slowly to rapid growth and may appear unresponsive to the needs of the community. Thus, the social problems and the time needed for institutional adjustments to them can result in a decline in trust in the local community. The level of confidence in local government should thus decline when an area experiences rapid growth.

Structural factors that specifically relate to suburban communities need to be analyzed. These are not considered by the pre–World War II urban theorists. One is the incorporated versus the unincorporated area. In the incorporated community, residents are represented by a municipal government. In the unincorporated area, no city government exists and political power resides outside the community, typically in county government. The difference between residents' own, single-purpose local government in one instance and a distant, multiple-role

108   Distrust in Local Government

local government in the other may influence feelings of trust. Residents of unincorporated areas may have less confidence.

Another important distinction is the older, residential suburb versus the newer, mixed-use suburban area with residential, commercial, and industrial activities. It is possible that this distinction influences trust. Individuals living in newer suburbs may view their governments as less responsive to the needs of residents and more responsive to the concerns of businesses than those in the older suburbs. Confidence in local government should thus be lower in newer developments.

Hypotheses

Community theories suggest a link between community characteristics and trust in local government. Four elements of trust in local governmnet seem especially pertinent. One is performance, or the degree to which citizens view their local government as able to solve problems that occur in the community. The second is efficiency, or the extent to which citizens perceive that their local government uses the resources at its disposal in a careful, unwasteful manner. The third is attention to citizens, or the perception among residents that government is responsive to individuals' needs and acts in ways to avoid political alienation among its constituency. The fourth is overall feelings of confidence in local government, a general measure of trust derived by summing the attitudes in the first three areas.

The research also suggests that community factors can influence trust in governments. The factors include size, density, social heterogeneity, rapid growth, incorporated status, and community age. Added to this are unique suburban community dimensions, such as incorporated status and single versus mixed land uses.

Two general hypotheses guide the analysis that follows. One is that trust in suburban governments is low when measured in terms of attention, efficiency, performance, or overall confidence.

The second hypothesis is that structural characteristics are related to lower trust in surburban government. Residents of large, dense, heterogeneous, rapidly growing, unincorporated, and new communities have less confidence in their government. It is assumed that the structural characteristics are generally associated with the attitudes toward local government but that more specific patterns of relationships may emerge.

Methods

Information is drawn from the 1983 Orange County Annual Survey. The interview included several questions regarding trust in local government. Survey items were partly based upon questions used in recent national surveys. They did, however, include important changes in wording. The survey interview also contained the necessary geographic codes to analyze the relationship between political attitudes and community characteristics.

Orange County has the appropriate resident characteristics and attributes of community structure for this investigation. The political fragmentation associated with the suburban metropolis is evident. The area lacks a core city dominating politics and decision-making. The 26 municipalities and 15 unincorporated areas within the county's borders represent diverse, semiautonomous communities. Demographic change and social variety are also present. The population increased by 500,000 people and grew at a rapid rate of 35 percent for the decade 1970 to 1980. Differences are found with respect to density, size, social heterogeneity, growth, politics, age, affluence, industrialization, and homeownership rates in different places within the county. The community characteristics are adequately varied for studying structural characteristics that influence personal trust in local government.

The attitude measures include three questions on trust in local government and a composite scale, all representing distinct issues.

A "local government performance" question was worded, "How would you rate the performance of your local government in solving problems in your community?" The scale was excellent, good, only fair, and poor. Fair and poor responses were collapsed into one category to form a three-point scale.

A "local government efficiency" question was worded, "In general, do you think that the people who run your local government waste a lot of money, waste some of the money, or waste very little of the money we pay in taxes?" The three-point scale was waste very little, waste some, and waste a lot. A "local government attention" scale was worded, "When your local government leaders decide what policies to adopt, how much attention do you think they pay to what the people think?" The three possible answers were: a lot of attention, some attention, and very little attention.

The items were then summed to form an "overall confidence" rating for local government. The possible scores were from 3 to 9, with higher scores indicating less confidence in local government. The composite scale has an alpha coefficient of .65.

The political attitude measures have been used with wording variations in other public opinion surveys. The "local government performance" variable had been used in the 1982 Orange County Annual Survey. The "local government efficiency" and "local government attention" variables were found in national surveys (see Lipset and Schneider 1983) as well as in California statewide polls (Field, 1979, 1981). These two items were modified to emphasize local government rather than government in general. Composite scales of the sort developed are frequently used to measure trust (see Barber 1983).

The causal variables are measures of community structure. They are density, population size, social heterogeneity, and growth. All four causal variables contain sufficient numbers in each of their two categories to pursue the analysis and are derived from the 1980 Census (U.S. Bureau of the Census 1981). Density is a two-category variable, high density versus low density. High density is the urban core of the metropolitan area, that is, Anaheim–Santa Ana–Garden Grove, as delineated by the U.S. Bureau of the Census (1981). Low density is the residual category involving all other places in Orange County.

Population size divides the sample into respondents living in large places, over 100,000 population, medium-size places, between 50,000 and 100,000, and small places, below 50,000 population.

Social heterogeneity separates the sample into those living in heterogeneous and those living in homogeneous places. Heterogeneous is defined as a place with a proportion of nonwhite and Hispanic population above the 22 percent countywide average. Homogeneous is defined as places with below-average nonwhite and Hispanic population.

Growth is defined using the population growth rates between 1970 and 1980. A rapid-growth place is one that grew faster than the 35 percent county average. A slow-growth place is one that grew at a below-average rate.

Other community features, considered as independent variables, have special significance for suburban counties. Residents living in incorporated places were distinguished from those living in unincorporated places. Residents living in older suburban communities are separated from those living in newer suburban communities. For this categorization, a north-south division of Orange County was used, with the Santa Ana River as the boundary. The older, north-county communities are adjacent to Los Angeles and are more predominantly bedroom communities, while the newer, south-county communities are more characteristic of recent suburbs that combine residential, commercial, and industrial activities in the proximate area. Again, these two variables have sufficient numbers in each category.

Since personal characteristics influence attitudes toward local government the statisical analysis included control variables. The relationship between urban structure and trust in local government is considered after controlling for the effects of age, education, homeownership status, length of residence, and family income. The statistical approach is to examine the mean differences in different categories of density, population size, social heterogeneity, and growth for each trust-in-government measure. Significance levels are examined on the basis of analyses of covariance that include the five control variables as covariates and each of the community-structure variables separately as main effects.

Since some of the structural variables are intercorrelated, further analyses were necessary to determine the most significant variables for each measure. For instance, population size is associated with density ($r = .57$). Thus, when analyzing the relationship between one community variable and the measures of trust in local government, it is necessary to control for all the other community variables. An analysis of covariance approach is used. The analysis thus identifies the characteristic significantly related to a trust-in-government question.

Findings

Table 4.1 presents the descriptive statistics for the measures of trust in local government. The mean scores for the three survey items and the overall rating indicate that the average responses are more negative than they are positive. The percentage distributions offer further evidence of this trend. Forty-four percent rated local government performance as fair or poor. Thirty-one percent said that local government wasted a lot of money. The local government attention item had 30 percent reporting very little attention by government to what people think. The overall confidence ratings indicate that 30 percent were in the two most negative categories (i.e., 8, 9). In all, a substantial proportion of the population distrusts local government.

There is evidence that trust in suburban governments is

Table 4.1 Trust in Local Government: Descriptive Statistics

	Percent	Mean
Overall confidence rating		
3 (all positive)	3	
4	6	
5	13	
6 (mid-point)	24	
7	24	
8	18	
9 (all negative)	12	
Total	100	6.61
Local government performance		
Excellent	8	
Good	48	
Fair or Poor	44	
Total	100	2.36
Local government efficiency		
Waste very little	19	
Waste some	50	
Waste a lot	31	
Total	100	2.12
Local government attention		
A lot of attention	15	
Some attention	55	
Very little attention	30	
Total	100	2.14

SOURCE is the 1983 Orange County Annual Survey. Higher means indicate lower trust.

weak. Whether there is more distrust in the suburbs today than elsewhere or in earlier times is difficult to determine. National survey questions do not specifically ask about local government. Statewide surveys do not have many comparable questions. Neither do local surveys, which would otherwise assist in determining whether suburban residents are becoming more distrustful. In sum, comparisons are limited because of the lack of consistency in question wording.

The next issue is to examine whether trust in suburban governments is influenced by community characteristics. The two specifically suburban characteristics did not explain variations in government trust. There were no significant attitude

Table 4.2 Trust in Local Government: The Effects of Personal Characteristics

	Overall Confidence		Performance		Efficiency		Attention	
	Mean	F, Sig	Mean	F, Sig	Mean	F, Sig	Mean	F, Sig
Density								
High	6.96	12.9;.001	2.45	4.6;.001	2.27	15.9;.001	2.24	3.2;.05
Low	6.46		2.33		2.03		2.10	
Population size								
Large	6.75	3.6;.05	2.39	1.1;NS	2.20	8.5;.001	2.16	1.5;NS
Medium	6.53		2.31		2.04		2.18	
Small	6.40		2.36		1.96		2.08	
Social heterogeneity								
Heterogeneous	6.92	16.1;.001	2.47	11.8;.001	2.23	14.0;.001	2.22	3.9;.05
Homogeneous	6.41		2.30		2.01		2.10	
Growth								
Rapid	6.76	9.0;.001	2.38	1.5;NS	2.15	7.2;.01	2.21	8.1;.01
Slow	6.39		2.32		2.00		2.06	

SOURCE is the 1983 Orange County Annual Survey. All means are adjusted and higher means indicate less trust in government. Adjusted means (F-scores) and significance levels are based upon analyses of covariance with covariates including age, education, homeownership, and family income.

differences between residents in unincorporated places as opposed to those in incorporated places, nor were residents in new and mixed-use suburbs distinct from those living in older and more residential suburbs. These suburban dimensions were simply not important in determining distrust in performance, efficiency, attention, and overall confidence.

Trust in local government is influenced by all four of the classic community variables. Table 4.2 presents the mean scores and the results of an analysis of variance. The overall confidence rating is affected by all the variables. So is the efficiency question. Performance and attention scores are affected by most of the community characteristics.

The significance levels and adjusted mean scores include the effects of personal factors that may influence the trust-in-government attitudes.[1] High-density places show lower overall confidence, performance ratings, efficiency ratings, and attention scores than do low-density places. Socially heterogeneous places also have lower scores in all four dimensions than do socially homogeneous places. Rapid growth results in more distrust than slow growth, except for distrust in performance. Finally, residents of large places express lower overall confidence and lower ratings of efficiency than residents in medium-size and especially small places. In all, there are 16 relationships examined in table 4.2. Thirteen of the 16 were significant. Eight relationships were significant at the .001 level or less. It appears, then, that size, growth, density, and diversity have created community conditions in some areas that limit trust in suburban governments. Like urban areas, then, the suburbs vary in trust because certain community characteristics limit positive feelings about community insititutions.

It is important which structural characteristic matters the most for which trust-in-government attitude. Table 4.3 reports the relationships between each structural characteristic and each attitude measure controling for all other structural characteristics. Only a few of the relationships are now significant.[2] Each attitude dimension is now related to only one place characteristic. Only 4 of the possible 16 relationships are

Table 4.3 Trust in Local Government: Controlling for Place Characteristics

	Overall Confidence		Performance		Efficiency		Attention	
	Mean	F, Sig	Mean	F, Sig	Mean	F, Sig	Mean	F, Sig
Density		0.2:NS		1.0:NS		0.0:NS		0.0:NS
High	6.53		2.30		2.08		2.14	
Low	6.64		2.40		2.11		2.14	
Population size		1.7:NS		1.5:NS		4.6:.01		1.5:NS
Large	6.76		2.41		2.21		2.14	
Medium	6.55		2.30		2.05		2.21	
Small	6.45		2.37		1.98		2.10	
Social heterogeneity		7.1:.01		10.0:.001		3.6:NS		1.2:NS
Heterogeneous	6.91		2.51		2.20		2.19	
Homogeneous	6.41		2.28		2.04		2.11	
Growth		0.5:NS		0.5:NS		0.0:NS		0.0:NS
Rapid	6.68		2.37		2.11		2.20	
Slow	6.58		2.40		2.11		2.07	

SOURCE is the 1983 Orange County Annual Survey. All means are adjusted and higher means indicate less trust in government. Adjusted means, F-scores and significance levels are based upon analyses of covariance that include the main effect and the covariates of density, population size, social heterogeneity, and social change.

significant. Overall confidence varies with social heterogeneity, and so do performance ratings. Efficiency scores decline with increasing size of place. Attention attitudes are related to the rate of growth.

It is interesting that density has no effect when the effects of other community factors are considered. In contrast, social heterogeneity is related to two trust-in-government attitudes, and growth and population size to one each. The overall results suggest that place characteristics are related to suburban distrust. The pattern, however, is that specific structural characteristics affect specific attitude dimensions.

Some support for each of the hypotheses was thus found. There is a problem with trust in local government in suburban areas. Beyond this, there is obviously a relationship between suburban place characteristics and distrust toward government.

Concluding Comments
on Suburban Distrust

The initial results of the empirical testing suggest that trust in local government is not strong in suburbia. One resident in twelve finds local government performance excellent, one in six thinks that local government pays a lot of attention to people, and one in five says that local government wastes very little tax money. About one in eleven finds local government consistently trustworthy according to the summed overall confidence rating. Exactly how good or bad these ratings are today, compared with past suburban times and other population bases, is hard to assess. Suffice it to say there is room for improvement in suburban trust.

Two major reasons can be suggested for the lack of trust in suburban governments. One is that the suburban transformation has created community characteristics, that is, size, density, heterogeneity, and rapid growth, which encourage distrust. The other is that suburbia's political structure breeds distrust because it is fragmented and unfocused. Political institutions are oriented toward a local level and lack influence in the broader region that, ultimately, has meaning for people's spheres of work and residence. One might assume that other formal institutions gain in legitimacy when suburban government fails. Organizations that ignore city boundaries and institutionalize the needs of their constituencies could fill the vacuum in decision-making and authority. Business associations, such as countywide chambers of commerce, can act in this manner. Citizen associations, such as consumer and homeowner advocates, can also wield power. Informal elite networks may also fill the need for regional decision-making and planning. One would assume, then, that no formal system of regional power is present. Rather, local government is weak and held in low regard by a substantial minority of residents.

If suburban governments are to assert more influence and, ultimately, increase their local esteem, new institutional forms must develop. City leagues and government associations today are more symbolic than meaningful. One possibility is to give county government more authority. This would certainly meet with disapproval from the municipalities. Another arrangement would be the superregional authority. This would be met with resistance by both the county and the municipal governments. An approach that might succeed is collapsing separate governments into fewer municipalities. This would concentrate decision-making in institutions that would have jurisdiction within more meaningful suburban boundaries.

A point worth exploring is whether citizens want a new form of suburban government. It is true that a substantial minority distrusts its suburban governments and that this attitude is partly a result of government's structure. But it does not naturally follow that citizens want their government to change. Residents of local communities may like the idea of a small government representing their interests. The current power of business and citizen activists may be seen as a positive phenomenon. In short, distrust in suburban government may remain if citizens are opposed to the further concentration of political power.

The analysis suggested that trust in suburban government declines when there is high density, large population size, social heterogeneity, and rapid growth. The classic theories which say that structural characteristics influence trust in local government are supported. The conclusion is that community features once characterized as urban have reached into suburbia. The same structural characteristics that limit trust in urban governments now also limit trust in suburban governments.

Four significant relationships emerged form the analytical process, one for each trust measure. Social heterogeneity was associated with less overall confidence. Social heterogeneity was also related to lower performance ratings. Rapid growth was related to perceptions that local government paid less attention to its citizens. Large population size was associated with lower efficiency ratings. These findings point to the need to refine existing theories. Structural features do affect trust in local government, but specific features influence specific dimensions of trust.

Several reasons are evident for the fact that socially heterogeneous places have lower performance ratings. Park (1925) and Wirth (1938) viewed socially diverse places as more conflict ridden. Differences exist in values, goals, and interests. Local government faces pressures from competing constituencies to follow different courses of action, resulting in fragmentation and a lack of consensus about what local government should do. This creates total inaction, or social groups unsatisfied with unmet needs. As a result, government performance is less highly rated in heterogeneous communities.

Wirth (1938) provides some insights as to why large places encourage the view that government is inefficient. Population size leads to more institutional differentiation, bureaucratization, and impersonality. As local governments become more bureaucratic and specialized, residents consider these institutions inflexible and overly complex. Under these conditions the view of government as wasteful would follow.

Rapid growth can cause residents to feel that local government is inattentive. The writings of Burgess (1925) and

McKenzie (1925) offer other clues relating to insititutional response to growth. There is necessary government response to rapid growth, including the development of new services, facilities, and infrastructure. Local institutions may respond slowly to change. This lag in response time can be the period in which negative attitudes toward government develop. Local government can be perceived as unresponsive to citizens and not attending to their needs.

The final issue is why social heterogeneity fosters less overall confidence. People may simply feel less trusting on various dimensions combined when there are different constituencies vying to control government actions. This is partly because the community groups themselves are not trusted by residents in heterogeneous areas. It is also because residents believe that local government may stray from its objective role and its clear course when it hears varying opinions. Overall confidence is thus lost when social diversity is present.

The evidence that suburban distrust is significant and partly influenced by classic community variables should encourage expansion, as well as replication, of current research. There could be more focus on other attitude dimensions. The rankings of elected leaders would be important. The ratings of specific institutions, such as planning and community development agencies, would also be instructive. Local government's perceived honesty, intelligence, concern with the general welfare, and malleability before business and special interests should also be explored. The many facets of powerlessness and political alienation need a comprehensive analysis. Future research ought also to consider several objective measures of suburban government activities. Further, residents' perceptions of the suburban system of government need to be considered. All these dimensions would now seem worth pursuing given the results reported here and the fact that the issues seem central to understanding suburban distrust.

The "suburban" structural features, which had no direct influence on trust in local government, deserve further attention. There is a need to caution against overinterpretation. Unincorporated versus incorporated status made no difference. In Orange County the unincorporated areas tend to be white and wealthy, and, further, small, low density, and homogeneous places. These community features may obscure the effects of political structure on trust. Age of community also had no effect on the attitudes toward government. Here again, the problem is that newer and mixed-activity places are low density, small, homogeneous, and more wealthy. These structural factors may counter the local government distrust in newer communities. Thus, a broader range of mixed-use and unincorporated suburban areas must be the foundation of future studies.

Suburban characteristics that may affect trust in local government need to be further pursued. Theories have simply lacked adequate attention to the suburban context. One is the number of municipal governments within a given region. Another is the density of governments, or the number of municipalities per area of a given size. A third is the degree to which a dominant suburban municipality, which acts as a focus for economic activity, political power, social institutions, and decision-making exists in the region. A fourth is the level of industrialization, measured in land use and employment. A last factor is the existence of specific community problems, such as crime, pollution, and traffic congestion, that may run counter to suburban expectations and result in distrust.

There is, in sum, adequate information to assume that corollaries of suburban rapid growth, industrialization, and political fragmentation will lower the suburban resident's trust in local government.

Notes

1. The analysis was repeated with ethnicity as a sixth covariate. The ethnicity variable was coded white and non-Hispanic versus all others. The significant effects are the same as those reported in table 4.2.

2. A multiple regression equation including the five personal characteristics in the footnote to table 4.2, the four structural characteristics in table 4.3, and the ethnicity variable was also examined. The results of the final equation generally confirmed the findings in table 4.3. Overall confidence was predicted only by social heterogeneity, performance only by social heterogeneity, and efficiency only by population size. Attention was not significantly predicted by rapid growth, but this is probably due to multicolinearity. The analysis also indicates that controlling for personal characteristics, including ethnicity, does not affect most of the significant relationships involving the structural characteristics.

CHAPTER FIVE

The Tax Revolt
and Fiscal Strain

What citizens prefer in the way of policies has been the focus of several studies. Citizen groups that favor certain forms of service spending have been examined (Hoffman and Clark 1979). The relationship between citizen attitudes and the formation of policy has been considered (Schumaker 1981). Citizen preferences have been viewed as important input for the process of policy review (Baldassare and Protash 1982; Hatry and Blair 1976). Some have even found that changes in public opinion correspond with changes in elected leader's decisions and policies (Kuklinski 1978, 1979; Page and Shapiro 1983). This chapter analyzes citizens' perceptions, elected leaders' attitudes, and elected leaders' views of their citizens' preferences on the issues of fiscal strain and the tax revolt.

Fiscal strain and the tax revolt have attracted so much discussion in recent years that the terms are in need of some clarification. Fiscal strain simply means that there is a gap between the funds needed to provide services in a community at their current level and the revenues which are currently available to support those services. Of course, fiscal strain is a relative term. Local governments can vary in the degree of mismatch between expenditures and funds (Clark and Ferguson 1983). There is obviously a subjective element in what is considered not enough money, and not enough services. Fiscal strain, for the purposes of this chapter, is the presence of residents and leaders who perceive service problems as seen either through poor service ratings or in a perceived need to increase service spending.

The tax revolt simply refers to the citizenry opposing any further increases in the tax burden. Clark and Ferguson (1983) refer to this as new fiscal populism, and others call it fiscal conservatism. There is evidence of the middle class supporting this movement. There are several indicators of the tax revolt, including voting for tax limitation initiatives, citizens' organizations that lobby for tax relief, public opinion swings against spending and taxing increases, and the election of so-called new fiscal populists. The tax revolt is, for our purposes, the existence of citizens opposed to tax increases or the recognition of citizen opposition by their leaders.

Fiscal strain and the tax revolt are by no means limited to the suburbs. Large central cities certainly had their share of fiscal problems during the late 1970s and early 1980s. But the rapid growth of suburban areas has further implications for the existence of fiscal strain. Local revenues do increase when new residents, industries, and commerce move into an area. But so do large infrastructure needs, which are very expensive. The existing network of schools, roads, sewers, police, and health and welfare agencies has to be expanded. New parks, libraries, and other public facilities expected in the suburbs must be developed. It is not surprising that sometimes service expansion cannot keep pace with service needs. More important, funding needs for early phases of rapid growth can be much more than the funding that is available (see Baldassare 1981).

There is a growing diversity in public service needs that has probably exacerbated suburban fiscal strain. Suburbs are industrializing, and localities must now provide services for the "daytime" work population as well as the resident population.

Also, as foreign immigrants and minorities move to the suburbs, there is a demand for more social services. For instance, schools and other institutions are pressed into new duties. Now that households are primarily nonfamily and also include many working couples, the facilities needed have changed. As another example, the lack of day care for the children of single parents and dual-career families is a major issue in many suburban areas. The presence of blue collar renters in suburban apartment complexes can stretch yet other facilities, including outdoor recreational sites and public parks. Further, the pockets of poverty and the elderly population have created diverse needs for police, health, and welfare services. A demand for not only more but more specialized services has emerged. In some instances suburban government is likely to be caught unprepared and short-funded. Industrialization and increasing diversity can, in an era of austerity, also add to fiscal strain.

Suburban areas have operated under a special disadvantage in seeking new revenues for services and infrastructure. When central cities needed new roads they were able to seek large grants from the federal government. Further, when the large influx of poor persons arrived in big cities there were substantial sums of money for social services forthcoming from federal and state sources. But suburban governments have been laboring to meet service needs in an era of fiscal austerity. The amount of funds available from state and federal sources is more limited because these governments are themselves operating under stricter budget constraints. New funds must come more often from local sources; but with a citizenry unwilling to increase local taxes, this solution becomes less feasible. Fiscal strain is thus heightened.

The tax revolt in suburbia is strong because of the values and interests expressed by residents. Clark and Ferguson (1983) have noted that the tax revolt is a middle class movement. The suburbs, of course, have a high concentration of middle class residents and thus a high potential for politically successful tax reduction programs. Other demographic features expand the support group. Homeowners are notoriously concerned about local taxes and government spending because of their property tax burden. Since the suburbs have a high concentration of homeowners and would-be homeowners, one would have to expect heightened interest in reducing local expenditures to maintain or decrease the taxes that residents pay. There are still substantial numbers of whites, families, middle-aged individuals, and professionals in the suburbs. These social features should translate into the traditional conservative and Republican supporters who, among other things, are against big government and taxes for social programs. Thus population qualities create support for the new fiscal conservatism as well as for the traditional conservative ideology. Together they form a strong political bloc against increased local taxes.

There are other social values predisposing suburban residents against tax increases. These involve the distrust in suburban governments discussed in the last chapter. One of the resultant attitudes is the view that local government is wasteful of tax dollars. Others include an inability of government to solve problems or listen to its constituents. Such perceptions can only fuel existing desires to reduce taxes and government spending. A structural composition that produces distrust would seem to be a solid base of support for the tax revolt.

Thus, the rapid growth and industrialization of the suburbs increases the opportunities for fiscal strain. Federal and state budgetary shortfalls mean that external solutions to fiscal strain are less forthcoming. Tax revolt sentiments, driven by suburbia's middle class values and distrust in government, mean that local solutions are also difficult to implement.

Studying Fiscal Strain
and the Tax Revolt

Since Proposition 13 passed in California in 1978 there have been many attempts to understand the tax revolt's causes and consequences (California 1980). This has proved to be a difficult task. Components involved include local, state, and federal issues that relate to revenues, expenditures, tax burdens, and service delivery. I have chosen to concentrate on the quality of local public services as perceived by residents, and on citizens' preferences regarding government spending and taxes. Further information is also offered on elected leaders' perceptions.

Some may argue that a more objective assessment of suburban service provision should be conducted. This would include a financial assessment of per capita spending for different public services. It might also involve an analysis of the gap between revenues and expenditures for each service, or the overall tax burden for the community's residents. Such approaches do have value but also have limits in predicting trends. Many different factors besides the budget can contribute to satisfaction with services (see Katz et al. 1975). In extreme cases, objective standards may have little to do with residents' needs and expectations. Attitude studies, further, allow one to pinpoint the groups with the clearest feelings toward fiscal strain and the tax revolt. Further, self-reports from residents are evidence of views which, even if unfounded, do have repercussions on local political, demographic, and economic trends (see Baldassare 1981; Marans and Wellman 1978; Morgan 1975).

There are many practical difficulties in responding to citizens' attitudes, particularly with regard to spending and taxes. Citizens are often found to want more spending in most of the areas they are asked about. They may be responding to a desire to increase the available services or improve some perceived deficit in the existing system. They may ask to cut back certain services and not others on the basis of personal experiences with bureaucracies and the individuals who hold positions in them. Most important, they may not recognize that, in an era of fiscal austerity, increased spending in one area may mean that taxes need to be increased or spending needs to be cut in another area. Thus, spending attitudes are not always accurate portrayals of policy preferences.

Several approaches have been used to improve citizens'

reports on spending preferences. Clark (1974) devised a "budget pie" method to elicit preferences within a limited budget, and other researchers have noted useful applications of this approach (McIver and Ostrom 1976; Scott 1976). The major conclusions drawn from these and other studies is, again, that citizens who are surveyed need in some way to be reminded of the practical implications of their spending decisions. The most salient method today is to confront citizens with the likelihood that their spending preferences can result in either tax increases or tax decreases.

The empirical evidence supports the need to distinguish service, spending, and taxing preferences. There is no link between spending preferences and the tax revolt. Nor does service quality seem to be a cause of fiscal conservatism. Many California voters who supported Proposition 13 actually wanted to see current levels of spending either maintained or increased for most services. Citrin (1979) thus noted that Californians were voting against high taxes, with little consideration of other issues, when they supported the reduction of property taxes. Ladd and Wilson (1982) found similar reasons behind the Proposition 2½ initiative in Massachusetts and offered further elaboration concerning the tax revolt. The major reason for support was the desire for lower taxes. Most voters wanted to maintain or increase the current level of government services and were in favor of drastically lowering spending only for welfare.

What links the seemingly impossible combination of decreasing taxes and possibly increasing services? It is the ideology that government is inefficient and wasteful. In other words, a tax cut may be a necessary incentive for government to use funds with greater care. Studies conducted after the Michigan tax initiative basically replicate the results reported thus far. The Michigan vote was yet another revolt against increasing taxes. In no way was it a serious statement in favor of spending reductions for public services (Courant, Gramlich, and Rubinfeld 1979, 1980; Gramlich, Rubinfeld, and Swift 1981).

Any approach to sorting out the issues involved in fiscal

strain and the tax revolt is thus necessarily complex. This chapter builds upon the experiences of previous researchers. The focusing of attitude questions on local services, and on several of them, is essential to understanding how individuals have responded to fiscal issues in the suburban community. Since one cannot rely upon citizens' spending preferences alone to understand either the tax revolt or fiscal strain, several types of attitude measures are used. The approach is to consider the overlapping attitude dimensions of public service ratings, spending preferences, tax sentiments, and political conservatism.

It is also important to know the perceptions suburbia's elected leaders have of their constituents. Policies designed to confront fiscal strain must be set in action by elected leaders who, ultimately, will react to their views of citizens' wishes.

Hypotheses

The first hypothesis to be studied here is that there is a conservative mood in the suburban area under study. It will be important to establish this fact, since political opinions underlie the tax revolt and, ultimately, affect the outcome of current fiscal strain. Evidence for a political orientation that is more conservative than liberal would be important. The gap between Republican and Democratic party affiliation would also be meaningful. The lack of a sizable Democratic-liberal coalition, which typically supports taxes and spending increases in large central cities, would be another essential proof of the hypothesis. Political distinctions between the suburban community and other places would be important verifications of the findings.

The second hypothesis is that fiscal strain exists on the local level. In public opinion surveys this will be evident in a substantial minority of residents giving low ratings to their services. Police, roads, schools, public health, and parks and recreation should have evident negative ratings. Further confirmation will exist if the suburban sample has more negative evaluations than those offered in other communities. There is no a priori view as to which services will receive the lowest ratings, nor which residents will have particularly negative ratings. These latter issues will be explored and considered later.

The third hypothesis is that residents will favor spending increases for services despite a suburban antitax sentiment. The spending preferences are a reflection of low service ratings and of fiscal strain. For this reason, services with the most negative evaluations will have the strongest preferences for spending increases. These prospending attitudes should be stronger in the suburbs than in other places. In addition, the resident characteristics associated with low service ratings will also be associated with high spending preferences.

The fourth hypothesis is that there will be evidence of tax revolt sentiment. Residents will be in favor of reducing the tax burden despite the implications for services. One would expect the antitax attitude to be stronger in suburban areas than in other places. One would also expect the support for reducing taxes to be strongest among the fiscal conservatives, that is, the middle class, homeowners, and the highly educated, as well as the traditional conservatives. Part of the evidence for the tax revolt will thus be derived from the attitudes of local residents. Further confirmation will be drawn from local elected leaders' views that citizens do not support spending increases for public services.

Methods

The major sources of information are the 1982 and 1983 Orange County Annual surveys. Other relevant data include a 1983 survey of California mayors. The 1982 survey asked residents about tax increases and about their ratings of 5 major public services. The 1983 survey of residents asked for spending preferences for the same 5 public services. The 1983 survey of mayors asked for impressions of citizens' spending preferences.

Other data are used to contrast Orange County with state and national trends in politics, service ratings, spending preferences, and tax attitudes.

Orange County possesses many appropriate characteristics for a study of fiscal strain and the tax revolt. State government revenues were reduced by Proposition 13 and an economic recession. Federal budget deficits and income tax cuts have reduced the flow of funds from higher levels of government. Fiscal austerity is thus at issue. Since Orange County and especially some of its individual communities have had rapid growth rates, there would seem to be pressure to increase the level of key public services. Fiscal strain may thus be present for demographic reasons. The population contains high proportions of homeowners and the middle class. The county's voting record also would seem to indicate tax revolt sentiments. The electorate overwhelmingly supported Proposition 13 in 1978, Ronald Reagan, George Deukmejian in 1982, and has sent mostly Republican conservatives to Congress, the state assembly, and the state senate. On all grounds, then, it is a good location to study fiscal strain and the tax revolt.

The 1982 and 1983 surveys asked the same questions about politics. One question was worded, "Are you currently registered as a Republican, Democrat, or Independent, or are you not registered to vote?" The other question was, "Would you consider yourself to be politically liberal, middle-of-the-road, or conservative?"

The 1982 survey had questions on public services which began with the introduction, "I'd like to ask you to rate some of the main public services you are supposed to receive." The services included roads, education, public health, police protection, and parks and recreation. The rankings included excellent, good, fair and poor. The fair and poor responses were again combined. For the purpose of calculating mean scores comparable to other surveys, three response categories were coded 1, 3, and 5. The questions and response categories are similar in wording to those used in national surveys and statewide polls.

Another question, which tapped support for the tax revolt, was worded, "Would you support further tax cuts in state and local taxes even if some government services would have to be cut back?" Answers were yes and no. The two response categories were coded as 1 and 5 to allow mean comparison.

In the 1983 survey questions involving spending preferences were prefaced by: "For each of these government services, tell me whether we should spend more money, less money, or no change." The services were the same as in the 1982 survey. The answers were coded again for purposes of comparison from 1 through 5.

The information concerning elected leaders' fiscal perceptions was gathered as part of the Fiscal Austerity and Urban Innovation Project, which sent a mail questionnaire to mayors and city managers throughout the nation.[1] The mailings for California cities over 25,000 commenced in April 1983. Several mail and telephone follow-ups were instituted to improve the response rate, and data collection ceased in June 1983.[2] The seven Orange County mayors who returned their questionnaires are analyzed.

One series of questions was used from the survey instrument. Mayors were asked, "Please estimate the preferences of the majority of voters in your city." They rated spending preferences for services on a scale from 1 through 5 including spend a lot less, spend somewhat less, spend the same, spend somewhat more, and spend a lot more. For the purposes of this analysis, the spending preferences for which there are comparable public opinion data were selected, which include education, roads, public health, parks and recreation, and police protection. It is thus possible to assess elected leaders' views of the tax revolt and to contrast mayors' perceptions of citizens' preferences with actual citizens' spending preferences.

The statistical approach allowed evidence to be established for each of the propositions. Orange County's political focus is examined through the proportions of conservative respondents in the two surveys. These numbers are then compared with state and national figures. Public service ratings, spending preferences, and tax attitudes in Orange County are analyzed through mean scores and percentages. These numbers are compared with available national and state statistics. The characteristics of Orange County respondents and their residential areas that predict these attitudes are then summarized. The results are based upon the significance levels achieved in chi-square tests including major demographic, economic, and political factors as the causal variables and all the public service attitude items as the dependent variables. The final task was to use the mayors' survey to indicate differences between the Orange County mayors' and their views of citizens' spending preferences, and differences between mayors' views of citizen preferences and actual citizens' preferences. The mean scores are compared and variations in mayors' views and citizens' preferences are determined. In sum, the analysis is a straightforward attempt to evaluate the suburbs' degree of conservatism, the ratings of public services and their causes, the need for spending increases and the determinants, and the extent to which individual citizens have especially antitax sentiments.

Findings

Much has been said about the conservative climate in suburban communities and particularly in Orange County. The 1982 and 1983 surveys asked respondents to define themselves as liberal, middle-of-the-road, or conservative. Data from the two years combined show 19 percent liberal, 45 percent moderate, and 36 percent conservative. Thus, fewer than one in five adults views himself or herself as liberal. Questions on party identification for the combined surveys showed that 77 percent defined themselves as registered voters. Of these, 49 percent were Republican, 40 percent were Democrat, and 11 percent were Independent or had other party memberships.

These proportions in themselves can be characterized as a conservative orientation. But consider, further, the different combinations of party and political orientation. Fifty-three percent of all Republicans, 25 percent of all Independents, and 22 percent of all Democrats label themselves as conservatives. Forty-eight percent of the Democrats, 47 percent of the Independents, and 38 percent of the Republicans call themselves middle of the road. Among the Democrats, only 30 percent call themselves liberals and among all registered voters only 12 percent are Democratic liberals. There is a sizable following for traditional, new fiscal populist, and Sunbelt conservatism. Little evidence exists for the urban coalitions that typically support spending and tax increases.

Orange County is clearly right of center in comparison with state and national figures. A 1982 national survey indicated 27 percent liberal and 54 percent Democratic, and 32 percent conservative and 32 percent Republican (Davis and Smith 1983). A California poll the same year showed 19 percent liberal and 51 percent Democrat (Field 1982). These political opinions need to be considered when viewing the public service ratings, spending preferences, and tax-related attitudes.

The next findings to consider are the public service ratings in 1982. The evaluations presented in table 5.1 point to several problem areas in Orange County. Education is the least highly rated of the five services. Only one in five rated the education system excellent while one in three noted that it was fair or poor. The evaluations of roads are not much better. Again, only one in five viewed the roads as excellent while a greater proportion rated them as fair or poor. Police protection received almost average ratings with about as many noting that it was excellent as indicating fair and poor. Parks and recreation and public health were given virtually identical ratings by the respondents. One-third rated each of these services as excellent, with 13 percent rating each as fair or poor.

These service ratings can be compared with statistics reported in a nationwide study (see Campbell et al. 1976). The education evaluations were more negative in Orange County than those reported in the national survey. The parks and recreation ratings were somewhat more positive than those

Table 5.1 Ratings of Public Services

	Percent	Mean
Roads		
Excellent	21	
Good	51	
Fair and Poor	28	
Total	100	3.13
Education		
Excellent	20	
Good	47	
Fair and Poor	33	
Total	100	3.28
Police Protection		
Excellent	24	
Good	55	
Fair and Poor	21	
Total	100	2.92
Parks and Recreation		
Excellent	35	
Good	52	
Fair and Poor	13	
Total	100	2.56
Public Health		
Excellent	36	
Good	51	
Fair and Poor	13	
Total	100	2.53

SOURCE is the 1982 Orange County Annual Survey. Higher means indicate more negative service evaluations.

found in the national survey. The better rating for parks and recreation is probably accounted for by the existence of private amusement parks (e.g., Disneyland, Knotts Berry Farm) and the ocean beaches, which are hardly attributable to public service provision. Evaluations of other services were fairly similar. It is interesting that only one service rating was better in Orange County than in the nation despite greater personal wealth.

Public service ratings were fairly uniform across demographic and economic groups. Schools and roads were rated similarly among the age, sex, income, family composition, and length-of-residence groups. Police and parks were rated some-

136   The Tax Revolt and Fiscal Strain

what more favorably by the high-status and older residents. Public health services are more positively rated by the long-term residents. One important difference is that the residents from the older, larger, and more diverse municipalities (i.e., Anaheim, Santa Ana, Garden Grove) had the worst ratings of public services. This is evidence that the demographic changes that have occurred in the suburbs do affect perceptions of public services.

The spending preferences—to spend more, spend less, or spend the same for the five public services which had been previously evaluated—are presented in table 5.2. Residents on average tend to want more spending in all instances, as shown

Table 5.2 Preferences for Service Spending

	Percent	Mean
Roads		
Less	6	
Same	48	
More	46	
Total	100	3.81
Education		
Less	5	
Same	21	
More	74	
Total	100	4.39
Police protection		
Less	2	
Same	32	
More	66	
Total	100	4.27
Parks and recreation		
Less	9	
Same	58	
More	33	
Total	100	3.47
Public health		
Less	12	
Same	47	
More	41	
Total	100	3.56

SOURCE is the 1983 Orange County Annual Survey. Higher means indicate preferences to spend more money.

in the mean scores. The proportion desiring less service spending is small in all five service categories. The preference to increase public spending, however, does vary across services. The strongest desire is to increase education spending, with nearly three of four residents wanting more spending. This is followed by police and then roads. The spending preferences for parks and public health are similar, and willingness to spend is comparatively weak.

To some extent the Orange County population does differ from the state as a whole in spending preferences. The suburban area is more prospending, as is evidenced with comparisons of the 1983 survey with a California poll conducted the same year (Field Institute 1983). Orange County residents were significantly more prospending with regard to education, roads, police protection, and parks and recreation. Their attitudes toward public health spending were very similar. Unfortunately, no comparable national questions are available.

A scale was created for overall attitudes toward spending increases in the study population. The scores were summed across the five service preference items. Rankings went from wanting to spend less on all the services (i.e., 5) to wanting to spend more on all of them (i.e., 15). There was no one who received a 5 ranking, and only 9 percent had scores of 6 through 9. This suggests that antispending sentiment is limited. But neither can the preference be described as one favoring across-the-board spending increases. Eight percent supported spending increases in all five service categories, and only 15 percent had ratings of 14 or 15. Half the respondents had scores of 10, 11, and 12, accounting for a mean score of 11.8. This indicates support for service spending increases in some categories but not all.

There is obviously a relationship between service evaluations and spending preferences. Roads, police protection, and education had the worst service ratings in Orange County and the strongest prospending attitudes. Parks and public health had the most favorable service ratings and the least support for increased spending. It appears, then, that residents are at least

partly responding to a need to improve services when they provide answers regarding their desire to increase government
spending. The preference for public spending may not be so
much a statement about political attitude, or an indicator of
actual policy preferences, as it is a partial perception of current
community conditions. It may thus lack an association with how
people are likely to respond to the need for increased taxes.

There are several demographic correlates with service
spending preferences. Renters and young adults tended to be
more favorable toward spending increases. Liberals were also
more willing to support efforts to spend more money for services. Women tended to favor increases more than men, offering further evidence of a gender gap that involved more liberal
views among women. However, none of these differences were
large, and in no way did they clearly differentiated who was in
favor of spending from who was seriously opposed. For instance, even two-thirds of the conservatives wanted more
spending for schools. Instead, individual characteristics distinguished degrees of support. Another factor of importance,
again, was residence in the older, larger, and more diverse
cities. Apparently the perceived quality of services in Anaheim–
Santa Ana–Garden Grove was reflected in the desire to increase spending.

A 1982 survey question shows the conflict between the
desire to increase spending and the willingness to minimize the
tax bill. Perhaps this is better described as a demonstration that
the need to improve services does not necessarily correspond
with attitudes toward the tax burden. On the question of more
local tax cuts even if services needed to be further reduced, 52
percent were in favor and 48 percent opposed. Thus, a slim
majority places tax cuts as a higher priority than maintaining the
current level of services. It is unlikely, given this attitude, that
there would be strong support for increasing taxes to pay for
increased spending for public services. People are dissatisfied
with current services, and seem willing to have spending increases, but their attitude toward current tax levels suggests they
will oppose tax increases. It is doubtful that residents view these

attitudes as contradictory. They probably believe that service spending can increase, and that services will improve, when local government learns to use existing funds more effectively.

The groups most in favor of reducing services in order to receive tax cuts were also identified. Republicanism and conservatism were notable influences. This is especially important since political variables had little impact on service evaluations or spending preferences. Approximately 60 percent of all Republicans and two-thirds of all conservatives favored tax cuts. The more advantaged were somewhat more inclined to accept service cuts than were the less advantaged. This was especially true with respect to family income and homeownership. Interestingly, the college-educated and women were less inclined to accept the notion of reducing services in order to reduce taxes. Maybe the most important findings of all are concerning the relationships between service evaluations and tax attitudes. Persons rating schools, police, roads, parks, and public health negatively are no more likely to reject further service and tax cuts. Service evaluations and tax preferences obviously exist in different attitude realms. Though impossible to test because the tax question was not repeated in the 1983 survey, it is likely that spending preferences also have little relationship to tax attitudes.

There is a large difference between the state and Orange County in attitudes toward taxes. California residents seem less eager to approve taxes to increase spending (Field Institute 1983). Here, it is probably question wording rather than political orientation that explains the difference. The California poll questioned whether tax increases should be imposed to avoid service spending cuts. The 1982 Orange County Annual Survey asked if tax cuts should be imposed even if it caused further spending cuts. Obviously, more antispending attitudes surface when tax increases are mentioned.

The 1983 California mayors' survey further corroborates the evidence already presented. The survey, again, was statewide, but analysis reported in table 5.3 is for Orange County mayors. Mayors were asked if their citizens favored spending less, spending the same, or spending more for various services.

Table 5.3. Citizens' Preferences for Spending: Mayors' Opinions and Public Opinions

Orange County Totals	Mayors' Opinions of Citizens' Preferences	Citizens' Preferences
Education	3.40	4.30
Public Health	2.71	3.69
Roads	3.57	3.83
Parks and Recreation	3.57	3.42
Police Protection	4.29	4.27
(N)	(7)	(301)

SOURCES are the 1983 Fiscal Austerity Survey and the 1983 Orange County Annual Survey. Citizens' preferences based upon the subsample of 301 who lived in the cities of the 7 mayors who responded. Higher means indicate preferences to spend more money.

The preferences regarding education, roads, public health, parks, and police protection are considered. Mayors believe that citizens are particularly antispending with regard to education and public health. These fit into the so-called "general welfare" services which have frequently been targeted by the middle class and fiscal conservatives. Feelings about roads and parks are somewhat more positive. Finally, mayors strongly believe that citizens want more money spent on police protection. The findings suggest that citizens' leaders tend to view citizens as antispending for most public services. This offers further evidence of a tax revolt in suburbia.

What is perhaps as interesting to consider is the mayors' impressions compared to actual citizen's preferences. In table 5.3 the spending preferences of the 301 individuals who lived in the same 7 cities as the mayors who responded are considered. The spending preferences for citizens in each of the 7 cities are separately aggregated, and then a mean is derived from the 7 scores for each spending preference. This is done because the number of interviews per city ranges dramatically. To calculate means based upon the subsample totals would heavily weight the findings toward one city which had the most respondents. It is interesting to note, first, that the means for the residents of these 7 cities are extremely close to the means for the total Orange

County sample reported in table 5.2. Most significant in table 5.3 are the discrepancies between the mayor's perceptions of citizens and actual citizens' preferences. Mayors view citizens as much more antispending with regard to education and public health than they actually are. There is more similarity with respect to roads and parks. Their views are almost identical with respect to police. The greatest differences, then, are in those very same "general welfare" services which mayors may believe are subject to the middle classes' greatest scrutiny. Mayors probably thought citizens tied their spending preferences for these services to their tax preferences and not, as they seem to more, their evaluations of services. The fact that mayors perceive a citizenry opposed to spending for several needed services is further evidence of the tax revolt.

In sum, a conservative mood was found, coincidental with a period of fiscal strain measured here in terms of significant numbers of people giving low ratings to public services. The negative feelings about local services seem the impetus for a desire to spend more money on specific services without much regard to existing fiscal conservatism. However, the suburban populace is still generally against tax increases and, when confronted with tax issues, seems to shy away from prospending orientations. Local government leaders are clearly aware of the antitax sentiments of the public at large. One can assume that this awareness would inhibit them from increasing service spending by raising taxes. There appears to be little room for maneuvering, given the suburban political climate, to improve local services.

Concluding Comments
on the Tax Revolt and Fiscal Strain

This study found evidence for conservatism, fiscal strain, and the tax revolt. All seem to be heightened by the suburban environment.

A substantial minority of Orange County residents had low ratings of several public services. Citizens also indicated a need to increase service spending. But efforts to address fiscal strain are evidently constrained by a conservative and antitax sentiment. Leaders also perceive the unpopularity of tax and spending increases to meet service needs. Fiscal strain could increase as spending needs are held down and service needs continue to increase. The local government's mission, as perceived by the people, is to better use existing monies and to find new sources of funds outside the locality. The extent to which suburban governments can accomplish these difficult tasks will probably determine the outcome of fiscal strain. The fiscal strain in suburbia is a by-product of years of rapid growth and industrialization coupled with an era of federal and state funding shortages. The tax revolt is a function of the suburb's middle class values and orientations and a substantial distrust in local governments.

There is evidence from the public opinion surveys that spending preferences reflect service evaluations rather than a willingness to commit new tax monies. This interpretation is noted with the caution that, as Clark (1974) indicates, many other factors account for spending preferences. Examples are present in the 1982 and the 1983 Orange County surveys. The services with the worst evaluations in the 1982 survey had on the whole the highest rankings for increased spending in the 1983 survey. There has also been a steady decline in perceived service quality, especially of schools, as measured over time in the California polls (Field Institute 1983b) coinciding with an increase from 1979 to the present in the proportion of California residents desiring spending increases for several service categories (Field Institute 1983a). Yet, there has been no significant change in the proportion of California citizens who favor spending reductions to avoid increased taxes: 60 percent in 1980 and 56 percent in 1983 opposed tax increases (Field Insititute 1983a). The desire for spending increases is not a measure of fiscal conservatism but, instead, of service problems. The fact that Orange County residents were more prospending than state residents indicates little about their political attitudes and much about Orange County's problems.

Another interesting pattern emerges with respect to public opinions concerning taxes. The California poll question asked citizens to trade off between a possible spending reduction and a tax increase to avoid a service reduction. The Orange County Annual Survey presented citizens with a choice between maintaining existing spending and service levels and a tax reduction that would decrease service levels. In both instances, a majority of the public approved the spending reductions, but the possibility of a tax increase led citizens to favor a reduction somewhat more than the possibility of a tax cut. This indicates that preferences for spending reductions are driven more by the fear of tax increases than by a desire for a tax cut. The finding corresponds with other evidence and is important information for suburban policy leaders to consider.

There are several explanations for the mayors' views that their citizens are opposed to new spending. Mayors obviously equate spending with taxes more readily than the public at large, probably because of their greater knowledge of the local budget process. This may also be because of their heightened sensitivity to the revolt through election campaigns (Kulkinski 1978). There are undoubtedly many informal, indirect means through which elected officials become aware of their citizens' preferences. City council meetings, public meetings, letters, and visits from private citizens and groups are examples.

The extent to which citizens' preferences actually affect policies is beyond the scope of this study. But mayors' views of citizens' preferences may influence mayors' fiscal actions. For instance, Orange County mayors' self-stated spending preferences were similar to what they perceived as citizens' spending preferences. In California as a whole, most of the mayors surveyed said that they often responded to their citizens' spending preferences. Elected officials may be moderating more pro-spending attitudes to accommodate their views of citizens' anti-spending attitudes. If so, fiscal strain cannot be fully addressed.

The discrepancies noted earlier between mayors' views

of citizens and citizens' actual opinions points to the possibility that elected leaders may misperceive their constitutents' spending preferences. Several factors may keep mayors in relative ignorance. One possibility is that leaders may mistake general preferences about spending and taxes as applying to specific policy decisions. Another is that past voting behaviors may be incorrectly extrapolated to current circumstances. Elected leaders may also hear the opinions of unrepresentative groups and develop their impressions in an insulated environment. It is fairly obvious, in any case, that elected officals need to be better informed about citizens' preferences. Systematic and current opinion polls are necessary for local leaders engaged in urban policy formation and policy review (Hatry and Blair 1976). This is especially important since elected leaders' views of citizens can affect their decisions.

Future research needs to specify citizens' reasons for service ratings and specific desires to improve services, pay more taxes, and increase spending in different service categories. To link citizens' preferences with local policies, comparable data should be collected from elected leaders. Specifically, leaders' attitudes toward service delivery and interest in improving services, increasing taxes, and increasing spending must be determined. As well, leaders' views on whether citizens want to do these things are essential.

Exactly how fiscal strain can be resolved in suburbia given the tax revolt is open to question. Perhaps these phenomena are merely temporary. Rapid growth could subside, thus taking pressure off service delivery problems. Sustained and slow growth could add substantially to existing local revenues. New funding from state and national governments could be freed and diverted to local services.

Most of these possibilities seem unlikely, and current trends will probably continue to some degree. Looking toward the future, greater variations between suburban communities are most likely. The affluent and organized communities will do well. They will deliver services and attract revenues with greater success than others. Residents who can will move to the "successful" areas and thus raise the status and prospects of those advantaged places. Further inequalities in status, goods, and services will evolve. Some suburban communities will gain in overall quality while others will lose. Where one lives and works in suburbia will become increasingly more important than whether one lives in the suburbs.

Notes

1. Ninety-three percent of the California cities with 25,000 or more population were thus included. The 11 excluded from the original mailing were in Terry Clark's "Permanent Community Sample" (see Clark and Ferguson 1983). These were Berkeley, Long Beach, Los Angeles, Palo Alto, Pasadena, San Diego, San Jose, San Francisco, and Santa Monica and the Orange County cities of Santa Ana and Fullerton.

2. The response rate throughout California was 33 percent or 50 responses from the original 150 mailings. A comparable proportion of responses was received from Orange County mayors.

CHAPTER SIX

Special Needs

Many new service needs emerged as housing, land use, and population composition changed as a result of industrialization and rapid growth. Transportation is exemplary of a special service need in the era of suburban transformation. Individuals who moved to the suburbs once believed that they were escaping the traffic congestion that plagued their trips to work. This was accurate when land use was residential, densities were low, and jobs were located in distant downtowns. But growth in population and in employment have combined to increase the daytime populations that fill suburban residential, industrial, and commercial districts.

The suburban ecology creates unique transportation needs. The physical layout of jobs and residences presents commuting flows which are not center to periphery, as in the Burgess model of urban development. Densities are moderate, and workplaces and residences are spread all over the suburban region. There is an ever increasing, sprawling distribution of homes and workplaces. Commuting traffic is not necessarily flowing in one direction at sunrise and in the opposite direction at sundown. Nor is it along a few major corridors. Traffic flows in all directions and to numerous mini-centers of jobs and homes. The commuter obviously has a difficult time in attempting to avoid daily congestion. The situation is equally problematic for the planner seeking to determine where new roads might help and where mass transit might work.

Traffic problems are aggravated by the social values which pervade suburbia. There is an unending attachment to the private vehicle with a solo driver as the mode of transportation. Individuals resist the use of carpooling, buses, and rail transit, despite increasing rush hour traffic and long delays in arriving at home or work. Traffic congestion and overused roadways are undesirable in any setting. But they run against the suburban image of uncrowded land, and residents are strongly bothered by their existence. Thus, suburban residents have high expectations about their transportation situation and have shown low tolerance for traffic problems.

Other suburban attitudes also inhibit actions to ameliorate transportation conditions. One is the tax revolt. It is likely that transportation improvements meet with resistance when residents oppose tax increases. The other is a general distrust of government planning capabilities. Suspicion of the public sector as a competent problem solver means that suburban residents will approach transportation proposals with skepticism.

Activity patterns have obviously changed in metropolitan areas as a result of industrialization. Rapid growth has led to the congestion of existing roads. This is part of the picture, though, since only home-to-work commutes have been considered. Consumer goods and services have found their place in the suburban landscape. Shopping malls, professional buildings, leisure centers, and recreational and cultural facilities have developed. This trend ensures that travels within suburban areas have become more frequent and trips to the downtown more rare. Commercial centers are also randomly distributed in the new suburbia. Thus consumer trips are also reliant upon the automobile and solo driving.

The industrialized suburbs show evidence of traffic congestion, overcrowding, and erratic commuting flows. That aside, residents' values and preferences regarding transportation have undoubtedly changed very little. Dissatisfaction with transportation and desire for improvement, however, must surely be present.

Transportation in Suburbia

The suburbs have developed special transportation patterns in this latest era. There is substantial evidence that most suburban residents tend to commute to jobs in the suburban area where they live rather than travel to the central city. According to the 1980 census figures, in the United States as a whole, 67 percent of the suburban employed residents are commuting to suburban workplaces. This involves 38 million suburban employed residents, of which 25 million have suburban jobs. This fact varies somewhat by region of the country but is pronounced everywhere: 76 percent for the Northeast, 67 percent for the North Central states, 59 percent for the South, and 66 percent for the West. The trend of combining suburban residence with suburban workplace varies directly with the size of the metropolitan area. Metropolises of over 3 million population have 76 percent of the suburban residents in suburban jobs, while the figures are 69 percent in metropolitan areas of 1–3 million, 61 percent for metropolitan places of 250,000–1 million, 56 percent for populations of 100,000–250,000, and 45 percent for metropolitan areas under 100,000. The larger the population, then, the more likely that the suburban area has developed a separate economy that involves suburban residents commuting to suburban jobs (U.S. Bureau of the Census 1984).

The majority of suburban jobs are also currently filled by suburban residents. According to the same census, 86 percent of suburban jobs in the United States were filled by suburban residents. That is, of the 30 million employed within the suburban area, there were 25 million from the suburbs, 4 million from the central city, and 1 million from outlying rural areas. There was again some variation by region of the country: 91 percent of the

northeastern jobs, 86 percent of the north central jobs, 85 percent of the southern jobs, and 80 percent of the western jobs
were filled by suburban residents. The proportion of suburban
jobs filled by suburban workers tended to decline by size of
place. The figures were 87 percent for metropolitan areas 1 million or more in population, 85 percent for 500,000–1 million, 81
percent for 100,000–500,000 population, and 69 percent for
under 100,000 population (U.S. Bureau of the Census 1984).
The Sunbelt regions and the smaller metropolitan areas tend to
have more central city residents commuting to suburban workplaces. This is indicative of trends in the new and developing
suburbs. The regional and size-of-place variations suggest that
suburban workplaces are increasingly popular in the metropolitan context. The findings also suggest that traffic congestion may
increase in suburban areas as city-to-suburb commutes combine
with existing suburb-to-suburb commutes.

Information concerning how suburban residents travel
to work is also important. The solo driver in the private vehicle
is the predominant mode. The 1980 census indicates that 69
percent of employed suburban residents drive alone to work.
Only 11 percent use carpools, and only 4 percent take public
transportation. There are minor variations in travel mode by
region of the country. Among suburban working residents in
the Northeast, 7 percent use public transit, almost twice the
proportion of the other regions' combined totals. Correspond-
ingly, 66 percent in the Northeast are solo drivers to work,
while the figures are 72 percent in the North Central states, 69
percent in the South, and 69 percent in the West. Another
relevant statistic is, among all those commuting in a private
vehicle, in every region of the country over 75 percent of the
suburban residents are driving alone. This proportion is basically unchanged since 1970, when 73 percent of suburban residents who commuted in a private vehicle drove alone (U.S.
Bureau of the Census 1972, 1983c). Suburban residents are
largely dependent upon the solo automobile commute to work.
They have not changed their travel habits as work within the
suburbs has become dominant.

Statistics on travel time to work show that suburban residents' commutes are as lengthy as central city residents' commutes. In each case, the mean travel time is 22 minutes. Those who commute for 45 minutes or more in the suburbs have 58 minutes average travel times, while their central city counterparts have 59 minute average commutes. Suburban residents' times to work vary somewhat from region to region. Mean minutes are 23 in the Northeast, 23 in the South, 22 in the West, and 21 in the North Central states. Interestingly, the suburban resident in the Northeast has a commute which is 5 minutes less than the central city resident's. This difference is probably due to the heavy traffic congestion and use of public transportation in older central cities. The trends suggest that suburban residents are commuting to local jobs rather than to central city jobs. Thus, their time to work is usually not different from those of others in the metropolitan area.

A more detailed picture of suburban commuting trends emerges when we consider two distinct suburban metropolitan areas. These are Orange County, California, and the adjacent counties of Nassau and Suffolk on Long Island, New York. They are the two large metropolises, both definitely suburban, which have emerged next to the largest central cities in the United States. The Orange County versus Nassau-Suffolk comparisons are interesting, since one area is in the North and the other is in the West. They represent both earlier and later suburban development patterns. The figure for total residents employed in 1980 is similar, at approximately 1 million residents.

The 1980 census indicates a similar reliance on the solo commute for private vehicle users. In Orange County 82 percent and in Nassau-Suffolk 78 percent drive alone if they use a private vehicle. Of all those residents who work, there are 75 percent who drive alone in Orange County and 64 percent who drive alone in Nassau-Suffolk. The difference in the means of transportation is almost totally accounted for by differences in public transportation use. In Nassau-Suffolk 12 percent use public transportation to get to work while 2 percent use this mode in Orange County (U.S. Bureau of the Census 1983c).

There are differences in commuting times in the two areas. The mean commute is 24 minutes in Orange County and 32 minutes in Nassau-Suffolk. For commutes of 45 minutes or more, the travel time is 59 minutes in Orange County and 69 minutes in Nassau-Suffolk. These differences are partly explained by use of public transportation. Both public transportation and the travel times are accounted for in reliance upon jobs outside the suburban area. For instance, about 2 in 10 Orange County employed residents worked outside the county. This is in contrast 4 in 10 of the Nassau County residents and 3 in 10 of the Suffolk County residents (U.S. Bureau of the Census 1983c). An analysis of the commuting flows in these areas indicates that many Nassau County residents travel to work in New York City. Few Suffolk County residents travel to a central city job. Even fewer Orange County residents commute to Los Angeles workplaces. A major distinction between Nassau-Suffolk and Orange County is that the former has more vestiges of earlier forms in which suburban residents traveled to central city jobs. The latter area has broken more clearly with the past, and thus Orange County has more reliance on solo driving and short commutes from suburban residence to suburban workplace.

There are some important similarities in the flow of suburban residents to suburban workplaces for Orange County and Nassau-Suffolk. There are trends evident that could not be uncovered in the national summary statistics. The major pattern is a lack of centrality of suburban workplaces. The largest places in population size do not tend to be where work is concentrated. Of the 700,000 who live and work in Orange County, few commute to jobs in the county's major cities. Only 83,000 work in Anaheim, 42,000 in Garden Grove, and 75,000 in Santa Ana. Similarly, of the 800,000 who live and work in Nassau-Suffolk, fewer than 25,000 work in the population centers of Hempstead and Freeport. The workplaces are thus thinly spread throughout the region.

Nor is there a distinctive pattern for residents to travel to work in their city of residence. There are 93,000 workers who live in Santa Ana. Only 30,000 of these work in Santa Ana. The trends are similar in Garden Grove, with 10,000 of the 59,000 workers commuting within the city. In Anaheim, only 37,000 of the 112,000 workers commute internally. The tendency to work away from the place of residence is even more obvious in Nassau-Suffolk. Fewer than 3,000 of the 19,000 Hempstead employed residents work in their city. In Freeport, only 4,000 of the 17,000 employed residents commute inside the city boundaries (U.S. Bureau of the Census 1984). Suburban residents obviously do not combine city of residence and city of workplace. These facts would tend to create difficulties for predicting traffic flow and planning transportation systems.

The following facts are evident in transportation patterns in suburbia. People are commuting to jobs within the suburbs rather than from suburb to city. Workers are commuting by automobile without passengers rather than carpooling or using public transit. The trips to work are of rather short duration. The work location for suburban residents is rarely in the city of residence and, more important, employment locations are not centralized but are spread out over the entire suburban region.

Hypotheses

The first hypothesis to be tested with Orange County residents concern the facts about travel to work in suburbia. It is expected that residents who work are now employed in the suburban area. The central city is thus a work destination for a relatively small proportion of residents. Travel times for many are relatively short. Further, the predominant travel mode is the private vehicle with one person, because of suburban preferences and because commuting flows are so diffuse. Related to the latter point, one would also expect substantial use of surface streets as well as freeways. It will be important to determine whether the long-distance commuters in suburbia represent a distinct subset of all workers, in particular the more affluent and those of high occupational status.

The second hypothesis involves the attitudes toward transportation. As a result of the new relationships between suburban work and suburban residence one would expect greater congestion to be perceived. The growth in the transportation system, further, has not kept pace with suburban population and industrial expansion, which would also tend to create more negative attitudes. Commuters would thus perceive problems during their travel to work and note that traffic has gotten worse in recent years. Among all residents there should be low levels of satisfaction with roadway conditions. Further, it could be expected that exposure to the traffic conditions would heighten the perception of transportation problems.

The third hypothesis pertains to support for transportation improvements. Given the problems as perceived by suburban residents, it is expected that there will be considerable support for new transportation projects. One would predict that many suburban residents would favor widening existing freeways, building new roads, and developing a mass transit system to alleviate the existing congestion. There may be support for increased spending and even taxes for road and transit projects given the seriousness of transportation needs. It will be important to determine whether support for specific projects, as well as spending and taxing initiatives, is in part determined by political and residential attitudes.

Methods

The sources of information are the 1982 and 1983 Orange County Annual Surveys. In particular, several questions concerned transportation facts, transportation perceptions, and attitudes toward transportation improvements. Orange County is an appropriate site for studying transportation patterns and attitudes for some of the reasons evident in the earlier analysis of census materials. Also, Orange County has had ballot initiatives, government commissions, and numerous public debates concerning the transportation system in recent years. The issue of transportation is thus salient for Orange County residents.

Four questions were used to establish transportation facts. These are all taken from the 1982 survey and are all asked of employed residents only. The first question was, "How do you usually commute to work?" The categories were drive by yourself, carpool with household member, carpool with a neighbor or friend, carpool with a stranger, public transits, vanpool through employer, or other. The next was worded, "Where do you work?" The choices were Orange County, Los Angeles, Riverside, San Diego, or someplace else. Following this question was one that asked, "On a typical day, about how long does it take you to get from your home to the place where you report to work?" The five categories were less than 10 minutes, 10–20 minutes, 21–30 minutes, 31–60 minutes, and more than 60 minutes. The last factual question was a yes or no item which asked, "Do you use a freeway in going to work?"

Three questions addressed attitudes toward the transportation system. One was asked of all respondents in the 1982 survey and then again in 1983: "Which of the following best describes how you feel about the freeways in Orange County: the current freeway system is satisfactory, more lanes should be added to the existing freeways but no new freeways should be built, or we need to build new freeways to prevent an increase in traffic congestion?"

Two questions were asked only of employed residents. The first was asked in the 1982 survey and repeated in 1983. It read, "On a typical day, how much of a problem is traffic congestion when you travel to and from work? Would you say it is no problem at all, a slight problem, or a great problem?" A question asked only in the 1982 survey was worded, "In the time that you have commuted along this route, do you think that the problem of traffic congestion has gotten better, worse, or is it about the same?"

Three questions in the 1983 survey asked about attitudes toward transportation improvements: "Are you in favor of expanding bus transportation?" "Are you in favor of building a local rail transportation system?" "Would you be willing to pay a one-percent higher sales tax to improve Orange County's road and public transportation system?" Answers were yes or no to all these questions.

The major focus of the analysis is descriptive, that is, to document the existence of special needs in the form of transportation patterns and attitudes, and preferences for transportation improvements. It is thus the purpose simply to establish certain facts and attitudes as prevalent in the Orange County setting.

There is also an analysis to determine which subpopulations use certain travel modes. For instance, there is an attempt to examine whether high-status residents tend to have longer commutes and are more likely to use the solo driver mode for travel. Thus, factors such as income, occupation, and prestige of the respondent's residence are considered.

When examining attitudes toward current transportation, several other potential causal factors are explored. It is expected that generally exposure to the transportation system will create more negative transportation attitudes. Therefore, work status and transportation facts such as commuting time, use of freeways, and number of years commuting are considered as affecting attitudes of residents and the commuter subgroups.

Finally, political and residential attitudes that may explain the desire for transportation improvements are considered. Party affiliation, political orientation, fiscal conservatism, attitudes toward growth, and confidence in local government may influence the interest in new projects and a willingness to spend and tax for new transportation programs. Commuting experiences, socioeconomic status, and residential area characteristics are also examined, since they, too, may account for the support for transportation improvements.

In sum, then, numerous factors are explored in order to consider the overall patterns and internal variations in the "special needs" for transportation expected in suburbia.

Findings

The 1982 survey asked several questions about the commute to work (see table 6.1). It is important, first, that 80 percent of resident workers commute to employment within the county. Only one in six resident workers commutes to Los Angeles. An even smaller proportion is employed in the less-developed surrounding counties. The intercounty commuters tend to be unique in their high income, high occupational status, and high prestige residential areas. The findings suggest that, for most, work and residence have now been combined in surburban counties.

There are some peculiarities in the suburban commute to work. Perhaps most surprising is that 51 percent of Orange County's resident workers use the freeways daily, while 49 percent do not. Of those resident workers using the freeways 30 percent are commuting to job destinations outside the county. This means that a majority of the intracounty commutes from home to work are on nonfreeway routes, a clear contradiction of the images of suburban commuting. It is accounted for by the current pattern of suburban industrialization. Rush-hour traffic in Orange County moves in multiple streams within and between municipalities.

The travel mode to work is, in contrast, no surprise. The

Table 6.1 Facts about the Commute to Work

Work location		Freeway use	
Orange County	80%	Yes	51%
Los Angeles	16	No	49
Other	4		
Travel time		Travel mode	
Less than 10 minutes	25%	Drive alone	82%
10 to 20 minutes	40	Carpool—family	5
21 to 30 minutes	18	Carpool—neighbor	6
31 to 60 minutes	14	Vanpool—employer's	1
More than 60 minutes	3	Bus	1
		Other	5

SOURCE is the 1982 Orange County Annual Survey.

1982 survey found that 82 percent of resident workers drove alone to work each day; 5 percent drove to work with a household member. Other transportation modes included 6 percent traveling by automobile with a neighbor, 1 percent using an employer vanpool, 5 percent using means including walking and bicycling, and 1 percent using public buses. The predominance of solo driving is partly explained by the overwhelming preferences among suburbanites for this form of travel. But, again, the form that suburban industrialization has taken partly shapes this modal choice.

Another important statistic is that two-thirds of all commutes are 20 minutes or less. This is, again, because the workplace is not centralized and is not highly segregated from places of residence. Short distances discourage use of mass transit, ridesharing, or vanpooling, since the scheduling of multiple passengers would probably lengthen trip time. Further, the commutes lasting more than 20 minutes are mostly taken by higher-income residents. The affluent are less likely to respond to the cost-saving aspects of the multiple passenger mode. Finally, the heavy use of surface streets suggests that the potential multiple-passenger commuter may not be easily accommodated. Resident preferences and land use patterns have thus seemingly locked suburbia into solo automobile commutes.

Many residents have negative attitudes toward commuting, indicating that traffic difficulties are common. The 1982 survey indicated that 40 percent felt that traffic problems had gotten worse. Only 2 percent felt that traffic problems had gotten better in recent years, while 58 percent felt they were the same. Freeway users, long-term commuters, and long-distance commuters were more negative in their evaluations of traffic trends. For instance, 43 percent of the freeway users, 50 percent of those noting traffic problems, and 61 percent commuting 5 years or more viewed the commute as "getting worse." Those working within Orange County were no more favorable than those working outside the area. This indicates that intrasuburban commutes have deteriorated.

Another question was whether traffic experienced dur-

158   Special Needs

ing daily commutes was typically no problem, a slight problem, or a great problem. In 1982, 53 percent indicated it was a great problem or a slight problem. The question was repeated in 1983 and, at that time, 59 percent indicated that traffic was a problem. The 1983 survey shows that 18 percent consider traffic a great problem, up from 13 percent in the 1982 survey. The residents who consider traffic during commuting as a problem hold similar characteristics, in most ways, to those who view the commute as getting worse. Thus on the basis of information gathered over time and traffic questions asking respondents for longitudinal perspective, there appeared to be a trend toward a worsening traffic situation (see table 6.2).

Satisfaction with the current freeway system was ascertained for all residents. In 1982, one in three was satisfied with the freeway system, while 42 percent felt that more lanes should be added to the current system, and 25 percent believed that new freeways should be built in Orange County. A trend is evident in examining the same question repeated in the 1983 survey. There is a 6 percent decline in satisfaction. Only 26

Table 6.2 Attitudes Toward the Transportation System

	Commuting perceptions	
	1982	1983
No problem	48%	41%
Slight problem	39	41
Great problem	13	18
	Freeway satisfaction	
	1982	1983
Satisfactory	32%	26%
Add lanes	43	46
Build freeways	25	28
	Change in traffic	
	1982	
Better	2%	
Worse	40	
Same	58	

SOURCES are the 1982 and 1983 Orange County Annual Surveys.

percent were satisfied, 46 percent wanted freeway lane additions, and 28 percent wanted new freeways built in Orange County. This is indicative of a deteriorating transportation system, not only for workers but for all residents in this county.

It is interesting to consider the differences between those who were satisfied with the current freeway system and those who were dissatisfied. Lower-income families and older residents were more satisfied. People who were younger and commuted to work each day were among the most dissatisfied. So were those workers who used the freeways and had longer commuting times. Suburbanites who are more active and more mobile thus complain more about the transportation situation.

There are some similarities and yet some differences among those who support lane additions as opposed to those who want new freeway construction. People who viewed traffic as getting worse were more supportive of both building new freeways and adding more lanes. Those who wanted to limit growth were less inclined to have new freeways built. No-growth advocates were, however, more likely than others to want new lanes added. Fiscal conservatives were no less likely than others to want freeway improvements. Those more distrustful of local government were not different from others in their desire for freeway additions or new construction. The transportation system is sufficiently bad that political considerations are overlooked to make some movement, at least conceptually, toward improvements.

Residents were also asked about their hopes and expectations for the future transportation system (see table 6.3). These are most interesting in light of the facts and attitudes already portrayed. The 1983 survey asked if there was support for expanding bus transportation: 70 percent said yes, 30 percent said no. Another transportation item concerned support for building a light rail commuter system: 63 percent said yes and 37 percent said no. The answers on alternative transportation modes are surprising given suburban values and the high ratio of solo drivers. The attitudes perhaps suggest a willingness to expand the suburban transportation system. But whether a

Table 6.3 Attitudes Toward Transportation Improvements

Support tax increase for transportation	
Yes	68%
No	32
Expand bus system	
Yes	70%
No	30
Develop light rail	
Yes	63%
No	37

SOURCE is the 1983 Orange County Annual Survey.

resident's support indicates that he or she will leave the solo drive to relieve congestion, or hopes that others will, is not known. The findings most definitely portray the depth of dissatisfaction with the current state of transportation.

In 1983, all respondents were also asked if they would be willing to pay a 1 percent sales tax to improve the road and public transportation system; 68 percent said yes and 32 percent said no. The strength of support is quite astonishing, given that the 1982 and 1983 surveys indicated a large proportion of Orange County residents are conservative, opposed to taxes, and distrustful of government. The recognition of the transportation problem and needs for immediate solutions is thus widespread.

The support for a transportation sales tax was further examined. Those who were Democrats, liberals, had greater confidence in government, and were "core" area residents (i.e., Anaheim–Santa Ana–Garden Grove) were more supportive. Interestingly, those favoring light rail and bus expansion were the strongest supporters of the tax increase. Central to public support for transportation, then, are solutions to the traffic problems that go beyond new roadways.

The issue for the future is the extent to which current values regarding travel, current travel modes, and the actual locations of work and residence can be stretched to accommodate a comprehensive transportation system. From the residents' perspectives, experimentation with alternatives seems on the surface to be desirable.

Orange County's Transportation Sales Tax Vote

Orange County voters were presented with a ballot initiative on June 5, 1984, which sought to raise funds for transportation projects. The specific proposal would have increased the sales tax from 6¢ to 7¢ on the dollar. The new revenues would be specifically designated for transportation. The average citizen's desire to improve the transportation system was evident in the 1982 and 1983 survey results. The preference to increase spending for transportation-related services has already been presented. Thus, the vote on the June ballot initiative, referred to locally as Proposition A, offers an example of what happens when citizens are asked to choose between their desire to improve existing services and their preference for no new tax burdens.

Voters rejected the sales tax increase by a 70 percent to 30 percent margin. The landslide victory against Proposition A appeared to contradict the 1982 and 1983 survey results. The vast majority of Orange County residents earlier noted dissatisfaction with the freeways and with commuting conditions. Most citizens wanted transportation improvements and increased spending to pay for a better system. The 1983 survey conducted 11 months before the election suggested that two-thirds of the county's adults supported a sales tax increase. The proponents of the sales tax spent nearly $2 million and enjoyed the support of large corporations, major business organizations, and a major newspaper. Few elected officials spoke against the sales tax. The opponents of the sales tax spent several hundred thousand dollars and included an uneasy coalition of automobile dealers, conservatives, libertarians, environmentalists, and no-growth advocates. In light of all these conditions, it would appear that a vote strongly in favor of a sales tax increase would have occurred. The actual outcome provides some insights into politics and public opinion in the modern suburbs.

Public attitudes toward transportation and the sales tax initiative were gathered in a survey conducted prior to the election.[1] Registered voters were reached through random digit dialing procedures. Once a household member was reached, he or she was asked, "Are you registered to vote?" and if not, "Is there anyone else in your household registered to vote?" Sample selection also relied upon a sex quota to ensure approximately half of the respondents were men and half were women, as with registered voters. Approximately 100 respondents per night were interviewed during the period May 27–May 30 and then June 1–June 4. The total number of interviews conducted was 824.

The central question in the survey was a verbatim presentation of Proposition A: "To improve, expand, construct, and operate the transportation system, this proposition authorizes the Orange County Transportation Commission to adopt a one percent sales tax solely for transportation purposes and/or to issue bonds payable from the proceeds of that sales tax and increase the appropriations limit." When asked how they would vote if the election were being held today, 50 percent said no, 14 percent said don't know, and 36 percent said yes. A low voter turnout and a late movement toward a no vote account for the difference between the survey results and the election results.

There was great interest in the election and sufficient knowledge about the ballot initiative. Ninety percent of the registered voters surveyed had heard of Proposition A. Two-thirds had heard radio advertisements or had seen television advertisements, most of which were in support of the sales tax increase. Over half had read about the proposition from their voting materials or from campaign mailings. Approximately one-third had been informed about Proposition A through the two local newspapers. One in four had discussed Proposition A with their friends and neighbors, an obvious indication of the importance attached to this proposal.

The lack of support for the sales tax increase was not indicative of registered voters' satisfaction with the transportation system. The problem recognition in the preelection surveys for transportation was stronger than for other issues, including rapid growth and development, the economy, and taxes and government spending. A low evaluation of transportation services was evident across most demographic and political groups.

The survey showed enthusiasm for most of the plans that would be initiated if Proposition A passed, even if there was sentiment against the tax increase itself. Sixty-nine percent approved the plans to widen the existing freeways, 66 percent favored improving surface streets, and 52 percent favored building new freeways. Mass transit was viewed less enthusiastically, with 39 percent favoring increased bus service and 36 percent approving a rail system.

Most residents also supported the actual plan to allocate the tax funds. Only one-third stated that they "didn't like" the fact that 50 percent of the funds were for highways, 20 percent for local streets, 20 percent for mass transit, and 10 percent for other transportation projects. In all, spending increases for transportation services were viewed favorably. Many voters who rejected the sales tax proposition supported the plan that had been devised by local government.

Reasons for support and opposition to Proposition A were probed through an open-ended question. A wide array of reasons was provided by those opposing the tax increase. One-fourth stated that they were opposed to all tax increases. Slightly fewer felt that other tax funds could be used to improve transportation services if government allocated and spent money more wisely. The next most popular reason was an unwillingness to increase taxes because of distrust in local government. Other infrequently noted concerns included antigrowth sentiment, anti–mass transit attitudes, the unfairness of the sales tax, and dislike of the planned transportation projects. Supporters noted their desire to improve transportation, relieve traffic congestion, and improve road conditions. A few residents noted the fairness of a sales tax and an interest in improving mass transit.

Opposition to the sales tax increase was evident across all major groups in the preelection survey. Neither the young, the middle aged, nor the elderly provided a majority in favor. Democrats and Republicans were against Proposition A. Men and women opposed the tax increase. Recent residents and long-term residents, short commutes and lengthy commutes, and growth cities and nongrowth cities did not distinguish supporters from the opposition. This broadly based rejection of Proposition A ensured its large defeat when the actual voting took place.

Several factors contributed to the lack of support for the sales tax increase. The lesson learned is that a desire to increase spending and improve transportation services is a necessary but not a sufficient condition. Sizable numbers of residents ultimately oppose tax increases for whatever purpose irrespective of needs. Another contributing factor to the defeat of this tax initiative was a lack of confidence in local government. Doubts about the need for new tax funds and their eventual use reflect on issues of competency, trustworthiness, and accountability. The extent of the defeat is indicative of the coalitions between liberal and conservative forces around issues of taxes, transportation, and growth. Voters with distinct ideologies found common ground in a no vote effort viewed as antitax, antigovernment, and antigrowth. Themes discussed elsewhere in this book, trust in government, the tax revolt, and the antigrowth coalition, are thus important in understanding why this suburban tax initiative failed. Perhaps most discouraging is the fact that political attitudes and attitudes toward government outweighed the problem recognition and acceptance of the new transportation projects.

Concluding Comments
on Special Needs

Suburban industrialization and growth have had many profound impacts. Land use is diversifying, higher population densities are occurring, and suburban space is used more intensively. This is all part of the suburban transformation. What is obvious from this chapter is that these changes have combined with unique suburban values and suburban ecology to special needs. This is quite evident in experiences, attitudes, and policy preferences in the realm of transportation.

The hypotheses concerning the transportation facts in current suburbia were confirmed in the recent census data and in the community survey information. The suburb-to-suburb commute is now the dominant trip pattern. Most people drive to work alone in their private vehicles. Their travel times are brief, which ensures that public transportation and ridesharing are avoided. There is little commonality in travel routes and travel destinations. Traffic is not concentrated on major roadways. It is instead spread out over freeways, major surface streets, and local roads.

Yet, there is a need to address transportation in suburbia, as evidenced in the deteriorating resident evaluations. Few residents are satisfied with the current freeway system, and the number dissatisfied is growing each year. A large proportion of commuters experience troubles in their travels, and this trend is also increasing over time. Many commuters also claim that commuting to work is getting worse over time. In all these findings it appears that the greater the exposure to the transportation system, the worse the perception of the problem. As the suburban transformation proceeds the residents who are most active note a deterioration in the delivery of transportation services.

Residents who were interviewed in Orange County seemed eager to see a more multifaceted system developed. This would include mass transit as well as new roadways to ease congestion. They even seemed willing in principal to pay for an expanded and improved system through increased taxes. But the recent vote on a transportation ballot initiative has dashed all hopes. Registered voters overwhelmingly rejected a comprehensive plan to improve roadways and mass transit in voting against a sales tax increase. Some of the reasons why voters were against the transportation proposal suggest that problem recognition and approval are necessary but not sufficient factors. Many residents are unwilling to take on new taxes, and distrustful of local government's actions, and fear that were transportation projects will encourage more rapid growth.

The current transportation facts and expressed attitudes, through voting and surveys, suggest that while there has been change in suburban home-to-work patterns and more congestion, there had been no shift in basic values. A solo driver preference for travel is dominant. Ridesharing and vanpooling are freak phenomena. Public transportation is used by so few that the sincerity of those who support it in concept must be doubted. In brief, then, a lack of change in people's values means that it will be even more difficult to solve the special transportation needs emerging in suburbia.

An issue which has not been fully considered in this chapter is the extent to which special needs have implications for distinct suburban populations. The analysis of "at risk" groups in the current system of transportation needs to be further explored. Solo driving is so heavily relied upon in suburbia that the experiences of those without automobiles would be important. Nonworking women without cars, the elderly, the poor, adolescents, and the handicapped probably have unique difficulties (see, for example, Wachs 1979). Those who spend more time traveling are more susceptible to negative experience. Residents who travel across city lines to work should be separately considered, inasmuch as the separation of city of work from city of residence may be an added irritant. Those who work in the commercial and industrial centers which are the quasidowntowns of suburbia should be considered. There are also the increasing numbers of suburban workers who commute from outside the area. Many of these people may prefer a suburban residence closer to work but have to commute because of housing costs and availability.

Other types of special needs are emerging as suburbia experiences rapid growth and industrialization. Schools are one of these. In chapter 5 it was noted that schools were given lower evaluations than any other public services in Orange County. This is a special consideration, since the predominantly middle class ethos of suburbia would place a high value on schools. The reasons for the schools' poor ratings were explored in the 1983 survey in questions asked only of parents with children in the public schools.[2] There was evidence that fiscal strain had affected school performance. Two out of three parents believed that budget cuts had adversely affected the schools' ability to teach students. There were also indications that increasing social heterogeneity may have lowered confidence in the school environment. More than half the parents worried about the types of friends their children had in schools, and the same proportion considered drug and alcohol abuse to be a problem. Performance ratings and attitudes were clearly distinct among different household types. Married parents were more likely to rate their child's school as excellent than were single, divorced, or separated parents. Working parents who said they had "heavy burdens from work" were more likely to rate the schools negatively than were others.

A number of recent events in suburbia are causing negative views about schools. A more ethnically, racially, and occupationally diverse population composition has caused many parents to worry about the schools' social atmosphere. Finally, a growth in non-nuclear-family households has meant that greater demands are made on schools. So has the increasing participation in the labor force. Budget problems in local government are another cause of public school's problems. Thus, the social and fiscal changes in suburbia have created for schools a new and challenging situation.

Reports about police and crime suggest other emerging "special needs" in suburbia. Residents are very sensitive to crime issues because, again, suburbia is so strongly associated in the public's mind wih safety, stability, and security. Crime protection has been strained as the population has grown, the suburban area has become more spread out, and an increasingly diverse population has materialized. One in five residents gave the police low ratings in the 1982 survey. Fear of crime was also evident among 20 percent of the population. Eighteen percent had experienced crime victimization. The people who fear crime tend to be in low income groups, the elderly, and renters. The people who are crime victims were more likely to be renters, low income, and low educational status residents. An increasing heterogeneity means that more suburbanites are in crime-prone areas and social groups. It should be noted that there is an excess of people who are fearful who have never been victimized. Fear of crime is present despite the fact that police-reported crimes in Orange County are well below those in other California metropolitan areas. But suburban residents may expect more safety than others and feel uncomfortable with even low crime rates. Attention to this "special need" in suburbia is thus important, since perceptions of police protection and crime safety are major factors in the quality of life.

As suburbia is transformed, then, special needs emerge. There are constants that also jeopardize the possibility for solutions. Some are the public's values, which constrain local leaders' ability to formulate and implement plans for improving services. Others are related to the geography of suburban work and residence. Problem recognition and the desire for improvement are increasingly apparent. But the task of providing for special needs will not be easy as evidenced by the current slowness of institutional responses to emerging special needs.

Notes

1. This study was completed by the author for the Santa Ana *Register,* as part of the *Register Poll.*

2. Ellen Greenberger prepared the survey questions on public schools discussed in this section.

CHAPTER SEVEN

Special Groups

The social homogeneity of the suburbs has always been overrated. Suburbs have been viewed as the bastions of white, middle class, family-oriented, and homeowner life-styles. This has always been more folklore than fact. Even in post–World War II metropolises, there were pockets of minorities, blue collar workers, singles, and renters. But one no longer has to search for exceptions to the stereotype. The population of suburbia has become more socially heterogeneous in the 1970s and 1980s.

The greater social diversity of suburbia can be traced to industrialization and rapid population expansion. The old migrants to suburbia were primarily white middle class families seeking housing. When suburbia became a major arena for business, commerce, and industry its resident pool changed. The people joining the suburban workforce were a diverse group. The employment opportunities that were forming in the suburbs were in manufacturing and services, high technology and light industry, and were low skilled and high skilled. The new population mixing in with the old could thus be minority as well as white, singles instead of nuclear families, blue collar as well as white collar, and lower middle income instead of upper middle income. The population shifts and trend toward industrial and commercial land use had consequences for new housing construction. Rentals, small homes, and high-density housing began to displace the usual planned owner-occupied, single-family homes on large lots. Thus, one of the most dramatic signs of the suburban transformation is now evident. There is a diversity in ethnicity, race, age, life cycle, marital status, employment characteristics, income, and housing heretofore not present.

The increasing social heterogeneity of the suburban population has presented new challenges. There are resident groups present on the suburban landscape that have special problems and potentially unique difficulties in adapting to suburban surroundings. Some have problems that would exist wherever they lived. The elderly and low-income population, for instance, are dependent upon certain services in cities, in suburbs, or in rural areas. Others may not fit well with the current suburban situation and experience added problems because of their place of residence. Singles and renters, for example, may find greater unhappiness in suburbia because their housing and life-cycle circumstances place them at odds with their surroundings. What all these special groups may have in common, then, is that they are miscast in suburbia.

There are several ways to examine the life circumstances of special groups in suburbia, one of which is emphasized here. It is possible to examine living conditions in terms of neighborhood, housing, household, and community attributes of certain subpopulations. One could also analyze whether special groups have higher rates of alcoholism, mental disorder, public dependency, or other unusual traits. The present study analyzes the distinction between suburbia's special groups and suburbia's general population in terms of perceived quality of life. It is most concerned with how residents in special groups differ from other suburbanites in their feelings about their surroundings and personal lives.

Social Groups in Suburbia

Numbers and types of suburban subpopulations have proliferated in recent years. This gives rise to concerns about special groups. Evidence from the 1980 census suggests that suburbs are moving further away from the white, middle class, family-oriented, and homeowner stereotype.

It is important to note the ethnic and racial characteristics of the suburbs. The 1980 census noted that 90 percent of the 100 million suburbanites were white. However, large numbers of ethnic and racial minorities were evident. There were 6.2 million blacks and 1.6 milliion Asians. Also there were 5.4 million Hispanics of white and nonwhite background. It is interesting that 50 percent of all the Asians living in metropolitan areas resided in the suburbs. Forty-two percent of all Hispanics and 29 percent of all blacks lived in suburbs. There is thus ethnic and racial diversity within suburban boundaries (U.S. Bureau of the Census 1983a, 1983b).

Perhaps equally significant is racial change in American suburbs. Here, the only reliable information involves white and black population figures. There has been a marked increase in both the numbers and the proportions of black suburbanites. In 1960, there were only 2.8 million blacks in the suburbs, or 4.6 percent of the total suburban population. There was a 32 percent increase in the black suburban population between 1960 and 1970, with a 3.6 million count by the 1970 census. In that year black suburbanites thus accounted for 4.8 percent of the total suburban population. The largest increase in blacks occurred between 1970 and 1980. This would be expected, given that this was the decade in which suburban industrialization took full hold. There was a 72 percent increase for a 6.2 percent 1980 black population. There were 2.6 million more blacks present in the suburbs in 1980 than in 1970. The black increase between 1960 and 1980 was 121 percent, or 3.4 million residents. Thus, dramatic racial changes serve as a backdrop to the new racial and ethnic diversity of suburban communities (U.S. Bureau of the Census 1971, 1983a).

There is age and life-cycle heterogeneity in today's suburbs. The 1980 census indicates that 10 percent of the total population is elderly. This amounts to approximately 10 million suburban residents who are 65 years of age or older. Even though a larger proportion of the central city population is elderly, that is, 12 percent, in actuality there are 2 million more elderly suburbanites the 8 million than central city elderly (U.S. Bureau of the Census 1983b).

There are approximately 9 million suburban households composed of married couples with children under 18 years of age; this is a substantial number but actually accounts for only 40 percent of all the housing units in suburbia. About 4 million households contain married couples with children under 6 years of age. Thus, about 18 percent of all housing units have nuclear families with young children (U.S. Bureau of the Census 1983c). There is thus evidence that suburbs are more diverse life-cycle character than their image allows.

Some information also suggests changing work and marriage roles within the suburban family household. In 52 percent of all married couples, both spouses are working full time. In about 30 percent of married couples one spouse only is working full time. In most instances that is the husband. In the remaining married households there is no one working full time, because of retirement, unemployment, or other reasons (U.S. Bureau of the Census 1983c). The one-wage-earner family is the exception for today's suburban marriages. The majority arrangement is both spouses in the labor force full time. In fact, two-thirds of all the dual-career marriages in metropolitan areas are in the suburbs. The outer realm of the metropolis thus appears to be leading this major change in work and family arrangements. This all suggests a deviation from earlier patterns.

There is diversity as well in today's housing circumstances. Seventy-one percent of all suburban housing units are owner occupied. This is, of course, a considerably higher proportion than the 49 percent owner-occupancy rate in the central cities. But the fact that there are 10.2 million housing units which are rented in suburbia is also important. This number amounts to 43 percent of all the rental housing units found in metropolitan areas (U.S. Census Bureau 1983b). A majority of suburban residents are homeowners, but it is increasingly evident that renting is not highly unusual.

Many social status differences still exist between the central cities and the suburbs. For instance, per capita income in 1979 was $7,234 in the central cities and $8,212 in the suburban areas. This amounts to a 13 percent advantage for the suburbs (U.S. Bureau of the Census 1983b). But this is not to say that the suburbs are only middle class and white collar. There are also 1.7 million families in poverty, 6 percent of all suburban families. There are 8.1 million persons in family and nonfamily households below the poverty level in the suburbs, or 8 percent of the total suburban population. The suburbs are thus not segregated to the extent that they exclude the poor.

Industrial and occupational diversity are also present in the suburbs. Almost 11 million suburbanites work in manufacturing, 24 percent of the employed workforce. In fact, about two-thirds of all the jobs in manufacturing in metropolitan areas are in the suburbs. There are 5.7 million manufacturing jobs in central cities or only about half as many as there are in the suburbs (U.S. Bureau of the Census 1983c).

Two of the largest suburban metropolitan areas are Orange County and the Nassau-Suffolk metropolitan area. Trends in these two regions are of interest for reasons discussed earlier (see chapter 6).

Both areas indicate racial change and increasing racial and ethnic heterogeneity. Orange County was 99 percent white in 1960, 97 percent in 1970, and 86 percent in 1980. A similar trend was evident in Nassau-Suffolk, with 96 percent white in 1960, 95 percent in 1970, and 92 percent in 1980. The form of racial change was distinct in the two areas. Black population has increased dramatically, more so in Nassau-Suffolk. Asian and especially Hispanic population has increased in Orange County. The differences in ethnic and racial change are indicative of suburban migration trends in the Northeast versus the

Southwest. Blacks are migrating from nearby central cities. Hispanics and Asians represent foreign immigrants and central city dwellers (U.S. Bureau of the Census 1973, 1983b).

There is also evidence that the two suburban areas, a continent dividing them, are experiencing very similar trends in age and life-cycle changes. A growing proportion of elderly are populating these suburbs. At this point, about 1 in 10 residents in these areas is elderly. Family status of the average household is also changing, as evidenced by the 1980 census. Only about one in three households was composed of married couples with children. One reason is the growing proportion of singles. Another reason is an increasing divorce rate in the suburbs. A final factor is that many married couples are simply delaying having children. Because of the number of single, divorced, and elderly widowed individuals there has also been a rapid increase in the number of persons living alone in these two suburban regions. These statistics, taken together, point to the diminishing predominance of the nuclear family in the suburbs (U.S. Bureau of the Census 1983b).

Indications of changes in land use and housing in these two areas are also evident. Both regions experienced a net decline in homeownership rates. This is during a time in which the population grew in both areas, thus indicating that new households were renter-oriented. New housing construction also points to the decreasing use of the single-family detached home. Multiple-family dwellings increasingly represent a greater proportion of new homes built in the suburbs. Density, housing type, and homeownership are all changing in Orange County and in Nassau-Suffolk (U.S. Bureau of the Census 1983b).

Another trend concerns the occupational and industrial diversity of these areas. These suburban residents are not employed in white collar jobs and industries. Further, in a time in which the nation as a whole was losing manufacturing jobs, these suburban areas held steady or slightly increased (U.S. Bureau of the Census 1983).There is thus evidence that the largest suburbs have become occupationally diverse and a viable place for blue collar work.

In sum, the suburbs throughout the United States show evidence of social heterogeneity. There is racial and ethnic change. Nuclear families are on the decline. There are increasing numbers of elderly and singles. Income and occupations are diversifying. Renting and apartment dwelling have become sizable social categories. Special groups thus exist in today's suburbia.

Special Groups and the Quality of Life

There is ample evidence in sociology that it is important to distinguish special groups from the general population. People in some social conditions are simply at higher risk for problems than are others. These so-called "vulnerable groups" are more likely to have health, mental health, and personal problems and to have a lower perceived quality of life. Some of these are special groups now on the rise in suburbia.

One reason to study special groups in suburbia is simply because there is now a "critical mass" for certain risk groups. Low income groups, for instance, typically have lower evaluations of their residence and lives in general (Campbell et al., 1976). Mental and physical health problems are more common in older groups and among singles and widows than in the general population (Dohrenwend and Dohrenwend 1969; Gurin 1960; Srole et al. 1962). Recent studies also suggest that married women have more anxious and depressive symptoms than married men (Rosenfield 1980). Social categories involving age, sex, ethnicity, income, occupation, and marital status have dominated the discussions of vulnerable groups. ·

There are increasing signs that certain community contexts create even more difficulties for special populations. A discussion of this phenomenon can be found in the "congruence" approach in urban sociology. Essentially, certain groups are supposed to fit better in certain environments than others (Michelson 1976). The elderly may be happier in age-homogeneous neighborhoods than in age-heterogeneous areas. Singles are better off in central city apartments than in single-family homes. Michelson (1977) found evidence of congruence and incongruence among apartment dwellers and single-family home residents in suburbia and the central city. The general idea, then, is that certain groups already at risk in terms of their attitudes and experiences can have even greater problems if they reside in specific residential contexts. Empirical evidence tends to support the view that when high-risk groups are placed in residential situations that are incongruent with their needs they experience more difficulties than other populations (Baldassare 1979, 1982b).

It is possible, then, that special groups in the suburban context may be subject to the incongruence phenomenon. In other words, some subpopulations may have even greater problems than they do elsewhere. The study of ethnic and racial groups and their employment, residential, and quality of life circumstances have tended to focus on problems in inner cities (Frisbie 1980; Morris and Winter 1978; Wilson and Portes 1980). Research on the special difficulties the elderly experience also tends to consider the inner-city aged. But the suburban landscape may also aggravate social and physical deficits. Reliance on the automobile for mobility, rather than walking or mass transit, may make the lives of the elderly and low income groups more difficult. The social values of suburbia may also create further stigma for vulnerable populations. Whatever physical inconveniences are associated with renting may be worsened by the feeling that an apartment dweller is a misfit in suburbia. Further, the family-oriented, middle class, and middle-aged adult image of suburbia may decrease feelings of personal happiness and self-worth.

There is another feature about special group status that should be considered. This is the fact that multiple special statuses may lead to even more personal problems and dissatisfaction. People do not only inhabit one role but fill many simultaneously. For instance, they are poor and elderly, or single and renting, or blue collar and nonwhite. For those who are in special groups that have difficulties, either in general or specific to the suburban landscape, then, we would expect a marked difference from those categorized by only one special group, or those in the general population.

One exemplary line of investigation concerning combined special group status is fear of crime among the elderly. This is because the elderly are heterogeneous and a growing proportion of the suburban population. Fear of crime is a major concern among all Americans (Baumer 1978; Erskine 1974; Furstenberg 1971), though variations in fear exist owing to urban residence, race, sex, age, victimization, and social status (see Clemente and Kleiman 1977). One of the most consistent findings is that the elderly report greater fear of crime than younger adults (Yin 1980).

The search for the causes of fear of crime among the elderly focused on many factors. It is generally believed that not age itself but some other factor associated with age, or perhaps age in combination with another factor, accounts for fearfulness. Relevant personal factors include sex, education, home-ownership, and income (Antunes et al. 1977; Baumer 1978; Braungart et al. 1980; Clemente and Kleiman 1976, 1977). Social factors including living arrangements, and housing conditions are also important (Clarke and Lewis 1982; Hartnagel 1979; Lebowitz 1975; Sundeen and Mathieu 1976). The community's crime rate and social character may cause fearfulness (Balkings 1979; Clarke and Lewis 1982; Lawton and Yaffe 1980). Finally, crime victimization and poor health and mental health ratings are significant (Antunes et al. 1977; Cook et al. 1978; Dowd et al. 1981; Lawton and Yaffe 1980; Ollenburger 1981).

In the case of the elderly, many features may combine with old age to heighten fears. One case in point is income, since there are low income as well as affluent elderly suburban residents. This area of investigation is worth pursuing, since it may explain why the elderly are so afraid. It may also provide evidence that multiple special group statuses exist in the suburbs and, more important, have meaning for important features of the quality of life.

Hypotheses

The major proposition guiding this analysis is that special groups have proliferated in numbers and size owing to suburban industrialization and population expansion. The focus here is on the consequences of the increasing suburban diversity. The main point to explore is that special groups have different life circumstances and thus different personal self reports than the more typical suburbanites. That is, they have a perceived lower quality of life.

Three special groups are represented in the hypotheses. These are renters, non-nuclear-family households, and the elderly. These do not, of course, comprise all the special groups in existence. They are exemplary of housing, family status, and age characteristics that distinguish certain subpopulations from what is considered typical for suburbia.

The first hypothesis is that renters will have lower satisfaction ratings than homeowners. This is partly because renters do probably live in less desirable homes and neighborhoods than homeowners. It is also because renters in suburbia are stigmatized as a group, and as individuals they recognize that they are not living in ideal housing. Renters thus feel somewhat out of place in the suburban setting and have unrealized expectations.

The next hypothesis is that non-nuclear-family households have more dissatisfaction with quality of life than nuclear family households. There are two reasons. First, single, widowed, and divorced people are generally more socially isolated and unintegrated in primary groups and, thus, more unhappy with general and specific features of their lives. Further, suburban location adds to these strains because the predominant culture of suburbia is built around the nuclear family. Feelings of alienation affect ratings of personal life and happiness. In essence, the non-nuclear-family household does not fit into the current suburban landscape.

The third hypothesis is that fear of crime ratings are higher among the elderly than in other groups. This association is usually found in central cities but should be present in the suburbs as well. However, it is expected that the combined status of old age and low income creates the greatest fear of crime.

Methods

The 1982 Orange County Annual Survey is used in the analysis of special groups and their quality of life circumstances in suburbia. Questions that elicit the demographic features of the resident and the household are used to define the special groups. Several other social and economic characteristics are available as control factors. Attitude questions concerning the residence, personal life, and safety from crime are also used in analysis.

Orange County's population of 2 million ensures that it contains sufficient social diversity for the study of special groups in suburbia. So does its industrialized character. Census figures reviewed earlier show that the population is diverse. The 26 municipalities within Orange County vary considerably in population and housing features, including age, income, ethnicity, occupation, number of children, and rental apartments.

Three special groups are examined: renters, non-nuclear-family households, and the elderly. The renters were distinguished from homeowners in the homeowner status question. Non-nuclear-family households were distinguished from nuclear family households through the combined analyses of two survey questions, current marital status and the presence of children in the dwelling. Respondents who are married and have at least one child living in the current dwelling are considered to be part of a nuclear family, while all remaining respondents comprise the non-nuclear-family or "other" group. The elderly group is separated from the nonelderly group by the age category question. Those 65 or older are considered elderly and all other age categories are collapsed.

The analysis of the elderly versus nonelderly group also involves a consideration of the combined effects of low income and age. The family income categories were collapsed to under $15,000, $15,000 to $35,000, and over $35,000.

Six questions were used to address quality of life for the homeowners versus renters and nuclear versus non-nuclear households. These were all in the form of residential or personal evaluations. Four questions were concerned with housing, neighborhood, leisure activities, and family life satisfaction. They were part of a section of the survey which asked, "How satisfied are you with each of the following?" and then listed several domains. Each item was answered on a 4-point scale including very satisfied, somewhat satisfied, somewhat dissatisfied, and very dissatisfied. Another question asked, "Would say your health, in general, is: excellent, good, only fair, or poor." The last item was worded, "Taken all together, how would you say things are these days? Would you say you're: very happy, somewhat happy, or not too happy."

Control variables are used in analyzing the relationship between special groups' status and personal and residential attitudes. These are all factors which may also be related to the quality of life perceptions. Five factors are considered in all the analyses that follow: sex, age, marital status (married versus other), education, and length of residence. Marital status was excluded when considering nuclear families versus others.

Another survey question was used to separately examine fear of crime in the elderly and nonelderly populations. The item was worded, "Would you say that it is safe to go out walking at night where you live?" Answers were yes and no.

The analytic approach was to examine whether resident attitudes differ for special groups in contrast to more typical suburbanites. Mean scores were compared for homeowners versus renters, nuclear families versus others, and elderly versus other adults. The significance of differences in mean scores was then established through analyses of variance and covariance that include the control variables.

The analysis of variance was also used to consider the main effects and interaction effect of age and income on feelings of personal safety. These statistics were examined in order to determine if the low-income elderly have more fear of crime.

Findings

There are sufficient proportions of the three special groups present in the 1982 survey sample. The renters amount to 36 percent. Thirty-three present of the total sample are in a nuclear family household. The age distribution is 89 percent under 65 years old and 11 percent who were are 65 or older. Thirty-five percent of the elderly have low incomes, that is, under $15,000 in annual family income.

Table 7.1 considers the quality of life ratings of renters and homeowners. The mean scores indicate that renters give worse ratings than homeowners to housing satisfaction, neighborhood satisfaction, leisure satisfaction, family satisfaction, and health satisfaction. Renters also report less overall happiness than homeowners. The largest discrepancies in ratings are with

Table 7.1 Homeowners Versus Renters: Quality of Life

	Means		Significance
	Own	Rent	
Housing satisfaction	1.26	1.54	.001
Neighborhood satisfaction	1.37	1.59	.001
Leisure satisfaction	1.35	1.38	NS
Family satisfaction	1.24	1.41	NS
Health satisfaction	1.56	1.65	.01
Overall happiness	1.71	1.85	.01

SOURCE is the 1982 Orange County Annual Survey. Higher means indicate more dissatisfaction. Significance levels are based upon analyses of covariance that include education, length of residence, marital status, sex, and age as control variables.

regard to the residential attitude variables. The analyses of co-variance confirm most of these descriptive trends. All the findings support the view that renters have different residential and personal evaluations than homeowners.

The respondents living in nuclear family households are next compared with those residents in other living arrangements. The mean scores indicate that those who are not in nuclear family households are more dissatisfied with their neighborhoods, their families, and their health (see table 7.2). Ratings of housing and leisure, as well as overall happiness, are similar for those in nuclear families and others. The analyses of covariance indicate three significant relationships. Family and health are evaluated more negatively by non-nuclear-family households than others. Also, those who are in non-nuclear-family households are somewhat more negative about their neighborhood, which may indicate a lack of fit with their social surroundings.

The elderly are next compared to younger age groups. Fear of crime ratings are reported in table 7.3. Calculating from the totals column for the mean scores shows that 20 percent of all respondents said they were fearful of crime and 8 percent said they were not fearful. These findings are comparable to nationwide metropolitan trends (see Campbell et al. 1976). Further, 30 percent of the elderly are fearful in contrast with 19 percent of respondents under 65 years of age. The analysis of

Table 7.2 Nuclear Families Versus Others: Quality of Life

	Means		Significance
	Nuclear families	Others	
Housing satisfaction	1.36	1.36	NS
Neighborhood satisfaction	1.41	1.47	.06
Leisure satisfaction	1.39	1.35	NS
Family satisfaction	1.16	1.35	.001
Health satisfaction	1.47	1.64	.01
Overall happiness	1.77	1.76	NS

SOURCE is the 1982 Orange County Annual Survey. Higher means indicate more dissatisfaction. Significance levels are based upon analyses of covariance that include education, length of residence, sex, and age as control variables.

Table 7.3 Age and Fear of Crime

Means

		Income		
	Under	*$15,000–*	*Over*	
Age	*$15,000*	*35,000*	*$35,000*	*Totals*
Under 65	1.25	1.22	1.12	1.19
65 and Over	1.48	1.10	1.10	1.30
Totals	1.31	1.21	1.11	1.20

	F-score	*Significance*
Analysis of variance: age only		
Main effect: age	7.3	.01
Analysis of variance: age and income		
Main effect: age	0.4	NS
Main effect: income	7.1	.001
Interaction effect: age × income	5.5	.01

SOURCE is the 1982 Orange County Annual Survey. Higher means indicate more fear of crime. F-scores and significance levels are derived from analysis of variance including age and then age and family income as main effects.

variance indicates that the mean score difference in age groups is significant. Thus, the greater fear of crime among the elderly population found in other studies is replicated in suburbia.

The effects of low income on the relationship between age and fear of crime were considered. When controlling for family income, the significant effect of age is negated. A significant interaction effect emerges between age and income. The mean scores in table 7.3 establish why the interaction effect occurs: the low-income elderly are especially fearful of crime. From this group 48 percent said that they were afraid to go out walking at night where they live. The low-income elderly are considerably more afraid of crime than the younger adults who have low incomes. They are also more fearful than the moderate- and higher-income older adults.

In sum, there is evidence for all the hypotheses. Special groups in suburbia do have lower quality of life ratings. Renters have distinguishing negative ratings in contrast to homeowners. Non-nuclear-family households are more dissatisfied with their neighborhoods and personal aspects than nuclear families. The elderly per se are not different, but the low-income elderly are particularly fearful of crime in contrast to other age and income groups. The last point suggests another fact about special groups in suburbia. Combinations of social features may define many relevant special groups.

Concluding Comments
About Special Groups

Suburban populations have become more socially diverse. With greater heterogeneity sizable and numerous special groups have emerged. The suburbs today are not only composed of middle-aged adults, homeowners, whites, and nuclear family households.

The experiences of special groups in suburbia may be distinct from those of the mainstream residents. Some groups, such as the poor, may have problems wherever they are. Others, such as apartment dwellers, may have additional difficulties because they are located in the suburban context. Either example speaks to new phenomena in suburbia, that is, greater diversity in life experiences and the perceived quality of life.

The 1982 Orange County Annual Survey indicated that renters, non-nuclear-family households, and the low-income elderly did have lower life quality ratings than their counterparts. Thus, the view that special groups are present in suburbia today was strongly confirmed.

The evidence presented on the low-income elderly suggests that analyses of special groups should include multiple social features. It may be that combined social deficits add up to serious problems. Consider the examples of combined personal features such as single nonwhites, new residents with blue collar occupations, and formerly married women with children. All may have less satisfaction with personal and residential circumstances than the suburban population as a whole. Consider also the possible combined effects of personal and housing conditions' on elderly apartment dwellers, singles in family-oriented areas, and low-income renters. All may, too, have lower ratings of life quality than others. Thus, many different features distinguish suburban residents, not only separately but in combination with one another.

Numerous special groups could be considered that were not reported earlier. Of those we could analyze, all confirmed the hypotheses about quality of life differences. One comparison was between those living in single-family homes and those in all other dwelling types. The findings paralleled those between renters and homeowners. The single-family-home dwellers had much more positive ratings of residential features. Another analysis contrasted white collar workers with blue collar workers. Personal ratings with regard to happiness, health, and family were worse for blue collar workers than others. Lower income suburbanites were also compared with the more affluent. Those with annual family incomes of $15,000 or less had less satisfaction in every category. Race and ethnicity could not be considered because as a group nonwhites were too heterogeneous, and individually the categories had too few cases. All the findings again reflect the importance of examining special groups.

Many special groups not explored here should be the focus of other studies. Some of them are very difficult to reach using standard community survey techniques, and in some cases the survey questions did not deal with the life circumstances of most importance to certain special groups. Subpopulations that need to be carefully considered in the future include foreign immigrants. The mentally and physically disabled would be especially interesting to study in the automobile-oriented suburban context. The poverty population and unskilled workers also need to be considered in suburbia. The distinctive life circumstances of the suburb's singles, nonemployed women, single parents, and adolescents should also be explored.

Unexpected special groups in suburbia will also be discovered. A case in point is found in the 1983 Orange County Annual Survey.[1] Age differences in mental health ratings were considered. Self-reported mental health symptoms such as trouble eating, trouble concentrating, problems with sleeping, self-esteem problems, and anxiety were analyzed. It was originally expected that older adults would have the poorest mental health ratings. In actuality, the 18–24 group fared the worst. The reasons for these unanticipated findings probably speak to some unique problems for young adults in suburbia including housing costs and low prospects for homeownership. It may be that the "suburban" generation has both high expectations about residential conditions and low expectations about realizing their residential goals. An analysis of special groups at risk in suburbia needs to go beyond conventional knowledge to explore unique subpopulations.

It is likely that the importance of special groups in suburbia will increase. The sizes of many special groups, such as the elderly, minorities, and renters, are likely to grow. The number of special groups is likely to multiply as suburban industrialization continues. The life circumstances and service needs of these subpopulations need to be considered as we come to grips with a more socially complex suburbia.

Notes

1. The discussion here is based upon survey questions and unpublished results by Sarah Rosenfield.

CHAPTER EIGHT

Suburbia and Its Future

Afundamental question about the implications of the
suburban transformation is whether suburbia's future
will be different from its past. Obviously, the question
with the most direct consequence for suburbia's future is
whether people will continue to move there, and whether
people who have already arrived in suburbia will continue to
stay. The issue, then, is whether suburbia will be bypassed or
deserted as these new realities continue to emerge.

Much of what can be said about suburbia and its future
hinges upon analyses of migration trends. There is evidence to
suggest the old moving trends no longer apply. If the stream of
new migrants is narrowed, and if a large proportion of new
residents want to leave, then only a rise in the rate of natural
increase, or suburban births over deaths, will provide for future
growth. It is as important to pay attention to exactly who
wants to move in and out of suburbia, and for what precise
reasons, as it is to consider the potential proportions lost and
gained. The characteristics of movers will help project the future composition of suburbia. The motivations for changing location will help in understanding how suburbia is viewed today. The past suburban migration discussed in earlier chapters

may be experiencing some deviations. There are possible ex-
tenuating circumstances in suburbs, cities, and the nation as a
whole that may be affecting current moving decisions. New and
relevant factors may have consequences for the numbers and
types of people who move to suburbia, and some circumstances
may result in a move out of suburbia.

The Move to Suburbia

The trend for city residents to move into suburbia extended
into the 1980s. Migration and the annexation of rural lands
continued. But growth within suburban areas is taking on new
dimensions. Who moves into the suburbs, and where they are
moving from, may be changing.

One begins with the fact that suburbia throughout most
of its history captured new residents through housing opportunities. In its early times the suburbs were the exclusive location
of the well-to-do exurbanite (see Burgess 1925). Roads and
public transit were limited. The average urban worker could
not afford an automobile and was not capable of paying the
cost of commuting each day from suburbs to city. The suburbs
began with mansions, estates, and palaces on large land hold-
ings. Long Island, New York, was the home of the "Great
Gatsbys," and Pasadena, California, was the home of early
screen stars. Large and affordable housing was not a suburban
prerequisite in those days. This all changed when the government built roads and trolley lines, the average citizen could buy
a car, the developers put up tract housing, and the banks had
easy lending terms. The suburbs became accessible to the
masses, the true site of "Middle America."

But recently the pendulum may have swung back to
more "exclusive" times. Housing costs became quite excessive
in the 1970s. High interest rates and tighter bank lending practices worked to the disadvantage of the average American.
These trends may eventually reduce the migration stream.

There were also adverse events in the energy realm. The price of utilities increased and, with it, the cost of heating, cooling, and simply living in a large home have changed. With higher petroleum costs, and large increases in the costs of maintaining an automobile, work commutes of any length are no longer inexpensive. The prospective mover to suburban locations must certainly be aware of all these facts. This is especially so for those wanting to purchase a large home. New suburban housing realities make the new migrants, like all the most recent residents, different from those who moved previously. More wealth and the potential for income advances are needed. Otherwise, better housing conditions in the suburbs than one had previously in the city are probably not possible.

What most new suburban residents receive upon arrival must also be quite distinct from what earlier suburban residents received upon their arrival. This also pertains particularly to housing. It would also include differences in the evaluative judgments. People in general are now receiving less housing for their money than they did before even in inflation-adjusted dollars. One would thus expect the new arrivals to have smaller homes, attached housing, fewer rooms, and more crowding. The fact that persons-per-room ratios have increased is most telling, since family size and the number of children have declined (Baldassare 1981). This reflects the extent to which housing costs have prohibited residence in large dwellings. The other housing factor that has probably changed over time for migrants is renting. Because costs prevent many newcomers from quickly if ever purchasing homes, the new migrants who rent perhaps far outnumber those who rented in the past.

Nonetheless, people are still moving to the suburbs. There are many upper middle income families and professional couples who can afford the higher costs of single-family homes. More important, people are moving to the suburbs because of job opportunities rather than housing choices, since the suburbs have increasingly been the sites for economic expansion (Kasarda 1978). Silicon Valley and the Irvine Industrial Complex are prime examples. Further, as individuals move to the suburbs for jobs, the migrant pool may be expanding geographically. The industrialized and commercialized suburbs draw people from thoughout their region, state, and even the nation. Suburban dependence on migrants from the urban core is thus more limited.

Related to changes in jobs and housing in the suburbs are the commuting patterns. Once people moved to the suburbs to purchase housing and then continued to commute to their city jobs. Today many of the movers into suburban areas are for jobs. Thus a large proportion of new migrants, like the rest of the community, are probably commuting to jobs within their suburban area rather than to the adjacent central city. The specific location of the residence within the suburban region becomes more important as a reason for moving.

Personal evaluations of new migrants probably also differ from earlier suburban movers. Since new migrants do not receive the quality and size of housing that older migrants had, their evaluations of residential conditions should be more negative. If people must pay so much more for the housing in which they live, reports of financial satisfaction should go down. Perhaps as a result personal happiness is lower among recent migrants.

In sum, the move to suburbia today differs from that in the past. Housing opportunities have diminished for most recent arrivals. New residents have different demographic characteristics and reasons for moving than past cohorts. The residential conditions and work locations are also different. Finally, the evaluations of home and personal life of newcomers would seem to be unique. It could be argued that these trends reshape and may even limit the future migration to suburbia.

The Move from Suburbia

Residential mobility is a regular part of American life. About one in five Americans moves each year, and every ten years most Americans have made one or more moves (Fischer et al. 1977). People frequently move from one house to another, or one neighborhood to an adjacent area. Sometimes people move to adjacent counties, as in the move from city to suburb. In other instances they move to far-off regions, as in the migration from the Northeast to the Sunbelt. The vast majority of moves are within a few miles of the present residence. Far fewer involve intercounty changes.

Long-distance and short-distance moves send different signals about the suburban community. Short-distance moves represent the least threat, as the population remains in the same sphere. The motivations for these moves are usually extraneous to community factors. A family may have outgrown its living quarters and moves to a larger house in the neighborhood (see Butler et al. 1969; Chevan 1971). An employee may decide to move closer to work or to some preferred amenities. Individuals may abandon an older house and neighborhood for a newer location. Families may increase their wealth, as their members are promoted to better jobs, and move to more prestigious areas. All these moves seem to be personal decisions, based on household resources and preferences rather than on the qualities of the suburban region.

The long-distance move has different connotations. In some way a given region has lost its attractiveness relative to some other region. People move across county lines for various reasons. They move away to seek jobs, go to school, join the military, or merely try out different life-styles. There is a common pattern in our society for these moves to be taken by young, highly educated, unmarried individuals and by childless couples (Long 1972, 1973). In short, they are seeking jobs and amenities in some other place that are more attractive than those found at home, a signal that a community has lost some of its relative economic advantages.

There are some housing reasons why people leave their region for an adjacent but fairly distant location. Decent housing in an area may become scarce or unaffordable, leading individuals to seek residences elsewhere and commute further from their jobs. This was the pattern that resulted in the original movement from city to suburb. Residents sometimes move not so much because life is better elsewhere as because life is unbearable in the current setting (see McAllister et al. 1971).

There is reason to believe that suburbia may now have features that cause residents to consider long-distance moves. The housing crisis noted in chapter 2 is such that people may consider moving beyond the conventional suburban area. The affordable first-time home purchase or the affordable larger home for the repeat buyer has become more difficult to find. As suburbia's land has become more expensive, jobs have begun to relocate even further out of the urban core. This draws residents out of the built-up suburban counties and into adjacent nonmetropolitan areas (see Long and DeAre 1981). These housing and job trends mean that the residents' desire to leave, and perhaps to actually move, may be substantial in suburbia.

There are other community features leading one to believe that suburbanites may be considering out-migration. The growth of suburbia has left some of the reasons for once moving from city to suburb in question. These include quiet, privacy, open space, and lack of crowding. The social problems once relevant as reasons to leave the inner city exist today in the suburbs. These include traffic, pollution, congestion, and fear of crime. A strong antigrowth sentiment expressed by many suburbanites and noted in chapter 3 is further evidence that some may not approve of the trend for the suburbs to take on a more urban character. Residents may disapprove of recent changes enough to seek another regional location.

A perception that government institutions cannot solve problems would seem to affect preferences to stay. Traffic problems are pervasive and, because of erratic commuting patterns, seem to defy the typical mass transit solutions. Schools have become burdened with a more heterogeneous population. Police are increasingly stretched in serving a complex population in a large geographic area. Lack of confidence in government and lack of sufficient funds to solve problems are notable in the suburbs. Residents may recognize that their "good government" reasons for moving to suburbia no longer apply and may be interested in moving elsewhere.

Thus a substantial proportion of suburban residents may want to move from their region, and not only those who fit the traditional demograhic profile of the "footloose" long-distance mover. Residents who are affected by an expensive housing market, shifting job opportunities, residential problems, and local government distrust are involved. The preference to move out is, in effect, an early warning signal. At some later point, such preferences may result in actual moves and a shift in suburban growth patterns.

Hypotheses

Several hypotheses are derived from the preceding discussion of potential changes in suburban migration patterns.

The first hypothesis is that migration into suburbia has changed over time, so that recent residents exhibit different characteristics and attitudes than past migrants. The new migrants should be of a distinctly higher income and include more dual-career couples, more individuals who work in the suburbs, and more childless households. Also evident among newcomers would be a lower rate of homeownership, fewer rooms per dwelling, more household crowding, and litte change in household space over the last dwelling. One would presume that newer migrants are more negative about their housing, neighborhood, and financial satisfaction.

Reasons for moving to suburbia should also have changed over time. Housing should be less important as a reason for moving for recent migrants than for earlier ones, owing to an increase in job opportunities in the suburbs and the decrease in housing choices. The significance of jobs and location would therefore have increased.

A related hypothesis concerns a specific group of migrants, the individuals who have moved from the urban core to

the nearby suburban region. This group is particularly important, since it caused most of suburbia's growth. It is assumed
that differences in personal and housing characteristics, in reasons for moving, and in resident attitudes should also be found
between recent and past city-to-suburban movers.

The next hypothesis concerns the move out of suburbia.
Here, we will examine the preference to migrate expressed by
current residents. The hypothesis is that the preference to move
out of suburbia is strong today. One would also expect that
renters and single-wage-earner couples are more common
among the potential out-migrants than others. The presence of
community problems would also figure in the desire to migrate
from suburbia. These include low ratings of services such as
schools and police and dissatisfaction with traffic, growth, and
local government performance. Reasons for moving out of suburbia would thus include housing and location issues.

A related hypothesis concerns those residents who want to
move to nearby, less-developed areas. These individuals represent the potential for metropolitan spillover. One would assume
the same propositions as for all would-be suburban movers.

Methods

The sources of information are the 1982 and 1983 Orange
County Annual Surveys. These surveys contained questions
about previous moves, moving preferences, reasons for moving,
resident attitudes, and demographic characteristics. Both moves
into suburbia and attitudes toward leaving suburbia could thus
be assessed.

The question about moves into Orange County followed
a length-of-residence item. All individuals who had lived at
their current residences for 10 years or less were asked, "Was
your last residence in Orange County, Los Angeles County,
Other California County, Other State, or Outside U.S.A." The
respondent was defined as a migrant to Orange County if his or

her last residence was outside Orange County. All migrants were analyzed and then only those migrants whose last residences were in Los Angeles, that is, in the large urban core area. Migrants were contrasted using three different length of residence categories. These were 2 years or less, 3–5 years, and 6–10 years at the current residence.

The migrants to suburbia at different time intervals were first examined for their personal and housing characteristics. Personal characteristics included whether there was a child present in the current dwelling, whether the respondent's workplace was in Orange County, the annual family income of the respondent, and whether the household was composed of a married couple with both spouses working. Housing features included whether the respondent owned or rented the current dwelling, how many rooms were in the current dwelling, how many persons per room were present, and whether there were more rooms in the current dwelling than in the last residence.

The migrants to suburbia were then considered for their resident attitudes to see if recent residents have different opinions than past cohorts who moved to suburbia. An open-ended question asked, "What are the primary reasons you decided to leave your last residence?" The interviewers were asked to probe for as many as three reasons. A follow-up open-ended question was worded, "What was the primary reason you chose your present community over some other places?" Again, instructions were to probe for up to three reasons. The open-ended answers were categorized into general reasons for moving. The three most popular reasons are considered in this study: housing, job, and area (or location) characteristics. A respondent was considered to have a "yes" response to housing as a reason, for instance, if housing was mentioned in one of the responses to the two questions and their probes. A "no" response would include no mention at all.

Three other residential evaluations were considered. These included the 4-point measures of satisfaction with the housing or apartment of residence, the neighborhood of residence, and finances.

The statistical analysis of migrants to suburbia concentrated on the mean scores over time. Analyses of covariance were then performed to indicate whether descriptive trends were significant after controlling for education, sex, married versus other, household size, and dwelling type. Two parallel analyses were conducted, one with all migrants to Orange County and then one which involved only migrants whose last residence was Los Angeles.

Two questions on moving preferences were from the 1982 survey. The first was, "At present, how interested are you in moving to a different residence?" The answers were not at all interested, somewhat interested, and very much interested. The second question was asked of everyone who was somewhat or very much interested in moving. It was worded, "Are you interested in moving outside Orange County?" Answers were yes and no.

The two questions were repeated in the 1983 survey, and people interested in moving outside Orange County were asked a third question: "Are you interested in moving to Riverside County or San Bernardino County?" Answers were yes or no. These are adjacent to Los Angeles County and Orange County and indicative of "metropolitan spillover."

Potential out-of-county movers and in-county movers were compared in terms of their personal characteristics, including age, marital status, education, family income, homeownership, children in the dwelling, and dual-career couples in the household. The resident attitudes contrasted were ratings of the public school system, streets and roads, police protection, commuting traffic congestion, and local government problem solving, along with the limit-growth preference.

Reasons for moving inside Orange County versus outside Orange County were also considered, on the basis of an open-ended question asked of all persons interested somewhat or very much in moving: "What are the primary reasons why you are interested in moving?" as in the case of migrants, the interviewers probed for up to three reasons. The three considered here are job, housing, and area (or location), which were the most common reasons given for the preference to move. If housing was mentioned any of the three times, the respondent's answer was coded "yes." No mention for all three times was coded "no."

The analysis of potential migrants compares those who want to move out of Orange County with those who want to move within Orange County, and then those who want to move to the Riverside–San Bernardino area with those who want to move elsewhere outside of Orange County. Mean differences for all groups are examined for personal, housing, and attitude characteristics. Analyses of covariance control for education, sex, age, married versus other, and length of residence in determining which relationships are significant.

Findings

The Move to Suburbia

All individuals who lived at their residence for 10 years or less, amounting to 34 percent, are considered. Forty-four percent of all respondents noted that their last residence was outside Orange County. Thus the majority of moves are now within the county. This indicates a maturing development pattern. Keeping existing residents, and forming new households from existing family units, has become an important source of growth.

For 44 percent the last residence was Los Angeles. The others arrived from other California counties (25 percent), from other states (27 percent), and a few from abroad (4 percent). This suggests that today suburbia does not only attract new residents from the urban core. Half, in this case, were from further away.

Table 8.1 presents the household characteristics of all suburban migrants. There are some important differences between the recent migrants and longer-term migrants. Many are similar to length-of-residence trends in chapter 2. The persons-

Table 8.1 Characteristics of In-Movers

	Means			
	2 years or less	3 to 5 years	6 to 10 years	Significance
Persons per room	0.74	0.69	0.61	.03
Number of rooms	3.90	4.77	5.19	.02
Renting	0.76	0.38	0.16	.001
Move for job	0.48	0.44	0.34	.09
Move for house	0.33	0.34	0.43	NS
Move for area	0.35	0.27	0.23	NS
Total (N = 336)	158	99	79	

SOURCE is the 1982 Orange County Annual Survey. Significance levels are based upon analyses of covariance that control for education, sex, marital status, household size, and dwelling type.

per-room ratio is highest in the more recent group. The number of rooms is considerably less among those who had moved to Orange County in the last two years. A highly significant factor is that three-fourths of new migrants rent their dwellings. In contrast, one in three residents of 3–5-years and one in six residents of 6–10 years rents a dwelling.

Other demographic factors were considered that are not reported in the table. Only one reached significance levels but all the trends are interesting and worth noting. The significant relationship was an increasing number of dual-career households. Of the suburban migrants of the last five years, 22 percent were dual-career households. This is in contrast to 14 percent in the 6–10 year category. Only one in four of the most recent migrants has more room now than in the previous housing unit. This contrasts with 38 percent for 3–5 years and 48 percent for 6–10 years. One-third of the most recent migrants had children, while 44 percent in the 3–5 year group and 45 percent in the 6–10 year group had children.

Work location and family income level did not show any length-of-residence trends. The proportion working in the suburbs, at least among all migrants, has not changed. Income differences are not marked among the length-of-residence groups. This is accounted for by the more advanced career stages of the older past migrants. In fact, one could argue that this is indirect evidence that relative income levels needed to migrate are rising.

The reasons for moving are also presented in table 8.1. Job reasons are more frequently noted among the most recent group in contrast to earlier cohorts. It is also interesting to note that "house" is somewhat less often noted as a major reason for moving in the last five years. Another trend is that "area" features are increasingly noted among the reasons for moving to a suburb.

There are no significant trends in the resident satisfaction measures. There are some indications, however, that later migrants have different evaluations of the immediate residence. Housing satisfaction has declined and neighborhood satisfaction is less among those migrants who have arrived most recently.

The analysis is replicated for the Los Angeles migrants and reported in table 8.2. Few of the trends are changed. Some lose significance because of the small sample size. The persons-per-room ratio indicates a trend toward less household space in recent years. So does the analysis of number of rooms over time. A large percentage of new migrants are renters, while a large percentage of earlier migrants are homeowners.

Other personal and housing characteristics of urban-core-to-suburb movers were considered. None indicated significant length-of-residence differences. These trends are worth

Table 8.2 Characteristics of Central City to Suburb Migrants

	Means			
	2 years or less	3 to 5 years	6 to 10 years	Significance
Persons per room	0.66	0.73	0.61	NS
Number of rooms	4.08	4.43	4.87	NS
Renting	0.71	0.35	0.15	.001
Move for job	0.44	0.37	0.16	.05
Move for house	0.41	0.44	0.46	NS
Move for area	0.34	0.29	0.22	NS
Total (N = 151)	64	48	39	

SOURCE is the 1982 Orange County Annual Survey. Significance levels are based upon analyses of covariance that control for education, sex, marital status, household size, and dwelling type.

reporting, since some replicate earlier results. More recent migrants from Los Angeles were somewhat more likely to be in dual-earner households than earlier groups. The recent migrants group, as with the previous results, more often did not have more room in their new dwelling than their previous one. Family income of Los Angeles migrants has changed very little over time.

Other trends did not replicate the results involving all migrants. The proportion of households with children has declined to 28 percent in the most recent group compared with 41 percent in the 3 years or more length-of-residence categories. Forty five percent of Los Angeles to Orange County migrants in the last 5 years have Orange County jobs contrasted with 34 percent in the 6–10 years group. The findings together indicate that members of the workforce rather than households with children characterize the new entrants to suburbia.

The findings concerning reasons for moving are basically the same as those from the total migrant pool (see table 8.2). The results of the length-of-residence comparisons involving moves for job reasons are even more dramatic: 44 percent of recent Los Angeles movers have mentioned job reasons, while of those who moved 6–10 years ago, only 16 percent mentioned job reasons. What is a new trend is that more and more Los Angeles residents are moving to their adjacent suburban county in pursuit of employment. Housing among new migrants is again less frequently mentioned as a reason for moving. In contrast, area is again noted more often.

The residential attitudes of migrants from Los Angeles were also analyzed. House and neighborhood evaluations of the recent urban movers are somewhat more negative than aong the earlier arrivals. Other attitudes have not changed over time. The findings are, again, that suburban migrants in more recent times not only have unique households, housing circumstances, and reasons for moving but also have lower residential satisfaction.

In brief, the household conditions of new migrants are distinct from those of past migrants. The findings for Los Angeles to Orange County migrants are similar. The most evident changes are related to housing. These include density, size, and ownership. Moving for job-related reasons is obviously on the increase. These trends indicate a shift from the suburbs offering large and inexpensive housing for city commuters to a trend toward suburbs offering smaller and more expensive housing and local employment. The necessity of two incomes is becoming more obvious among recent movers. There seem to have been some changes in reported satisfaction with residential conditions.[1]

The Move from Suburbia

The next questions from the 1982 survey measure the stated preference to leave the immediate area for some other region. The first moving preference item rated interest in moving from not at all to very much interested. About 70 percent of all respondents were not at all interested in moving. Of the remaining, 15 percent were somewhat interested and 15 percent were very much interested. This is fairly typical of national trends (Campbell et al. 1976).

Orange County residents who had already admitted to "some" or "much" interest in moving were then asked if they wanted to move out of the county. The short-distance move was by far the most preferred. Forty percent wanted to move out while 60 percent wanted to remain in the county. In all, one in nine persons interviewed wanted to move out of this suburban county.

What do these moving preferences imply? Most studies indicate that the large majority of movers want to relocate a few miles from their present address (see Butler et al. 1969). Short-distance moves generally comprise anywhere between 70 percent and 85 percent of all urban moves (Fischer et al. 1977; Goodman 1978). There is then evidence of a desire for out-migration that is larger than the previous moving trends.

Table 8.3 Attitudes of Potential Out-Movers

	Means		Significance
	Move out of county	Move within county	
School ratings	2.69	2.25	.01
Street ratings	2.38	2.06	.001
Police ratings	2.23	1.99	.02
Traffic perceptions	1.50	1.34	.01
Local government ratings	2.84	2.48	.001
Limit growth preference	0.79	0.67	.03
Total (N = 283)	111	172	

SOURCE is the 1982 Orange County Annual Survey. Significance levels are based upon analyses of covariance which control for education, sex, age, marital status, and length of residence. Higher mean scores indicate less satisfaction with community conditions.

Table 8.3 reports that self-reports about the region among those who wish to leave are more negative. Those who want to move from Orange County are contrasted with those who wish to move within Orange County. Comparing those who want to move out with all others gives even more dramatic differences. The potential out-migrants are dissatisfied with schools and roadway conditions. They complain more about the traffic. They rate police protection more negatively than those who want to move within the county. They are more in favor of limiting growth. They are also more likely to report that local government has performed poorly in solving the community's problems.

Also considered were the reasons people gave for wanting to move. There were no significant differences between within-county movers and out-of-county movers. But, as expected, jobs figure prominently in preferences for long-distance moves. One out of four would-be long-distance movers cited "housing" as a reason. This is a clear indication of unfulfilled wishes in the local area. Almost one of three potential out-of-county movers note that area's features were determining factors. This indicates a dislike of many evolving features in suburbia.

The characteristics of the individuals who want to move out of the county were also considered. Some are similar to long-distance movers everywhere: younger and better educated than others and unmarried. Forty-nine percent are renters compared with one-third of the total population. The potential long distance migrants are also different from the short distance movers. They are less likely to have children, more often in single wage-earner households, and have lower incomes. The trends suggest that lower-status and nonfamily households are feeling the push factors.

Statistics gathered in the 1983 survey further elaborate the findings. There was little change in desire to move or preference to move from Orange County. Of those wanting to move from Orange County 24 percent said that nearby Riverside–San Bernardino was their preference. This is important, since housing costs there are about half of those in Orange County. The statistics imply that housing is no longer a large pull factor in the developed suburb. In fact, it may be becoming a push factor.

Of all the outmovers, those wanting to leave for nearby Riverside–San Bernardino were more likely to have housing which was small, which they had lived in for only a short time, and which they rented. They tended to be less affluent than those wanting to migrate longer distances. These are thus the frustrated new apartment dwellers who are probably working in Orange County but need to find affordable housing outside the area. These data would seem to suggest the makings of an out-migration. But in fact the move to an adjacent region eventually results in more suburban domination.

In sum, some residents in Orange County are considering leaving this affluent suburban county. The housing market and an increasing awareness of community problems figure heavily in potential out-migrants' inclinations. They held surprisingly negative residential evaluations given the image of suburbia. They rated their public institutions poorly, complained about traffic, were distrustful of local governments' capabilities, and were fearful of growth. These opinions send an early warning signal. The suburbs may have trouble not only in attracting new people, as indicated in the earlier results, but in maintaining those who are there.

Concluding Comments
on Suburbia's Future

This chapter presents some evidence that the challenges which reflect the suburban transformation have implications for suburbia's future. Changes in housing opportunities seem to be particularly noteworthy in their consequences. But other changes evident in attitudes toward growth, transportation, and local government and its services are also important. In brief, the movement into and out of suburbia is changing as a result of new circumstances.

The patterns of recent moves into Orange County in contrast with earlier moves is enlightening. Housing size and quality seem to be on the decline. Recent movers in comparison with past movers are more crowded, have fewer rooms, are more likely to be renting, and are less likely to have experienced a gain in household space as a result of their suburban migration. They are, not surprisingly, less happy with their residence than the previous migrants.

The move for job reasons seems to be growing in popularity while the move for housing reasons is somewhat declining, for two reasons. Jobs are a more prominent feature of the new and industrialized suburb and have thus become a major draw. Housing has become more expensive and is in fact creating obstacles to employment migration.

The analysis of movers from Los Angeles provides an interesting portrait of changes in the traditional central-city-to-suburb migration. In a dramatic turnabout in the classical relationship between city and suburb, residents are now moving from the urban core to the suburbs for jobs. In fact, high proportions of new migrants already have suburban jobs. Few will move to suburbia and commute back to city jobs. Housing prices in the suburbs are not as dramatically different from city prices as they once were. Suburban housing advantages are thus difficult for new migrants to achieve. Housing, in brief, is becoming less of a reason to move.

One can think of several possible consequences of the new migration trends. If housing is less of a reason to move to suburbia, then perhaps growth rates due to migration will decline. After all, the major reason for suburbia's growth has been its housing opportunities. But one would have to reject that possibility because as housing choices have declined, job opportunities have increased. The reason for moving perhaps more than the numbers moving is changing.

One might also expect that as housing becomes more expensive, a higher-class resident pool will comprise the suburban migration, since only wealthy individuals would be able to afford a suburban residence. This possibility is also rejected, again for employment reasons. A variety of peoples will have to move to the suburbs because that is where they will find their jobs relocated or new employment locating. This will mean that some who move to the suburbs will experience deficits in regard to their own expectations and actual housing conditions.

The preference to move out of suburbia indicates the extent to which suburbia is maintaining its attractiveness as it continues its transformation. The information provided in the surveys does not offer overwhelmingly positive reviews. Forty percent who preferred to move wanted to leave suburbia, or about one in nine of all residents. This is a higher proportion of intercounty movers than is found in other regional and national surveys.

A direct link between the suburban challenges noted throughout the book and the desire to leave suburbia is evident. This suggests that the suburban transformation has reached a stage at which its emerging problems are felt by residents. Those who wanted to move from suburbia were more negative in residential and personal attitudes than the general population. The potential out-movers were also more dissatisfied than others who want to move inside suburbia. Those wishing to leave were more negative about public services, including police and schools, than those who wanted to stay. The potential out-migrants were also more negative about traffic conditions and roads, were more antigrowth, and lacked confidence in local government. In brief, specific suburban problems are central to residents' thoughts about whether to stay in an area.

Of special interest is the attractiveness of rural but "metropolitan spillover" communities. One in four potential outmovers noted a desire to move to the Riverside–San Bernardino "Inland Empire." A certain type of suburbanite preferred this sort of out-migration. These were people whose housing circumstances in suburbia were more desperate than others'. They tended to rent and to live in small homes. They were young families and blue collar workers. They had not been in suburbia for long but were apparently there long enough to realize that their housing expectations were not to be realized. A possibility thus exists that built-up suburban communities, such as Orange County, may someday be places in which the more wealthy live and to which the less affluent commute. This can result in greater traffic problems as time and distance on the freeways rise.

What does the preference to leave a suburban area say about its future? First, no one knows exactly how many of those who state a preference to leave will actually go. And, of course, some with no desire to leave may have found job and housing circumstances that force them to leave. Let us assume one likely scenario, that one in nine moves out and the rate of natural increase is steady. Growth would slow down in suburbia even if the migration flow into the area was the same. Invasion and succession processes also begin to develop if substantial population turnover occurs. The population remaining in suburbia could change. They may be the wealthy who can afford suburban homeownership and the poor who cannot afford long commutes to work.

Final Thoughts
on the Suburban Transformation

This book began by presenting three distinct visions of suburbia today. The evidence presented throughout allows for some clarification about the current state of affairs.

There is little evidence that a utopian image of suburbia is realistic, because the suburban challenges do exist. There is a housing crisis, as evidenced by several factors. These include a decline in homeownership, increases in the cost of owning a home, and lowered expectations of future homeownership by renters. The social values of the single-family, owner-occupied home are still evident but increasingly unfulfilled.

There are growth controversies that leave communities divided about future development. Many residents want growth halted and believe their governments have not been careful enough in their monitoring of in-migration. But even among those who agree on the need to limit growth, there is no consensus as to why this is needed or how to implement policies.

There are also fiscal problems that are not easily solved. Many services that suburbia has prided itself on delivering in a more satisfactory way than the cities are in disrepair. Schools, roads, and police are of utmost importance to average citizens. All have substantial negative ratings today. There are no easy ways to improve these services today, since external funds are limited and a fiscally conservative populace has asked government for further sacrifices.

These is a crisis in confidence in local governments. As suburbs have become larger, more dense, and more diverse, substantial numbers of residents have come to distrust their public institutions. This suburban distrust is experienced in questions about the efficiency, performance, and responsiveness of local government. The belief that local government works and is respected in the suburbs seems no longer to apply.

The proposition that an urban contagion was responsible for any problems in the suburbs also has no basis in the evidence considered. The challenges seem best explained by industrialization and rapid growth coupled with the unique social values, political structure, and geography of the suburbs. The issues in suburbia are thus not merely extensions of ongoing trends in the central cities.

The suburban transformation calls into question the future of suburbia. Two scenarios are likely given the current trends. They are to a large extent overlapping. One is that there will be a further diffusion of the suburban movement into the nearby countryside, the so-called metropolitan spillover phenomenon. It is probable that some residents and industries will move from the developed suburbs to the developing adjacent suburban areas. People will move out to find less expensive housing and fewer community problems. Industry will move for many of the same reasons as residents. In a sense, people will be escaping the suburbs today in search of some earlier vision. But the move to spillover areas is only a temporary escape from the new suburban reality. In a matter of time the places outside the suburban orbit will be filled in. The spaces between developed and undeveloped areas will shrink. A larger suburban region will then take the place of a smaller one.

The other scenario that is likely to occur is increasing suburban differentiation.[2] There will be more inequality between residents and between suburban communities as suburbanization evolves. Some individuals will be able to achieve all that they believe they should have from their suburban community. This includes single-family homeownership, the exclusion of unwanted growth, good public service delivery, and a local government that can be trusted. Such dreams will be fulfilled when the residents can afford to live in suburbs that provide the desired amenities. As the advantaged residents congregate in such areas, the communities themselves will become more powerful and resourceful than others in a region.

What this amounts to is a more rigid class system in suburbia. Some individuals will take root in preferred areas and others will be driven out. Some suburbs will flourish while others face insolvency and daily crises.

The attainment of high status in suburbia by some residents and communities is not, even for the most advantaged, a long-term solution. No community is an island. Nor can any resident survive only in the community of residence. Problems in nearby areas impinge upon the life of a community and its residents. Even if population growth or industrial development is halted in some places, there is congestion, pollution, noise, crime, and social pressures surrounding those places. Internal differentiation may give small comfort. In the long run, it is a "head in the sand" approach to suburban problem solving.

The conclusion, then, is that a new approach to the suburban transformation must occur. Metropolitan spillover and increasing social differentiation result in an extension of the status quo. In order for adverse conditions to be relieved, suburban Americans must come to realize that they and their residential communities are part of a larger area. This, in itself, requires a change in values and orientations. Residents of a suburban region ultimately pay the price, financially and in life quality, for the events occurring throughout an area. Local governments must be coerced to work in concert with other local governments, higher levels of government, the private sector, and citizen groups to ensure sound planning for suburban regions. Only then will the challenges of industrialization and rapid growth, and the influences of suburban geography and suburban values, be considered in a broad enough perspective and with appropriate resources. It is unlikely that local government will take the initiative to act. Suburban citizens who have shown the strength to react to local issues must thus take a more enlightened perspective and ask for a regional approach to community problems.

Notes

1. Some migrants in the last ten years have obviously been excluded, since the selection process defined migrant as "anyone whose previous residence was outside the county." For instance, someone who was a migrant five years ago but moved to a second Orange County location two years ago would be excluded from the category of migrants in the last ten years.

2. I am grateful to Gerald Suttles who, in a personal communication, elaborated upon some of these ideas. Also, the research of John Logan is consistent with these concerns.

APPENDIX

Survey Questions

1982 Orange County Annual Survey

First, I'd like to ask you some questions about where you presently live.

1. Is the place where you currently live a:
   1 = single family detached house
   2 = single family attached house
   3 = apartment
   4 = mobile home
   5 = other (specify)
2. How many rooms do you have in hour home, not counting hall-ways, kitchen, and bathrooms? [CODE DIRECTLY]
3. How long have you lived at your current residence?
   1 = less than a year
   2 = 1 to 2 years
   3 = 3 to 5 years
   4 = 6 to 10 years
   5 = 11 to 20 years (Skip to Q. 11)
   6 = more than 20 years (Skip to Q. 11)
4. What was the primary reason you decided to leave your last residence? (List up to three: probe)

5. What was the primary reason you chose your present community over some other places? (List up to three: probe)
6. Was your last residence in:
   1 = Orange County
   2 = Los Angeles County
   3 = other California county
   4 = other state
   5 = outside USA
7. Did you own or rent your previous residence?
8. How many persons, including yourself, lived in your last residence? [CODE DIRECTLY]
9. How many rooms did you have in your previous residence, not counting hallways, kitchen, and bathrooms? [CODE DIRECTLY]
10. Counting your move to your present residence, how many times have you moved in the last five years?
    0 = didn't move in last 5 years
    1 = one
    2 = two
    3 = three
    4 = four
    5 = five or more
11. At present, how interested are you in moving to a different residence?
    1 = not at all interested (Skip to Q.14)
    2 = somewhat interested
    3 = very much interested
12. What are the primary reasons why you are interested in moving? (List up to three: probe)
13. Are you interested in moving outside Orange County?
    1 = yes
    2 = no
14. Do you own or rent your present residence?
    1 = own (Skip to Q.17)
    2 = rent
15. Do you hope to someday own a home?
    1 = yes
    2 = no (Skip to Q.17)
16. Realistically, how likely is it that within the next three years you will own your own home?
    1 = very likely

2 = somewhat likely
3 = not at all likely
17. If you had your choice, what type of dwelling would you *prefer* to live in?
    1 = single family detached house
    2 = single family attached house
    3 = apartment
    4 = mobile home
    5 = other (specify)
18. Are you active in any local group, such as homeowners' association, a block club, or other sort of neighborhood organization?
    1 = yes
    2 = no
19. How often do you socialize with friends and relatives who live in your neighborhood?
    1 = several times a week
    2 = about once a week
    3 = several times a month
    4 = about once a month
    5 = several times a year
    6 = almost never
    7 = never
20. Would you say it is safe to go out walking at night where you live?
    1 = yes
    2 = no
21. In the last year have you or anyone in your immediate family been the victim of a crime—such as a burglary, auto theft, mugging, stickup, or threat—in your neighborhood?
    1 = yes
    2 = no
22. Now I'd like to ask you about smog in your neighborhood. Would you say in the past week there was:
    1 = little or no smog
    2 = some smog
    3 = quite a bit of smog
    4 = extreme smog
23. What about the level of noise from cars, airplanes, and neighbors in your neighborhood. Would you say in the past week there was:

1 = little or no noise
2 = some noise
3 = quite a bit of noise
4 =extreme noise

24. In the last three years do you think the population in your city or
town has been:
1 = growing rapidly
2 = growing slowly
3 = staying about the same
4 = losing population

I'd like to ask you how you would rate some of the main public
services you are supposed to receive.

(Categories for Q. 25 to Q. 30)
1 = excellent
2 = good
3 = only fair
4 = poor

25. The way streets and roads are kept up. Would you say this is:
26. The public school system. Would you say this is:
27. Police protection. Would you say this is:
28. Parks and other public recreational facilities. Would you say these
are:
29. Grocery stores and shopping centers. Would you say these are:
30. Hospitals and health clinics. Would you say these are:

31. Do you think that growth and development in your city should
be limited?
1 = yes
2 = no (Skip to Q. 36)

I am going to read you a list of reasons why some people want to
limit growth. For each one tell me if this is a reason why you would
like to limit growth.

(Categories for Q. 32 to Q. 35)
1 = yes
2 = no

32. To avoid increase in government spending and local taxes.
33. To prevent the environment from deteriorating.

34. To prevent an increase in traffic congestion and overcrowding.
35. To maintain present property values.

36. Do you think that government regulations in your city aimed at controlling growth are:
    1 = too strict
    2 = about right
    3 = not strict enough
37. How would you rate the performance of your city government in solving problems in your community?
    1 = excellent
    2 = good
    3 = only fair
    4 = poor
38. Would you support further cuts in state and local taxes even if some government services would have to be cut back?
    1 = yes
    2 = no
39. Which of the following best describes how you feel about the freeways in Orange County?
    1 = The current freeway system is satisfactory. (Skip to Q. 41)
    2 = More lanes should be added to the existing freeways but no new freeways should be built. (Skip to Q. 41)
    3 = We need to build new freeways to prevent an increase in traffic congestion. (Ask Q. 40)
40. Would you be willing to pay slightly higher county taxes to support the construction of new freeways in Orange County?
    1 = yes
    2 = no

How satisfied are you with each of the following?

    (Categories for Q. 41 to Q. 47)
    1 = very satisfied
    2 = somewhat satisfied
    3 = dissatisfied
    4 = very dissatisfied
41. The house or apartment in which you live.
42. The neighborhood in which you live.
43. Your job.
44. Your non-working activities like hobbies.

45. Your family life.
46. Your friendships.
47. Your financial situation.

48. Would you say your own health, in general, is:
    1 = excellent
    2 = good
    3 = only fair
    4 = poor
49. Do you have a chronic disability or illness that limits your ability to get around?
    1 = yes
    2 = no
50. How many times were you ill or injured in the past three months, that is, since Memorial Day?
    0 = not at all
    1 = once
    2 = twice
    3 = three times
    4 = four or more times
51. In general, would you say that your spirits lately have been:
    1 = excellent
    2 = good
    3 = only fair
    4 = poor
52. Taken all together, how would you say things are these days—would you say you are:
    1 = very happy
    2 = pretty happy
    3 = not too happy
53. What is your current work status?
    1 = full-time employed (30 hours a week or more)
    2 = part-time employed
    3 = unemployed, looking for work (Skip to Q. 62)
    4 = unemployed, not looking, but interested (Skip to Q. 62)
    5 = unemployed, not looking, not interested (Skip to Q. 62)
    6 = retired (Skip to Q. 62)
    7 = keeping house (Skip to Q. 62)
    8 = other (specify) (Skip to Q. 62)

54. What is your current occupation (the job you do, not who you work for)? (specify)
55. How do you usually commute to work?
    1 = drive by yourself
    2 = carpool—household member
    3 = carpool—neighbor, friend
    4 = carpool—stranger
    5 = public transit
    6 = vanpool through employer
    7 = other (specify)
56. Where do you work?
    1 = in Orange County
    2 = in Los Angeles
    3 = Riverside
    4 = San Diego
    5 = some place else (specify)
57. On a typical day, about how long does it take you to get from your home to the place where you report to work? (just your best estimate)
    1 = less than 10 minutes
    2 = 10 to 20 minutes
    3 = 21 to 30 minutes
    4 = 31 to 60 minutes
    5 = more than 60 minutes
58. Do you use a freeway in going to work?
    1 = yes
    2 = no
59. On a typical day, how much of a problem is traffic congestion when you travel to and from work? Would you say it is:
    1 = no problem at all
    2 = a slight problem
    3 = a great problem
60. For how long have you commuted along this route to work?
    1 = less than a year
    2 = 1 to 2 years
    3 = 3 to 5 years
    4 = 6 to 10 years
    5 = 10 to 20 years
    6 = more than 20 years
61. In the time you have commuted along this route, do you think

that the problem of traffic congestion has gotten better, worse, or is it about the same?
1 = better
2 = worse
3 = same

Finally, I have some questions about your household and present circumstances.

62. How many persons, including yourself, live in your household? [CODE DIRECTLY]
63. How many children 5 and under are there? [CODE DIRECTLY]
64. How many children from 6 to 13? [CODE DIRECTLY]
65. How many children from 14 to 18? [CODE DIRECTLY]
66. What was the last grade of school that you completed?
    1 = some high school or less
    2 = high school graduate
    3 = some college
    4 = college graduate or more
67. What is your current marital status?
    1 = married (Ask Q. 68)
    2 = divorced
    3 = separated
    4 = widowed   } Skip to Q. 69
    5 = single (never married)
68. What is the current work status of your spouse?
    1 = full-time employed (30 hours a week or more)
    2 = part-time employed
    3 = unemployed, looking for work
    4 = unemployed, not looking, but interested
    5 = unemployed, not looking, not interested
    6 = retired
    7 = keeping house
    8 = other (specify)
69. What is your age category?
    1 = under 25
    2 = 25 to 34
    3 = 35 to 44
    4 = 45 to 54
    5 = 55 to 64
    6 = 65 or older

70. What is the zip code of your present residence? (city, if not known) [CODE DIRECTLY]
71. What is the category of your total family income for 1981?
    1 = under $15,000
    2 = $15,000 to $25,000
    3 = $26,000 to $35,000
    4 = $36,000 to $50,000
    5 = over $50,000
72. What is the category of your personal income for 1981?
    1 = under $15,000
    2 = $15,000 to $25,000
    3 = $26,000 to $35,000
    4 = $36,000 to $50,000
    5 = over $50,000
    6 = no personal income
73. How would you describe your ethnicity or race?
    1 = Asian
    2 = Black
    3 = Hispanic
    4 = White
    5 = Other (specify)
74. Were you born in Orange County, in Los Angeles County, in another California county, in another state, or outside the U.S.?
    1 = Orange County
    2 = Los Angeles County
    3 = other California county
    4 = other state
    5 = outside U.S.
75. Would you consider yourself to be politically:
    1 = liberal
    2 = middle-of-the-road
    3 = conservative
76. Are you currently registered as a Republican, Democrat, or Independent, or are you not registered to vote?
    1 = Republican
    2 = Democrat
    3 = Independent
    4 = Not registered
77. What is your sex?
    1 = male   2 = female

78. Would you be willing to participate in a follow-up interview at a later date?

    1 = yes   2 = no

1983 Orange County Annual Survey

First, I'd like to ask you some questions about where you presently live.

1. Is the place where you currently live a:
   1 = single family house not attached to any other
   2 = single family house attached to another
   3 = apartment
   4 = mobile home
   5 = other (specify)
2. How many rooms do you have in your home, not counting hallways, kitchen, and bathrooms? [CODE DIRECTLY]
3. How long have you lived at your current residence?
   1 = less than a year
   2 = 1 to 2 years
   3 = 3 to 5 years
   4 = 6 to 10 years
   5 = 11 to 20 years
   6 = more than 20 years
4. Was your last residence in:
   1 = Orange County
   2 = Los Angeles County
   3 = other California county
   4 = other state
   5 = outside U.S.
5. At present, how interested are you in moving to a different residence?
   1 = not at all interested (Skip to Q. 18)
   2 = somewhat interested
   3 = very much interested
6. Are you interested in moving outside Orange County?
   1 = yes
   2 = no (Skip to Q. 8)
7. Are you interested in moving to Riverside County or San Bernardino County?
   1 = yes
   2 = no
8. Do you own or rent your present residence?

1 = own (Skip to Q. 11)
2 = rent
9. Would you buy a small home in Orange County if you could afford the monthly payments?
1 = yes
2 = no
10. What is your monthly rental payment?
1 = under $250
2 = $251 to $500
3 = $501 to $750   }   Skip to Q. 12
4 = $751 to $1,000
5 = more than $1,000
11. What is the category of your monthly mortgage payment (not including taxes and insurance)?
1 = under $350
2 = $351 to $500
3 = $501 to $750
4 = $751 to $1,000
5 = $1,001 to $1,250
6 = $1,251 to $2,000
7 = more than $2,000
12. In the last three years do you think the population in your city or town has been:
1 = growing rapidly
2 = growing slowly
3 = staying about the same
4 = losing population

I am going to read you a list of ways cities try to limit growth. For each one, tell me if this is an approach you favor very much, somewhat, or not at all.

(Categories for Q. 13 to Q. 16)
1 = very much
2 = somewhat
3 = not at all
13. Limit the number of new apartment buildings.
14. Limit the number of new industries moving in.
15. Limit the building of roads and freeways.
16. Limit the number of high rise buildings.

17. How would you rate the performance of your local government in solving problems in your community?
    1 = excellent
    2 = good
    3 = only fair
    4 =poor
18. In general do you think that the people who run your local government:
    1 = waste a lot of the money we pay in taxes.
    2 = waste some of the money we pay in taxes.
    3 = waste very little of the money we pay in taxes.
19. When your local government leaders decide what policies to adopt, how much attention do you think they pay to what the people think?
    1 = a lot of attention
    2 = some attention
    3 = very little attention
20. In the future do you think that Orange County will be:
    1 = a better place to live than it is now.
    2 = a worse place to live than it is now.
    3 = no change.

For each of these government services, tell me whether you think we should:

        (Categories for Q. 21 to Q. 25)
        1 = spend more money
        2 = spend less money
        3 = no change
21. Schools
22. Police protection
23. Hospitals and clinics
24. Parks and recreation
25. Streets and roads

26. Which of the following best describes how you feel about the freeways in Orange County?
    1 = The current system is satisfactory
    2 = More lanes should be added to the existing freeways but no new freeways should be built.

  3 = We need to build new freeways to prevent an increase in traffic congestion.
27. Are you in favor of expanding bus transportation?
  1 = yes 2 = no
28. Are you in favor of building a local rail transportation system?
  1 = yes 2 = no
29. Would you be willing to pay a one percent higher sales tax to improve Orange County's road and public transportation system?
  1 = yes 2 = no
30. Do you have children currently enrolled in public schools in Orange County?
  1 = yes 2 = no (skip to Q. 45)

I'd like to ask some questions about the public school which your oldest child attended this year. First of all,
31. Was that school an:
  1 = elementary school
  2 = intermediate or junior high school
  3 = high school

Now I'll be asking whether you agree or disagree with several statements about your oldest child's school.

  (Categories for Q. 32 to Q. 38)
  1 = agree 2 = disagree
32. The most up-to-date textbooks are used.
33. The teachers provide a high quality of instruction.
34. Some of your children's school friends are a bad influence.
35. Drugs or alcohol are problems at school.
36. The teacher assigns too little homework.
37. Budget cuts have had bad effects on the curriculum.
38. Too much attention is given to children with special learning needs.

The following statements are about your own attitudes and activities concerning your oldest child in school.

  (Categories for Q. 39 to Q. 43)
  1 = A lot of the time
  2 = some of the time

3 = rarely
4 = never
39. How often do you ask to see your child's homework?
40. How often do your child's needs interfere with doing things for yourself?
41. How often do you feel that you are not doing enough as a parent?
42. How often do you give specific advice about your child's daily concerns? /
43. Aside from being a parent, how often do you feel heavy burdens from work and other responsibilities?

44. Overall, how would you rate your oldest child's school?
    1 = excellent
    2 = good
    3 = fair
    4 = poor
45. In the last week how often have you gotten together with people just to socialize?
    1 = every day
    2 = several times
    3 = once
    4 = You didn't have a chance to socialize with anyone this week.
46. In the last week how often have you spoken with someone about a personal matter?
    1 = every day
    2 = several times
    3 = once
    4 = You didn't talk to anyone this week about a personal matter.
47. In the last week how often has someone helped you with a practical problem or chore?
    1 = every day
    2 = several times
    3 = once
    4 = No one helped you with a practical problem this week.

I am going to read you a list of the ways you might have felt or behaved. During the past week how often did you feel this way:

(Categories for Q. 48 to Q. 55)
1 = most of the time
2 = occasionally
3 = rarely
4 = never
48. You did not feel like eating.
49. You had trouble keeping your mind on what you were doing.
50. You felt depressed.
51. You felt hopeful about the future.
52. Your sleep was restless.
53. You felt lonely.
54. You were under a lot of stress.
55. You felt bored.
56. Would you say your own health, in general, is:
1 = excellent
2 = good
3 = only fair
4 = poor
57. We are also interested in whether people have diabetes. Do you happen to have diabetes?
1 = yes   2 = no (Skip to Q. 59)
58. Do you take insulin?
1 = yes   2 = no
59. If the medical profession wanted to provide additional medical care in your community, which type of care would be the most useful to you?
1 = care for the newborn
2 = care for elementary school aged children
3 = care for adolescents
4 = care for young and middle aged adults
5 = care for the elderly
60. What is your age category?
1 = 18 to 24
2 = 25 to 34
3 = 35 to 44   } Skip to Q. 70
4 = 45 to 64
5 = 55 to 64
6 = 65 or older   (Ask Q. 61)
61. How satisfied are you with your friendships?
1 = very satisfied

2 = satisfied
3 = dissatisfied
4 = very dissatisfied
62. How satisfied are you with your family life?
   1 = very satisfied
   2 = satisfied
   3 = dissatisfied
   4 = very dissatisfied
63. Do you think that in your community there are enough good places for you to meet new people or get together with friends?
   1 = yes
   2 = no
64. In general, how difficult is it for you to make friends with the people in your community?
   1 = very difficult
   2 = somewhat difficult
   3 = not too difficult
65. In general, when you meet new people how difficult is it for you to strike up a conversation?
   1 = very difficult
   2 = somewhat difficult
   3 = not too difficult
66. Considering where most of your friends and relatives live, how easy is it to get together with them?
   1 = very easy
   2 = easy
   3 = hard
   4 = very hard
67. Because of crime some people are afraid to go out at night to get together with friends and relatives. How often do you feel this way?
   1 = frequently
   2 = sometimes
   3 = rarely
   4 = never
68. How often do health problems prevent you from getting together with friends and relatives?
   1 = frequently
   2 = sometimes
   3 = rarely
   4 = never

69. How often do you have a personal disagreement with a friend or relative?
    1 = frequently
    2 = sometimes
    3 = rarely
    4 = never
70. What is your current work status?
    1 = full-time employed (30
        hours a week or more)
    2 = part-time employed
    3 = unemployed and actively
        looking for work
    4 = unemployed and not
        actively looking for work } Skip to Q.75
    5 = student
    6 = retired
    7 = keeping house
    8 = other (specify)
71. Some people work overtime or beyond what is required. On the average, how many additional hours per week do you work?
    1 = none
    2 = less than 5 hours
    3 = 6 to 10 hours
    4 = more than 10 hours
72. What is your current occupation (the job you do—not who you work for)? (specify)
73. Where do you work?
    1 = in Orange County
    2 = in Los Angeles
    3 = Riverside–San Bernardino
    4 = San Diego
    5 = some place else (specify)
74. On a typical day, how much of a problem is traffic congestion when you travel to and from work? Would you say it is:
    1 = no problem at all
    2 = a slight problem
    3 = a great problem
75. How many persons, including yourself, live in your household? [CODE DIRECTLY]
76. How many adult full time workers are in your household? [CODE DIRECTLY]

77. Do you live with your parents?
    1 = yes   2 = no
78. How many children 5 and under are there? [CODE DIRECTLY]
79. How many children from 6 to 13? [CODE DIRECTLY]
80. How many children from 14 to 17? [CODE DIRECTLY]
81. What was the last grade of school that you completed?
    1 = some high school or less
    2 = high school graduate
    3 = some college
    4 = college graduate or more
82. What is your current marital status?
    1 = married (Ask Q. 83)
    2 = divorced
    3 = separated   ⎫
    4 = widowed   ⎬ Skip to Q.85
    5 = single (never married) ⎭
83. What is the current work status of your spouse?
    1 = full-time employed (30
         hours a week or more)
    2 = part-time employed
    3 = unemployed and actively ⎫
         looking for work
    4 = unemployed and not
         actively looking for work ⎬ Skip to Q.85
    5 = student
    6 = retired
    7 = keeping house
    8 = other (specify)   ⎭
84. What is your spouse's current occupation? (specify)
85. What is the zip code of your present residence? (city, if not known) [CODE DIRECTLY]
86. What is the category of your total household or family income for 1982?
    1 = under $15,000
    2 = $15,000 to $25,000
    3 = $26,000 to $35,000
    4 = $36,000 to $50,000
    5 = $51,000 to $75,000
    6 = over $75,000
87. Would you consider yourself to be politically:
    1 = liberal

2 = middle-of-the-road
3 = conservative

88. Are you currently registered as a Republican, Democrat, Independent, another party, or are you not registered to vote?
    1 = Republican
    2 = Democrat
    3 = Independent or other party
    4 = not registered

89. How would you describe your ethnicity or race?
    1 = Asian
    2 = Black
    3 = Hispanic
    4 = White
    5 = other (specify)

90. What is your sex?
    1 = male
    2 = female

References

Abramson, P. and A. Finifter. 1981. "On the Meaning of Political Trust: New Evidence from Items Introduced in 1978." *American Journal of Political Science*, 25:297–307.

Alonso, W. 1973. "Urban Zero Population Growth." *Daedalus*, 102:191–206.

Antunes, G., F. Cook, and W. Skogan. 1977. "Patterns of Personal Crime Against the Elderly: Findings from a National Survey." *The Gerontologist*, 4:321–27.

Baldassare, M. 1979. *Residential Crowding in Urban America*. Berkeley: University of California Press.

—— 1981. *The Growth Dilemma*. Berkeley: University of California Press.

—— 1982a. "Evidence for Neighborhood Revitalization: Manhattan in the 1970s." *Journal of Urban Affairs*, 4:25–37.

—— 1982b. "The Effects of Neighborhood Density and Social Control on Resident Satisfaction." *Sociological Quarterly*, 23:95–105.

—— 1984. "Predicting Local Concern about Growth: The Roots of Citizen Discontent." *Journal of Urban Affairs* 6(4):39–50.

—— 1985. "The Suburban Movement to Limit Growth: Reasons for Support in Orange County." *Policy Studies Review*, forthcoming.

——, ed. 1983. *Cities and Urban Living*. Introduction. New York: Columbia University Press.

Baldassare, M. and W. Protash. 1982. "Growth Controls, Population Growth, and Community Satisfaction." *American Sociological Review*, 47:339–46.

Balkins, S. 1979. "Victimization Rates, Safety, and Fear of Crime." *Social Problems*, 26:343–58.

Barber, B. 1983. *The Logic and Limits of Trust.* New Brunswick, N.J.: Rutgers University Press.

Baumer, T. 1978. "Research on Fear of Crime in the United States." *Victimology,* 3:254–64.

Beale, C. 1975. "The Revival of Population Growth in Nonmetropolitan America." ERS-605. Washington, D.C.: U.S. Department of Agriculture.

Bell, D. 1973. *The Coming of Post Industrial Society.* New York: Basic Books.

Berger, B. 1960. *Working Class Suburb.* Berkeley: University of California Press.

—— 1961. "The Myth of Suburbia." *Journal of Social Issues,* 17:38–49.

Braungart, M., R. Braungart, and W. Hoyer. 1980. "Age, Sex, and Social Factors in Fear of Crime." *Sociological Focus,* 13:55–66.

Bridgeland, W. and A. Sofranko. 1975. "Community Structure and Issue-Specific Influences: Community Mobilization over Environmental Quality." *Urban Affairs Quarterly,* 11(2):186–214

Burgess, E. 1925 (1967). "The Growth of the City: An Introduction to a Research Project." In R. E. Park, E. W. Burgess, and R. D. McKenzie, eds., *The City,* pp. 47–62. Chicago: University of Chicago Press.

Burrows, L. 1978. *Growth Management: Issues, Techniques, and Policy Implications.* New Brunswick, N.J.: Center for Urban Policy Research.

Butler, E. et al. 1969. *Moving Behavior and Residential Choice.* Chapel Hill, N.C.: Center for Urban and Regional Studies.

Buttel, F. and W. Flynn. 1978. "Social Class and Environmental Beliefs: A Reconsideration." *Environment and Behavior,* 10(3):433–50.

California. 1979. *Economic Report of the Governor.* Sacramento: State of California.

—— 1980. "The Growth Revolt: Aftershock of Proposition 13?" Office of Planning and Research, Sacramento. Mimeo.

—— 1983. *Economic Report of the Governor.* Sacramento: State of California.

Campbell, A., F. Converse, and W. Rodgers. 1976. *The Quality of American Life.* New York: Russell Sage Foundation.

Castells, M. 1976. "Theory and Ideology in Urban Sociology." In C. G. Pickvance, ed., *Urban Sociology,* pp. 60–84. New York: St. Martin's Press.

Center for Ecomomic Research. 1983. "Housing Prices in Orange County: Is the Big Crash Coming?" Report Number 12. Orange: Chapman College.

Chevan, A. 1971. ' Family Growth, Housing Density, and Moving." *Demography,* 8:451–58.

Citrin, J. 1974. "The Political Relevance of Trust in Government." *American Political Science Review,* 68:973–88.

—— 1979. "Do People Want Something for Nothing? Public Opinion on Taxes and Government Spending." *National Tax Journal,* 32:113–29.

Clark, T. 1979. *Blacks in Suburbs.* New Brunswick, N.J.: Center for Urban Policy Research.

Clark, T. N. 1974. "Can You Cut a Budget Pie?" *Policy and Politics,* 3:3–31.

—— 1981. "Community Development and Fiscal Strain." *Urban Affairs Papers*, 3(2):1–12.

Clark, T. N. and L. C. Ferguson. 1983. *City Money: Political Processes, Fiscal Strain, and Retrenchment*. New York: Columbia University Press.

Clarke, A. and M. Lewis. 1982. "Fear of Crime Among the Elderly." *British Journal of Criminology*, 22(1):49–62.

Clemente, F. and M. Kleinman. 1976. "Fear of Crime Among the Aged." *The Gerontologist*, 16(3):207–10.

—— 1977. "Fear of Crime in the United States: A Multi-Variate Analysis." *Social Forces*, 56:519–31.

Cook, F., W. Skogan, T. Cook, and G. Antunes. 1978. "Criminal Victimization of the Elderly: The Physical and Economic Consequences." *The Gerontologist*, 18(4):338–49.

Courant, P., E. Gramlich, and D. Rubinfeld. 1979. "Tax Limitations and the Demand for Public Services in Michigan." *National Tax Journal*, 32:147–57.

—— 1980. "Why Voters Support Tax Limitations Amendments: The Michigan Case." *National Tax Journal*, 33:1–20.

Danielson, M. 1976. *The Politics of Exclusion*. New York: Columbia University Press.

Danielson, M. and J. Doig. 1982. *New York: The Politics of Urban Regional Development*. Berkeley: University of California Press.

Davis, J. and T. Smith. 1983. *General Social Survey Cumulative File, 1972–1982*. Ann Arbor: Unviersity of Michigan.

Dawson, G. 1977. *No Little Plans*. Washington, D.C.: Urban Institute.

Devall, W. 1970. "Conservation: An Upper Middle Class Social Movement: A Replication." *Journal of Leisure Research*, 2:122–26.

Dobriner, W. 1958. *The Suburban Community*. New York: G. Putnam.

Dohrenwend, D. and B. Dohrenwend. 1969. *Social Status and Psychological Disorder*. New York: John Wiley.

Dolce, P. C. 1976. *Suburbia: The American Dream and Dilemma*. New York: Anchor Books.

Donaldson, S. 1969. *The Suburban Myth*. New York: Columbia University Press.

Dowall, D. 1980. "An Examination of Population-Growth-Managing Communities." *Policy Studies Journal* 9(3):414–27.

Dowd, J., R. Sisson, and D. Kern. 1981. "Socialization to Violence Among the Aged." *Journal of Gerontology*, 36(3):350–61.

Durkheim, E. 1893 (1933). *The Division of Labor in Society*. New York: Free Press.

Easton, D. 1975. "A Reassessment of the Concept of Political Support." *British Journal of Political Science*, 3:435–57.

Ehrlich, P. 1968. *The Population Bomb*. New York: Ballantine.

Ellickson, R. 1977. "Suburban Growth Controls: An Economic and Legal Analysis." *Yale Law Journal*, 86(2):385–511.

Erskine, H. 1974. "The Polls: Fear of Violence and Crime." *Public Opinion Quarterly*, 38:131–48.

Faris, R. and M. Dunham. 1939 (1967). *Mental Disorders in Urban Areas*. Chicago: University of Chicago Press.

Farley, R. 1976. "Components of Suburban Population Growth." In B. Schwartz, ed., *The Changing Face of the Suburbs*, pp. 3–38. Chicago: University of Chicago Press.

Feldman, S. 1983. "The Measurement and Meaning of Trust in Government." *Political Methodology*, 9:341–54.

Field, M. 1979. *California Poll*. San Francisco: Field Institute.

—— 1981. *California Poll*. San Francisco: Field Institute.

—— 1982. *California Poll*. San Francisco: Field Institute.

Field Institute. 1983a. "Taxes and Government Spending." *California Opinion Index, April*. San Francisco: California Poll.

—— 1983b. "California's Public Schools." *California Opinion Index, July*. San Francisco: California Poll.

Firey, W. 1946. "Ecological Considerations in Planning for Suburban Fringes." *American Sociological Review*, 11:411–23.

Fischer, C. S. 1975. "The City and Political Psychology." *American Political Science Review*, 69(2):559–71.

—— 1981. "The Public and Private Worlds of City Life." *American Sociological Review*, 46(3):306–16.

—— 1984. *The Urban Experience*. New York: Harcourt, Brace, Jovanovich.

Fischer, C. S., R. Jackson, C. Stueve, K. Gerson, L. Jones, and M. Baldassare. 1977. *Networks and Places*. New York: Free Press.

Foley, D. 1972. *Governing the London Region*. Berkeley: University of California Press.

Freudenberg, W. 1979. "People in the Impact Zone: The Human and Social Consequences of Energy Boomtown Growth in Four Western Colorado Communities." Unpublished manuscript.

Frey, J. 1983. *Survey Research by Telephone*. Beverly Hills: Sage Publications.

Frey, W. 1979. "Central-City White Flight." *American Sociological Review*, 44:425–48.

—— 1980. "Black In-Migration and White Flight: Economic Effects." *American Journal of Sociology*, 85:1396–1417.

Frieden, B. 1979. *The Environmental Protection Hustle*. Cambridge, Mass.: MIT Press.

Frisbie, W. P. 1980. "U.S. Urban Sociology." *American Behavioral Scientist*, 24:177–214.

Fuguitt, G. and J. Zuiches. 1975. "Residential Preferences and Population Distribution." *Demography*, 12:491–504.

Furstenberg, F. 1971. "Public Reactions to Crime in the Streets." *American Scholar*, 56:176–93.

Gale, D. 1979. "Middle Class Resettlement in Older Urban Neighborhoods: The Evidence and the Implications." *Journal of the American Planning Association,* 45:293–304.

Gramlich, E., D. Rubinfeld, and D. Swift. 1981. "Why Voters Turn Out for Tax Limitation Votes." *National Tax Journal,* 34:115–24.

Gans, H. 1962. "Urbanism and Suburbanism as Ways of Life: A Re-evaluation of Definitions." In Arnold Rose, ed., *Human Behavior and Social Processes,* pp. 625–48. Boston: Houghton Mifflin.

—— 1967. *The Levittowners.* New York: Pantheon.

Garkovich, L. 1982. "Land Use Planning as a Response to Rapid Population Growth and Community Change." *Rural Sociology,* 47(1):47–67.

Goddschalk, D. 1977. *Constitutional Issues of Growth Management.* Chicago: ASPO Press.

Goodman, J. 1978. *Urban Residential Mobility.* Washington, D.C.: Urban Institute.

Gottdiener, M. and M. Neiman. 1981. "Characteristics of Support for Local Growth Control." *Urban Affairs Quarterly,* 17:55–73.

Groves, R. and R. Kahn. 1979. *Surveys by Telephone.* New York: Academic Press.

Gurin, G. 1960. *Americans View Their Mental Health.* New York: Basic Books.

Hall, P. 1977. *World Cities.* New York: McGraw-Hill.

Harry, J., R. Gale, and J. Hendee. 1969. "Conservation: An Upper Middle Class Movement." *Journal of Leisure Research,* 1:246–54.

Hartnagel, T. 1979. "The Perception and Fear of Crime: Implications for Neighborhood Cohesion, Social Activity, and Community Affect." *Social Forces,* 58:176–93.

Harvey, D. 1973. *Social Justice and the City.* London: Edward Arnold.

Hatry, H. and L. Blair. 1976. "Citizen Surveys for Local Government: A Cop-out Manipulative Tool, or a Policy Guidance and Analysis Tool?" In Terry N. Clark, ed., *Citizen Preferences and Urban Public Policy,* pp. 129–40. Beverly Hills: Sage Publications.

Hawley, A. 1950. *Human Ecology: A Theory of Community Structure.* New York: Ronald Press.

Henretta, J. 1984. "Parental Status and Child's Homeownership." *American Sociological Review,* 49:131–40.

Hirsch, F. 1976. *Social Limits to Growth.* Cambridge, Mass.: Harvard University Press.

Hoffman, W. and T. N. Clark. 1979. "Citizens' Preferences and Urban Policy Types." In J. Blair and D. Nachmias, eds., *Fiscal Retrenchment and Urban Policy,* pp. 85–105. Beverly Hills: Sage Publications.

House, J. and W. Mason. 1975. "Political alienation in America, 1952–1968." *American Sociological Review* 40(2):123–147.

Jordan, L., A. Marcus, and L. Reeder. 1980. "Response Styles in Telephone and Household Interviewing: A Field Experiment." *Public Opinion Quarterly*, 44:210–22.

Kasarda, J. 1972. "The Impact of Suburban Population Growth in Central City Service Functions." *American Journal of Sociology*, 77:1111–24.

—— 1976. "The Changing Occupational Structure of the American Metropolis: Apropos the Urban Problem." In B. Schwartz, ed., *The Changing Face of the Suburbs*, pp. 113–36. Chicago: University of Chicago Press.

—— 1978. "Urbanization, Community, and the Metropolitan Problem." In D. Street, ed., *Handbook of Contemporary Urban Life*, pp. 27–57. San Francisco: Jossey Bass.

—— 1980. "The Implications of Contemporary Distribution Trends for National Urban Policy." *Social Science Quarterly*, 61:373–400.

Katz, D., B. Gutek, R. Kahn, and E. Barton. 1975. *Bureaucratic Encounters.* Ann Arbor: Institute for Social Research.

Kramer, J. 1972. *North American Suburbs.* Berkeley: Glendessary Press.

Kuklinski, J. 1978. "Representativeness and Elections: A Policy Analysis." *American Political Science Review*, 72:165–77.

—— 1979. "Political Participation and Government Responsiveness: The Behavior of California Supreme Courts." *American Political Science Review*, 73:1090–99.

Ladd, H. and J. Wilson. 1982. "Why Voters Support Tax Limitations: Evidence from Massachusetts Proposition 2½." *National Tax Journal*, 35:121–48.

Lake, W. 1981. *The New Suburbanites: Race and Housing in the Suburbs.* New Brunswick, N.J.: Center for Urban Policy Research.

Lawton, M. and S. Yaffe, 1980. "Victimization and Fear of Crime in Elderly Public Housing Tenants." *Journal of Gerontology*, 35(3):768–79.

Lebowitz, B. 1975. "Age and Fearfulness: Personal and Situational Factors." *Journal of Gerontology*, 30:696–700.

Levin, M. 1960. *The Alienated Voter.* New York: Holt, Rinehart, and Winston.

Lipset, S. and W. Schneider. 1983. *The Confidence Gap.* New York: Free Press.

Listokin, D. and W. Beaton. 1983. *Revitalizing the Older Suburb.* New Brunswick, N.J.: Center for Urban Policy Research.

Logan, J. 1978. "Growth, Politics, and the Stratification of Places." *American Journal of Sociology*, 84:404–16.

Logan, J. and O. A. Collver. 1983. "Residents' Perceptions of Suburban Community Differences." *American Sociological Review*, 48:428–33.

Logan, J. and M. Schneider. 1981. "The Stratification of Metropolitan Suburbs, 1960–1970." *American Sociological Review*, 46:175–86.

Logan, J. and M. Semyonov. 1980. "Growth and Succession in Suburban Communities." *Sociological Quarterly*, 21:93–105.

Long, L. 1972. "The Influence of Number and Ages of Children on Residential Mobility." *Demography*, 9:371–82.

—— 1973. "Migration Differential by Education and Occupation." *Demography*, 10:243–58.

—— 1980. "Back to the Countryside and Back to the City in the Same Decade." In S. Laske and D. Spain, eds., *Back to the City: Issues in Neighborhood Renovation*, pp. 61–76. New York: Pergamon Press.

Long, L. and D. DeAre. 1981. "Population Redistribution, 1960 to 1980." Washington, D.C.: U.S. Bureau of the Census.

Lyon, L., L. Felice, and M. Perryman. 1981. "Community Power and Population Increase: An Empirical Test of the Growth Machine Model." *American Journal of Sociology*, 86:1387–1400.

McAllister, R., E. Kaiser, and E. Butler. 1971. "Residential Mobility of Blacks and Whites: A Longitudinal Survey." *American Journal of Sociology*, 77:445–56.

McKenzie, R. 1925 (1967). "The Ecological Approach to the Study of the Human Community." In R. E. Park, E. W. Burgess, and R. D. McKenzie, eds., *The City*, pp. 63–69. Chicago: University of Chicago Press.

McIver, J. and E. Ostrom. 1976. "Using Budget Pies to Reveal Preferences: Validation of a Survey Instrument." In T. N. Clark, ed., *Citizen Preference and Urban Public Policy*, pp. 87–110. Beverly Hills: Sage Publications.

Marando, V. and R. Thomas. 1977. "County Commissioners' Attitudes Towards Growth: A Two-State Comparison." *Social Science Quarterly*, 58(1):128–38.

Marans, R. and J. Wellman. 1978. *The Quality of Nonmetropolitan Living*. Ann Arbor: Institue for Social Research.

Massotti, L. 1973. *The Urbanization of the Suburbs*. Beverly Hills: Sage Publications.

Maurer, R. and J. Christenson. 1982. "Growth and Nongrowth Orientations of Urban, Suburban, and Rural Mayors: Reflections on the City as a Growth Machine." *Social Science Quarterly*, 63(2):350–58.

Michelson, W. 1976. *Man and His Urban Environment*. Reading, Mass.: Addison Wesley.

—— 1977. *Environmental Choice, Human Behavior, and Residential Satisfaction*. New York: Oxford University Press.

Miller, A. H. 1974. "Political Issues and Trust in Government, 1964–1970." *American Political Science Review*, 68:951–72.

Molotch, H. 1976. "The City as a Growth Machine: Toward a Political Economy of Place." *American Journal of Sociology*, 82:309–32.

Morgan, D. 1975. "Subjective Indicators of the Quality of Life in U.S. Communities." Unpublished report, University of Chicago.

Morris, E. W. and M. Winter. 1975. "A Theory of Family Housing Adjustment." *Journal of Marriage and the Family*, 37:79–88.

—— 1978. *Housing, Family, and Society*. New York: Wiley Press.

Morrison, P. 1977. "Migration and rights of Access: New Public Concerns of the 1970s." Rand Series P-5785 (March), Santa Monica, Calif.

Naisbitt, J. 1982. *Megatrends.* New York: Warner Books.

Neiman, M. 1980. "Zoning Policy, Income Clustering, and Suburban Change." *Social Science Quarterly,* 61(3,4):666–75.

Neiman, M. and R. Loveridge. 1981. "Environmentalism and Local Growth Control: A Probe into the Class Bias Thesis." *Environment and Behavior,* 13(6):759–72.

Ollenburger, J. 1981. "Criminal Victimization and Fear of Crime." *Research on Aging,* 3(1):101–18.

Page, B. and R. Shapiro. 1983. "Effects of Public Opinion on Policy." *American Political Science Review,* 77:175–80.

Park, R. 1925 (1967). "The City: Suggestions for the Study of Human Behavior in the Urban Environment." In R. E. Park, E. W. Burgess, and R. D. McKenzie, eds., *The City,* pp. 1–46. Chicago: University of Chicago Press.

Perin, C. 1977. *Everything in Its Place.* Princeton, N.J.: Princeton University Press.

Perry, D. and A. Watkins. 1977. *The Rise of the Sunbelt Cities.* Beverly Hills: Sage Publications.

Ploch, D. 1980. "The Effects of Turnaround Migration on Community Structure in Maine." In D. Brown and J. Wardell, eds., *New Directions in Urban-Rural Migrations,* pp. 291–312. New York: Academic Press.

Protash, W. and M. Baldassare. 1983. "Growth Policies and Community Status: A Test and Modification of Logan's Theory." *Urban Affairs Quarterly,* 18:397–412.

Rogers, T. 1978. "Interviews by Telephone and in Person: Quality of Responses and Field Performance." *Public Opinion Quarterly,* 40:51–65.

Rosenbaum, N. 1978. "Growth and Its Discontents: Origins of Local Population Controls." In A. Wildavsky and J. May, eds., *The Policy Cycle,* pp. 43–61. Beverly Hills: Sage Publications.

Rosenfield, S. 1980. "Sex Differences in Depression: Do Women Always Have Higher Rates?" *Journal of Health and Social Behavior,* 22:33–42.

Rossi, P. 1956. *Why Families Move.* Glencoe, Ill.: Free Press.

Schnore, L., C. Andre, and H. Sharp. 1976. "Balck Suburbanization, 1930–1970." In B. Schwartz, ed., *The Changing Face of the Suburbs,* pp. 69–94. Chicago: University of Chicago Press.

Schumacher, E. F. 1973. *Small Is Beautiful.* London: Blond and Briggs.

Schumaker, D. 1981. "Citizen Preferences and Policy Responsiveness." In T. N. Clark, ed., *Urban Policy Analysis,* pp. 227–43. Beverly Hills: Sage Publications.

Schwartz, S. and R. Johnston. 1983. "Inclusionary Housing Programs." *Journal of the American Planning Association,* 49:3–21.

Scott, D. 1976. "Measures of Citizens' Evaluations of Local Government Services." In T. N. Clark, ed., *Citizen Preferences and Urban Public Policy,* pp. 111–28. Beverly Hills: Sage Publications.

Scott, R., D. Brower, and D. Miner. 1975. *Management and Control of Growth,* Vol. 1. Washington, D.C.: Urban Land Institute.

Shaw, C. and H. McKay. 1929 (1969). *Juvenile Delinquency in Urban Areas.* Chicago: University of Chicago Press.

Simmel, G. 1905 (1969). "The Metropolis and Mental Life." In R. Sennett, ed., *Classic Essays on the Culture of Cities,* pp. 47–60. New York: Appleton.

Spain, D., J. Reed, and L. Long. 1980. "Housing Succession Among Blacks and Whites in Cities and Suburbs." Current Population Reports, January. Washington, D.C.: U.S. Government Printing Office.

Srole, L., et al. 1962. *Mental Health in the Metropolis.* New York: Harper Press.

Sundeen, A. and J. Mathieu. 1976. "The Fear of Crime and Its Consequences Among Elderly in Three Urban Communities." *The Gerontologist,* 16:211–19.

Suttles, G. 1969. *The Social Order of the Slum.* Chicago: University of Chicago Press.

Thurow, L. 1980. *Zero Sum Society.* New York: Basic Books.

Tremblay, K. and D. Dillman. 1983. *Beyond the American Housing Dream.* New York: University Press of America.

Troldahl, V. and R. Carter. 1964. "Random Selection of Respondents Within Households in Phone Surveys." *Journal of Marketing Research,* 1:71–76.

U.S. Bureau of the Census. 1971. *Statistical Abstracts of the United States, 1970.* Washington, D.C.: U.S. Government Printing Office.

—— 1972. *General Social and Economic Characteristics, 1970.* Washington, D.C.: U.S. Government Printing Office.

—— 1973. *County and City Data Book, 1972.* Washington, D.C.: U.S. Government Printing Office.

—— 1981. "California: Final Population and Housing Counts." Washington, D.C.: U.S. Department of Commerce.

—— 1982. *County and City Data Book, 1982.* Washington, D.C.: U.S. Government Printing Office.

—— 1983a. *Statistical Abstract of the United States: 1982–1983.* Washington, D.C.: U.S. Government Printing Office.

—— 1983b. *State and Metrpolitan Area Data Book, 1982.* Washington, D.C.: U.S. Government Printing Office.

—— 1983c. *General Social and Economic Characteristics, 1980: United States Summary.* Washington, D.C.: U.S. Government Printing Office.

—— 1984. *Journey to Work, 1980.* Washington, D.C.: U.S. Department of Commerce.

U.S. League of Savings. 1984. *Homeownership: Celebratin the American Dream.* Washington, D.C.: U.S. League of Savings.

Van Liere, K. and R. Dunlap. 1980. "The Social Bases of Environmental

Concern: A Review of Hypotheses, Explanations, and Empirical Evidence." *Public Opinion Quarterly*, 44:181–97.

Voss, P. 1980. "A Test of the 'Gangplank Syndrome' Among Recent Migrants to the Upper Great Lakes Region." *Journal of the Community Development Society*, 11:95–111.

Wachs, M. 1979. *Transportation for the Elderly*. Berkeley: University of California Press.

Whyte, W. H. 1956. *The Organization Man*. New York: Simon and Schuster.

——1968. *The Last Landscape*. New York: Doubleday.

Wilson, K. and A. Portes. 1980. "Immigrant Enclaves: An Analysis of the Labor Market Experience of Cubans in Miami." *American Journal of Sociology*, 86:295–319.

Wirth, L. 1938. "Urbanism as a Way of Life." *American Journal of Sociology*, 44:1–24.

Yin, P. 1980. "Fear of Crime Among the Elderly: Some Issues and Suggestions." *Social Problems*, 27(4):492–504.

Zimmer, B. 1975. "The Urban Centrifugal Drift." In A. Hawley and V. Rock, eds., *Metropolitan America in Contemporary Perspective*, pp. 23–92. New York: John Wiley.

Zuiches, J. 1981. "Residential Preferences and Rural Population Growth." In A. Hawley and S. Mazie, eds., *Toward an Understanding of Nonmetropolitan Growth*, pp. 72–115. Chapel Hill: University of North Carolina Press.

Zuiches, J. and G. Fuguitt. 1972. "Residential Preferences: Implications for Population Redistribution in Nonmetropolitan Areas." In S. Mazie, ed., *Population, Distribution, and Policy*, Vol. 5, pp. 617–30. Washington, D.C.: U.S. Government Printing Office.

Index

250INDEX